Bible
Speaks
today

the message of

THE KINGDOM
OF GOD

Series editors:
Alec Motyer (OT)
John Stott (NT)
Derek Tidball (Bible Themes)

'Tracing the story of God's kingdom from the words "in the beginning" to the last and great "Amen", Alexander serves as a faithful guide in this work of biblical theology. Along the way, we learn how the kingdom of God has progressively revealed itself through the course of redemptive history to the bright future of its fulfilment, all the while centred on the king.'
Matthew Boswell, hymn writer and Assistant Professor of Church Music and Worship, Southern Baptist Theological Seminary

'Kings and kingdoms can seem to be merely the fodder of fairy tales for some, while for myriad others, especially those who have lived under cruel kings in corrupt kingdoms, kings and kingdoms are seen primarily as perpetrators of oppression and violence. This is why we need the story the Bible presents to us, and which Desi Alexander has so capably expounded on for us in *The Message of the Kingdom of God*. This book connects all of the biblical dots for us, so that we can see not only how God is answering our prayers for his kingdom of justice and righteousness to come, but also the beauty of the king who has come and will come again.'
Nancy Guthrie, Bible teacher and author of *Even Better than Eden: Nine Ways the Bible's Story Changes Everything About Your Story*

the message of

THE KINGDOM
OF GOD

T. Desmond Alexander

INTER-VARSITY PRESS
SPCK Group, Studio 101, The Record Hall, 16–16A Baldwin's Gardens,
London EC1N 7RJ, England
Email: ivp@ivpbooks.com
Website: www.ivpbooks.com

First published 2024

British Library Cataloguing-in-Publication Data
A catalogue record for this book is available from the British Library.

ISBN: 978–1–78974–382–1
eBook ISBN: 978–1–78974–383–8

Set in 9.5/13pt Karmina
Typeset in Great Britain by CRB Associates, Potterhanworth, Lincolnshire
Printed in Great Britain by Ashford Colour Press Ltd, Gosport, Hampshire

Produced on paper from sustainable sources

*Inter-Varsity Press publishes Christian books that are true to the Bible
and that communicate the gospel, develop discipleship and strengthen the church
for its mission in the world.*

*IVP originated within the Inter-Varsity Fellowship, now the Universities and Colleges
Christian Fellowship, a student movement connecting Christian Unions in universities
and colleges throughout Great Britain, and a member movement of the International
Fellowship of Evangelical Students. Website: www.uccf.org.uk. That historic association
is maintained, and all senior IVP staff and committee members subscribe
to the UCCF Basis of Faith.*

To Paul and Helen McQueen

Contents

Bible Speaks today

GENERAL PREFACE

The Bible Speaks Today describes three series of expositions, based on the books of the Old and New Testaments, and on Bible themes that run through the whole of Scripture. Each series is characterized by a threefold ideal:

- to expound the biblical text with accuracy
- to relate it to contemporary life, and
- to be readable.

These books are, therefore, not 'commentaries', for the commentary seeks rather to elucidate the text than to apply it, and tends to be a work rather of reference than of literature. Nor, on the other hand, do they contain the kinds of 'sermons' that attempt to be contemporary and readable without taking Scripture seriously enough. The contributors to The Bible Speaks Today series are all united in their convictions that God still speaks through what he has spoken, and that nothing is more necessary for the life, health and growth of Christians than that they should hear what the Spirit is saying to them through his ancient – yet ever modern – Word.

ALEC MOTYER
JOHN STOTT
DEREK TIDBALL
Series editors

Author's preface

The writings of John Stott have been exceptionally influential in shaping the lives of many Christians. As a young Christian, I read with great benefit his books in The Bible Speaks Today series. For this reason, I count it a great honour to be able to contribute in a small way to the series that he edited for many years. For the invitation to write on the kingdom of God I am indebted to Derek Tidball and Phil Duce. To be entrusted with explaining such an important biblical topic is both an amazing privilege and a serious responsibility.

For over forty years, my university and college teaching has allowed me to explore the Scriptures from many angles. This has been a remarkable experience, for which I am deeply grateful. In my studies I have encountered the writings of numerous scholars, from all kinds of theological backgrounds and none. I do not accept unquestioningly everything that others write, but their ideas have often challenged my thinking and sharpened my understanding of what the Bible says. No-one is an island. These influences are too many and too varied to acknowledge here. If by God's grace I see things more clearly, it is because I stand on the shoulders of others. For opening the door to these resources, I am indebted to several generations of librarians at the Queen's University of Belfast and Union Theological College. For their assistance with the writing of this book, my sincere thanks go to Joy Conkey and Margaret Ollivier. Their efficiency in supporting academic staff and students deserves special mention.

No book arrives with a publisher fully formed in its first draft. My thanks go to Dr Rita Cefalu for her constructive feedback on an early draft of the manuscript. For their editorial advice and guidance, I wish to thank most sincerely Derek Tidball and Tom Creedy. Writing for this series has been something of a challenge and I have tried my best to respond appropriately to their many helpful suggestions. It is difficult, however, to teach an old dog new tricks. The failings and shortcomings that remain are entirely my responsibility.

As a husband, I receive generous and unending support from my wife, Anne. With self-giving patience, she has lovingly created time for me to research and write. Her prayerful encouragement continues to be exceptionally important. I also value greatly the love of our children, Jane and David, their respective spouses, Ross and Alana, and our grandchildren, Martha, Maggie and Gregor. It is my prayer that this book may help them and others to be 'kingdom people'. With appreciation for their friendship, this book is dedicated to Paul and Helen McQueen.

SOLI DEO GLORIA.

T. DESMOND ALEXANDER

Chief abbreviations

AUSS	*Andrews University Seminary Studies*
BAR	*Biblical Archaeology Review*
CSB	Christian Standard Bible
ESV	English Standard Version
IECOT	International Exegetical Commentary on the Old Testament
JBL	*Journal of Biblical Literature*
JETS	*Journal of the Evangelical Theological Society*
JPS	Jewish Publication Society (1917)
JSOT	*Journal for the Study of the Old Testament*
JSOTSup	Journal for the Study of the Old Testament Supplement Series
KJV	King James Version
LHB/OTS	Library of Hebrew Bible/Old Testament Studies
NAC	The New American Commentary
NET	New English Translation
NETS	A. Pietersma and B. G. Wright (eds.), *A New English Translation of the Septuagint* (New York: Oxford University Press, 2007)
NICNT	New International Commentary on the New Testament
NICOT	New International Commentary on the Old Testament
NIDOTTE	W. A. VanGemeren (ed.), *New International Dictionary of Old Testament Theology and Exegesis*, 5 vols. (Grand Rapids: Zondervan, 1997)
NIV	New International Version
NJB	New Jerusalem Bible

NJPS	*Tanakh: The Holy Scriptures: The New JPS Translation according to the Traditional Hebrew Text* (1985)
NovTSup	Supplements to Novum Testamentum
NRSV	New Revised Standard Version
OTS	Old Testament Studies
RBS	Resources for Biblical Study
REB	Revised English Bible
SJOT	*Scandinavian Journal of the Old Testament*
SNTSMS	Society for New Testament Studies Monograph Series
TDNT	G. Kittel and G. Friedrich (eds.), tr. G. W. Bromiley, *Theological Dictionary of the New Testament*, 10 vols. (Grand Rapids: Eerdmans, 1964–67)
TWOT	R. L. Harris (ed.), *Theological Wordbook of the Old Testament*, 2 vols. (Chicago: Moody, 1980)
VTSup	Supplements to Vetus Testamentum
WTJ	*Westminster Theological Journal*

Select bibliography

Abernethy, A. T., and G. Goswell, *God's Messiah in the Old Testament: Expectations of a Coming King* (Grand Rapids: Baker Academic, 2020).

Adams, E., 'The Coming of the Son of Man in Mark's Gospel', *Tyndale Bulletin* 56 (2005), pp. 39–61.

Alexander, T. D., 'Book of the Covenant', in T. D. Alexander and D. W. Baker (eds.), *Dictionary of the Old Testament: Pentateuch* (Leicester: Inter-Varsity Press, 2003), pp. 94–101.

——, *The City of God and the Goal of Creation*, Short Studies in Biblical Theology (Wheaton: Crossway, 2018).

——, *Discovering Jesus: Four Gospels, One Person* (Nottingham: Inter-Varsity Press, 2010).

——, *Exodus*, Apollos OT Commentary 2 (London: Apollos, 2017).

——, *Face to Face with God: A Biblical Theology of Christ as Priest and Mediator*, Essential Studies in Biblical Theology (Downers Grove: InterVarsity Press, 2021).

——, *From Paradise to the Promised Land: An Introduction to the Pentateuch*, 4th edn (Grand Rapids: Baker Academic, 2022).

——, 'Further Observations of the Term "Seed" in Genesis', *Tyndale Bulletin* 48 (1997), pp. 363–367.

——, 'Genesis 22 and the Covenant of Circumcision', *JSOT* 25 (1983), pp. 17–22.

——, 'Pentateuch', in A. Johnston (ed.), *T&T Clark Companion to Atonement* (London: Bloomsbury T&T Clark, 2017), pp. 677–684.

——, 'The Regal Dimension of the תלדות־יעקב: Recovering the Literary Context of Genesis 37 – 50', in J. G. McConville and K. Möller (eds.), *Reading the Law: Studies in Honour of Gordon J. Wenham*, LHB/OTS 461 (Edinburgh: T&T Clark, 2007), pp. 196–212.

Alter, R., *The Art of Biblical Poetry* (New York: Basic Books, 1985).

——, *Genesis* (New York: W. W. Norton, 1996).

Attridge, H. W., 'Pollution, Sin, Atonement, Salvation', in S. I. Johnston (ed.), *Ancient Religions* (Cambridge, MA; London: Belknap, 2007), pp. 71–83.

Baldwin, J. G., *1 and 2 Samuel: An Introduction and Commentary*, Tyndale Old Testament Commentaries 8 (Leicester: Inter-Varsity Press, 1988).

——, *Daniel: An Introduction and Commentary*, Tyndale Old Testament Commentaries (Downers Grove: InterVarsity Press, 1978).

Barber, D. C., and R. A. Peterson, *Life Everlasting: The Unfolding Story of Heaven*, Explorations in Biblical Theology (Phillipsburg: P&R, 2012).

Barnes, W. H., *1 – 2 Kings*, Cornerstone Biblical Commentary 4b (Carol Stream: Tyndale House, 2012).

Bartholomew, C. G., 'The Theology of Place in Genesis 1 – 3', in J. G. McConville and K. Möller (eds.), *Reading the Law: Studies in Honour of Gordon J. Wenham*, LHB/OTS 461 (Edinburgh: T&T Clark, 2007), pp. 173–195.

Bauer, D. R., 'Son of David', in J. B. Green et al. (eds.), *Dictionary of Jesus and the Gospels* (Downers Grove: InterVarsity Press, 1992), pp. 766–769.

——, 'Son of God', in J. B. Green et al. (eds.), *Dictionary of Jesus and the Gospels* (Downers Grove: InterVarsity Press, 1992), pp. 769–775.

Beale, G. K., *Revelation: A Shorter Commentary* (Grand Rapids: William B. Eerdmans, 2015).

Beckwith, R. T., *The Old Testament Canon of the New Testament Church and Its Background in Early Judaism* (London: SPCK, 1985).

Bergen, R. D., *1, 2 Samuel* (Nashville: Broadman & Holman, 1996).

Bietak, M., *Avaris: The Capital of the Hyksos; Recent Excavations at Tell El-Dab'a* (London: British Museum Press, 1996).

Bird, M. F., 'The Crucifixion of Jesus as the Fulfillment of Mark 9:1', *Trinity Journal* 24 (2003), pp. 23–36.

——, *Jesus Is the Christ: The Messianic Testimony of the Gospels* (Milton Keynes: Paternoster, 2012).

Blocher, H., *In the Beginning: The Opening Chapters of Genesis* (Leicester: Inter-Varsity Press, 1984).

Block, D. I., *Judges, Ruth*, NAC 6 (Nashville: Broadman & Holman, 1999).

Bock, D. L., 'Son of Man', in J. B. Green et al. (eds.), *Dictionary of Jesus and the Gospels*, 2nd edn (Nottingham: Inter-Varsity Press, 2013), pp. 894–900.

Boda, M. J., '"Declare His Glory among the Nations": The Psalter as Missional Collection', in S. E. Porter and C. L. Westfall (eds.), *Christian Mission: Old Testament Foundations and New Testament Developments*, McMaster New Testament Studies (Eugene: Pickwick, 2010), pp. 13–41.

Breasted, J. H., *Ancient Records of Egypt: The Nineteenth Dynasty*, 4 vols. (Chicago: University of Chicago Press, 1906).

Brettler, M. Z., *God Is King: Understanding an Israelite Metaphor*, JSOTSup 76 (Sheffield: JSOT Press, 1989).

Bright, J., *The Kingdom of God: The Biblical Concept and Its Meaning for the Church* (Nashville: Abingdon Press, 1953).

Burkett, D., *The Son of Man Debate: A History and Evaluation*, SNTSMS 107 (Cambridge: Cambridge University Press, 1999).

Calvin, J., *Commentary on a Harmony of the Evangelists, Matthew, Mark and Luke*, 3 vols. (Edinburgh: Calvin Translation Society, 1845).

Carson, D. A., *The Sermon on the Mount: An Evangelical Exposition of Matthew 5 – 7* (Grand Rapids: Baker, 1982).

Carson, D. A., et al., *The Expositor's Bible Commentary: Matthew–Mark*, rev. edn (Grand Rapids: Zondervan, 2010).

Charles, J. D. (ed.), *Reading Genesis 1 – 2: An Evangelical Conversation* (Peabody: Hendrickson, 2013).

Chrupcala, L. D., 'The Kingdom of God: A Bibliography of 20th Century Research. Update', last modified 11 November 2019, accessed 10 May 2022, <https://www.academia.edu/download/61549144/The_Kingdom_of_God_A_Bibliography_of_20th_Century_Research_Update20191218-80011-1unyaxe.pdf>.

Clarke, T. A., 'Complete v. Incomplete Conquest: A Re-Examination of Three Passages in Joshua', *Tyndale Bulletin* 61 (2010), pp. 89–104.

Clines, D. J. A., 'The Image of God in Man', *Tyndale Bulletin* (1968), pp. 53–103.

Coleson, J., et al., *Joshua, Judges, Ruth*, Cornerstone Biblical Commentary (Carol Stream: Tyndale House, 2012).

Copan, P., *Is God a Moral Monster? Making Sense of the Old Testament God* (Grand Rapids: Baker, 2011).

Copan, P., and M. Flannagan, *Did God Really Command Genocide? Coming to Terms with the Justice of God* (Grand Rapids: Baker, 2014).

Currid, J. D., 'Genesis', in M. V. Van Pelt (ed.), *A Biblical-Theological Introduction to the Old Testament: The Gospel Promised* (Wheaton: Crossway, 2016), pp. 37–63.

Dalrymple, S., 'Ephraim or Judah: Divine Sovereignty and the Potential for Kingship in Joshua–Judges', in P. R. Williamson and R. F. Cefalu (eds.), *The Seed of Promise: The Sufferings and Glory of the Messiah; Essays in Honor of T. Desmond Alexander*, GlossaHouse Festschrift Series 3 (Wilmore: GlossaHouse, 2020), pp. 50–73.

Davies, J. A., *A Royal Priesthood: Literary and Intertextual Perspectives on an Image of Israel in Exodus 19.6*, JSOTSup 395 (London: T&T Clark International, 2004).

Davis, D. R., *The Message of Daniel: His Kingdom Cannot Fail*, The Bible Speaks Today (Nottingham: Inter-Varsity Press, 2013).

Dempster, S. G., *Dominion and Dynasty: A Biblical Theology of the Hebrew Bible*, New Studies in Biblical Theology 15 (Leicester: Apollos, 2003).

———, 'The End of History and the Last Man', in P. R. Williamson and R. F. Cefalu (eds.), *The Seed of Promise: The Sufferings and Glory of the Messiah; Essays in Honor of T. Desmond Alexander*, GlossaHouse Festschrift Series 3 (Wilmore: GlossaHouse, 2020), pp. 113–141.

———, 'Hannah's Song, a New World Order and the Right Side of History', in M. A. G. Haykin et al. (eds.), *Ecclesia Semper Reformanda Est – The Church Is Always Reforming: A Festschrift on Ecclesiology in Honour of Stanley K. Fowler* (Dundas: Joshua Press, 2016), pp. 3–32.

DeRouchie, J. S., 'Counting Stars with Abraham and the Prophets: New Covenant Ecclesiology in OT Perspective', *JETS* 58 (2015), pp. 445–485.

Dumbrell, W. J., *Covenant and Creation: An Old Testament Covenantal Theology* (Exeter: Paternoster, 1984).

———, *The End of the Beginning: Revelation 21 – 22 and the Old Testament* (Grand Rapids: Baker, 1985).

Edwards, J. R., *The Gospel According to Mark*, The Pillar New Testament Commentary (Grand Rapids: Eerdmans, 2002).

Emadi, M. H., *The Royal Priest: Psalm 110 in Biblical Theology*, New Studies in Biblical Theology 60 (London: Apollos, 2022).

Evans, C. A., 'Inaugurating the Kingdom of God and Defeating the Kingdom of Satan', *Bulletin for Biblical Research* 15 (2005), pp. 49–75.

Fee, G. D., *The First Epistle to the Corinthians*, NICNT (Grand Rapids: W. B. Eerdmans, 1987).

Firth, D. G., *1 & 2 Samuel* (Nottingham: Apollos, 2009).

——, *Including the Stranger: Foreigners in the Former Prophets*, New Studies in Biblical Theology 50 (Nottingham: Apollos, 2019).

——, *Joshua*, Evangelical Biblical Theology Commentary (Bellingham: Lexham Academic, 2021).

Fishbane, M. A., *Text and Texture: Close Readings of Selected Biblical Texts* (New York: Schocken Books, 1979).

Flew, A., and R. A. Varghese, *There Is a God: How the World's Most Notorious Atheist Changed His Mind* (New York: HarperOne, 2007).

Ford, W. A., '"Dispossessing" the Canaanites in Deuteronomy', in M. Spalione and H. Paynter (eds.), *Map or Compass? The Bible on Violence*, Bible in the Modern World 79 (Sheffield: Sheffield Phoenix, 2022), pp. 56–71.

France, R. T., *Matthew: An Introduction and Commentary* (Nottingham: Inter-Varsity Press, 1985).

Gane, R., *Cult and Character: Purification Offerings, Day of Atonement, and Theodicy* (Winona Lake: Eisenbrauns, 2005).

Gentry, P. J., and S. J. Wellum, *Kingdom through Covenant: A Biblical-Theological Understanding of the Covenants* (Wheaton: Crossway, 2012).

Goldsworthy, G., *Christ-Centred Biblical Theology: Hermeneutical Foundations and Principles* (Nottingham: Apollos, 2012).

Gordon, R. P., *I & II Samuel: A Commentary* (Grand Rapids: Zondervan, 1986).

Gowan, D. E., *Eschatology in the Old Testament* (Philadelphia: Fortress, 1986).

Green, G. L., *The Letters to the Thessalonians*, The Pillar New Testament Commentary (Grand Rapids: Eerdmans, 2002).

Grindheim, S., *Living in the Kingdom of God: A Biblical Theology for the Life of the Church* (Grand Rapids: Baker Academic, 2018).

Groves, J. A., 'Zion Traditions', in Bill T. Arnold and H. G. M. Williamson, *Dictionary of the Old Testament: Historical Books* (Downers Grove: InterVarsity Press, 2005), pp. 1019–1025.

Gurney, R. J. M., 'The Four Kingdoms of Daniel 2 and 7', *Themelios* 2 (1977), pp. 42–45.

Habel, N. C., *Literary Criticism of the Old Testament* (Philadelphia: Fortress, 1971).

Hagner, D. A., *Hebrews*, New International Biblical Commentary (Peabody: Hendrickson, 1983).

Hahn, S., *Kinship by Covenant: A Canonical Approach to the Fulfillment of God's Saving Promises*, The Anchor Yale Bible Reference Library (New Haven: Yale University Press, 2009).

Hamilton, J. M., *With the Clouds of Heaven: The Book of Daniel in Biblical Theology*, New Studies in Biblical Theology 32 (Nottingham: Apollos; Downers Grove: InterVarsity Press, 2014).

Hamilton, V. P., *The Book of Genesis: Chapters 1–17*, NICOT (Grand Rapids: Eerdmans, 1990).

Harmon, M. S., *Galatians*, Evangelical Biblical Theology Commentary (Bellingham: Lexham Academic Press, 2021).

——, *The Servant of the Lord and His Servant People: Tracing a Biblical Theme through the Canon*, New Studies in Biblical Theology 54 (London: Apollos, 2020).

Hart, I., 'Genesis 1:1 – 2:3 as a Prologue to the Book of Genesis', *Tyndale Bulletin* 46 (1995), pp. 315–336.

Hasel, G. F., 'Meaning of "Let Us" in Gn 1:26', *AUSS* 13 (1975), pp. 58–66.

Hassler, M. A., 'The Identity of the Little Horn in Daniel 8: Antiochus IV Epiphanes, Rome, or the Antichrist?', *The Master's Seminary Journal* 27 (2016), pp. 33–44.

Hess, R. S., *Joshua*, Tyndale Old Testament Commentaries (Leicester: Inter-Varsity Press, 1996).

——, 'The Roles of the Woman and the Man in Genesis 3', *Themelios* 18 (1993), pp. 15–19.

——, 'Splitting the Adam: The Usage of 'ādām in Genesis i – v', in J. A. Emerton (ed.), *Studies in the Pentateuch*, VTSup 41 (Leiden: Brill, 1990), pp. 1–15.

Hoekema, A. A., *The Bible and the Future* (Grand Rapids: Eerdmans, 1979).

Hoffmeier, J. K., *Israel in Egypt: The Evidence for the Authenticity of the Exodus Tradition* (New York: Oxford University Press, 1997).

——, 'Out of Egypt: The Archaeological Context of the Exodus', *BAR* 33 (2007), pp. 30–41, 77.

Hubbard, R. L., 'גאל (g'l)', *NIDOTTE* 1:789–794.

Jackson, J., 'The Bows of the Mighty Are Broken: The "Fall" of the Proud and the Exaltation of the Humble in 1 Samuel', *Themelios* 46 (2021), pp. 290–305.

Jenkins, S., 'The Antiquity of Psalter Shape Efforts', *Tyndale Bulletin* 71 (2020), pp. 161–190.

Jipp, J. W., *Christ Is King: Paul's Royal Ideology* (Minneapolis: Fortress, 2015).

Johnson, A. F., *1 Corinthians* (Downers Grove: IVP Academic, 2004).

Keener, C. S., *Matthew*, The IVP New Testament Commentary Series (Downers Grove: InterVarsity Press, 1997).

Keiser, T. A., 'The Divine Plural: A Literary-Contextual Argument of Plurality in the Godhead', *JSOT* 34 (2009), pp. 131–146.

Koorevaar, H. J., 'De Opbouw van het Boek Jozua' (PhD diss., University of Brussels, 1990).

Ladd, G. E., *A Theology of the New Testament*, rev. edn (Grand Rapids: Eerdmans, 1993).

Lee, C.-C., 'גים [sic] in Genesis 35:11 and the Abrahamic Promise of Blessings for the Nations', *JETS* 52 (2009), pp. 467–482.

Lewis, C. S., *The Last Battle* (London: The Bodley Head, 1956).

Lincoln, A. T., 'The Lazarus Story: A Literary Perspective', in R. Bauckham and C. Mosser (eds.), *The Gospel of John and Christian Theology* (Grand Rapids: William B. Eerdmans, 2008), pp. 211–232.

Long, V. P., *1 and 2 Samuel: An Introduction and Commentary*, Tyndale Old Testament Commentaries (London: Inter-Varsity Press, 2020).

Longman, T., III, and D. G. Reid, *God Is a Warrior*, Studies in Old Testament Biblical Theology (Grand Rapids: Zondervan, 1995).

McCartney, D. G., 'Ecce Homo: The Coming of the Kingdom as the Restoration of Human Vicegerency', *WTJ* 56 (1994), pp. 1–21.

McComiskey, T. E., *The Covenants of Promise: A Theology of the Old Testament Covenants* (Nottingham: Inter-Varsity Press, 1985).

McConville, J. G., *Grace in the End* (Carlisle: Paternoster, 1993).

McKeown, J., *Genesis*, Two Horizons Old Testament Commentary 1 (Grand Rapids: Eerdmans, 2008).

Marcus, J., 'Crucifixion as Parodic Exaltation', *JBL* 125 (2006), pp. 73–87.

———, *Mark 8 – 16: A New Translation with Introduction and Commentary*, The Anchor Yale Bible 27A (New Haven: Yale University Press, 2009).

Marshall, C. D., *Faith as a Theme in Mark's Narrative*, SNTSMS 64 (Cambridge: Cambridge University Press, 1989).

Marshall, I. H., 'The Hope of a New Age: The Kingdom of God in the New Testament', in *Jesus the Saviour: Studies in New Testament Theology* (London: SPCK, 1990), pp. 213–238.

Mathews, K. A., *Genesis 1 – 11:26*, NAC 1A (Nashville: Broadman & Holman, 1995).

———, *Joshua*, Teach the Text Commentary (Grand Rapids: Baker, 2016).

Meyers, C. L., 'Gender Roles and Genesis 3:16 Revisited', in C. L. Meyers and K. M. O'Connor (eds.), *The Word of the Lord Shall Go Forth: Essays in Honor of David Noel Freedman* (Winona Lake: Eisenbrauns, 1983), pp. 337–354.

Miano, D., *Shadow on the Steps: Time Measurement in Ancient Israel*, RBS 64 (Atlanta: Society of Biblical Literature, 2010).

Middleton, J. R., *The Liberating Image: The Imago Dei in Genesis 1* (Grand Rapids: Brazos, 2005).

———, *A New Heaven and a New Earth: Reclaiming Biblical Eschatology* (Grand Rapids: Baker, 2014).

Milgrom, J., *Leviticus 1 – 16: A New Translation with Introduction and Commentary*, Anchor Bible 3A (New York: Doubleday, 1991).

Millar, J. G., ' "We Three Kings . . ." – An Examination of the Messianic Trajectory of the Book of Kings with Special Reference to Solomon, Hezekiah, and Josiah', in P. R. Williamson and R. F. Cefalu (eds.), *The Seed of Promise: The Sufferings and Glory of the Messiah; Essays in Honor of T. Desmond Alexander*, GlossaHouse Festschrift Series 3 (Wilmore: GlossaHouse, 2020), pp. 90–112.

Miller, S. R., *Daniel*, NAC 18 (Nashville: Broadman & Holman, 1994).

Mitchell, D. C., 'Lord, Remember David: G H Wilson and the Message of the Psalter', *Vetus Testamentum* 56 (2006), pp. 526–548.

———, *The Message of the Psalter: An Eschatological Programme in the Book of Psalms*, JSOTSup 252 (Sheffield: Sheffield Academic Press, 1997).

———, *Messiah ben Joseph* (Newton Mearns: Campbell Publications, 2016).

Möller, K., 'Images of God and Creation in Genesis 1 – 2', in J. A. Grant et al. (eds.), *A God of Faithfulness: Essays in Honour of J. Gordon McConville on His 60th Birthday*, LHB/OTS 538 (New York: T&T Clark, 2011), pp. 3–29.

Morales, L. M., 'Atonement in Ancient Israel: The Whole Burnt Offering as Central to Israel's Cult', in J. C. Laansma et al. (eds.), *So Great a*

Salvation: A Dialogue on the Atonement in Hebrews, Library of New Testament Studies (London: T&T Clark, 2019), pp. 27–39.

——, *Exodus Old and New: A Biblical Theology of Redemption*, Essential Studies in Biblical Theology (Downers Grove: IVP Academic, 2020).

Morgan, C. W., and R. A. Peterson (eds.), *Heaven*, Theology in Community (Wheaton: Crossway, 2014).

Morris, L., *1 Corinthians: An Introduction and Commentary* (Leicester: Inter-Varsity Press, 1985).

——, *The Gospel According to Matthew*, The Pillar New Testament Commentary (Grand Rapids: Eerdmans, 1992).

——, *Revelation: An Introduction and Commentary*, Tyndale New Testament Commentaries 20 (Leicester: Inter-Varsity Press; Downers Grove: InterVarsity Press, 1987).

Motyer, J. A., *Isaiah: An Introduction and Commentary*, Tyndale Old Testament Commentaries 20 (Leicester: Inter-Varsity Press, 1999).

Müller, M., *The Expression 'Son of Man' and the Development of Christology: A History of Interpretation*, Copenhagen International Seminar (London: Equinox, 2008).

Neusner, J., et al. (eds.), *Judaisms and Their Messiahs at the Turn of the Christian Era* (Cambridge: Cambridge University Press, 1987).

O'Connell, R. H., *The Rhetoric of the Book of Judges*, VTSup (Leiden: E. J. Brill, 1995).

Ollenburger, B., 'Creation and Peace: Creator and Creature in Genesis 1 – 11', in J. M. Isaak (ed.), *The Old Testament in the Life of God's People: Essays in Honor of Elmer A. Martens* (Winona Lake: Eisenbrauns, 2009), pp. 143–158.

Paul, S. M., *Isaiah 40 – 66: Translation and Commentary* (Grand Rapids/ Cambridge: William B. Eerdmans, 2012).

Payne, J. B., 'אבה (*'bh*)', *TWOT* 1:5–6.

Pennington, J. T., *Heaven and Earth in the Gospel of Matthew*, NovTSup 126 (Leiden: Brill, 2007).

——, *The Sermon on the Mount and Human Flourishing: A Theological Commentary* (Grand Rapids: Baker Academic, 2017).

Peterson, D. G., *The Acts of the Apostles*, The Pillar New Testament Commentary (Grand Rapids: William B. Eerdmans, 2009).

Polhill, J. B., *Acts*, NAC 26 (Nashville: Broadman, 1992).

Postman, N., 'Science and the Story That We Need', *First Things* (1997), pp. 29–32.

Poythress, V. S., *Christian Interpretations of Genesis 1*, Christian Answers to Hard Questions (Philadelphia: P&R, 2013).

Provan, I. W., *1 and 2 Kings*, New International Biblical Commentary Old Testament Series (Peabody: Hendrickson; Carlisle: Paternoster, 1995).

———, *Discovering Genesis: Content, Interpretation, Reception*, Discovering Biblical Texts (London: SPCK, 2015).

Quarles, C. L., *Matthew*, Evangelical Biblical Theology Commentary (Bellingham: Lexham Academic, 2022).

Rooker, M. F., *Leviticus*, NAC 3A (Nashville: Broadman & Holman, 2000).

Schaffner, A. K., 'What Is Humility & Why Is It Important?', PositivePsychology.com, 27 August 2020, accessed 25 September 2023 <https://positivepsychology.com/humility/>.

Schreiner, P., *The Kingdom of God and the Glory of the Cross*, Short Studies in Biblical Theology (Wheaton: Crossway, 2018).

Seesemann, H., 'πειρα', *TDNT* 6:23–36.

Shreckhise, R., 'The Rhetoric of the Expressions in the Song by the Sea (Exodus 15,1–18)', *SJOT* 21 (2007), pp. 201–217.

Sklar, J., *Leviticus: An Introduction and Commentary*, Tyndale Old Testament Commentaries 3 (Nottingham: Inter-Varsity Press, 2013).

———, *Sin, Impurity, Sacrifice, Atonement: The Priestly Conceptions*, Hebrew Bible Monographs 2 (Sheffield: Sheffield Phoenix Press, 2005).

Smith, G. V., 'Isaiah 65 – 66: The Destiny of God's Servants in a New Creation', *Bibliotheca Sacra* 171 (2014), pp. 42–51.

Sommer, B. D., *The Bodies of God and the World of Ancient Israel* (Cambridge: Cambridge University Press, 2009).

Sprinkle, J. M., *Daniel*, Evangelical Biblical Theology Commentary (Bellingham: Lexham Academic, 2020).

Sproston North, W. E., *The Lazarus Story within the Johannine Tradition* (Sheffield: Sheffield Academic Press, 2001).

Stott, J. R. W., *The Message of the Sermon on the Mount: Christian Counter-Culture*, The Bible Speaks Today, rev. edn (London: Inter-Varsity Press, 2020).

Tannehill, R. C., *The Narrative Unity of Luke–Acts: A Literary Interpretation*, Vol. 2: *The Acts of the Apostles* (Minneapolis: Fortress, 1990).

Taylor, M., *1 Corinthians*, NAC 28 (Nashville: B&H, 2014).

Thiselton, A. C., *The Living Paul: An Introduction to the Apostle and His Thought* (London: SPCK, 2009).

Thomas, D. W. H., *Heaven on Earth: What the Bible Teaches about Life to Come* (Fearn: Christian Focus, 2018).

Thompson, B., 'Pride and Kingship: A Literary Reading of 1 and 2 Samuel Considering the Role of the Poetry in Shaping the Characterisation of the Kings' (PhD diss., Queen's University Belfast, 2021).

Thompson, M. M., 'The Raising of Lazarus in John 11: A Theological Reading', in R. Bauckham and C. Mosser (eds.), *The Gospel of John and Christian Theology* (Grand Rapids: William B. Eerdmans, 2008), pp. 233–244.

Treat, J. R., *The Crucified King: Atonement and Kingdom in Biblical and Systematic Theology* (Grand Rapids: Zondervan, 2014).

Tsumura, D. T., *Creation and Destruction: A Reappraisal of the Chaoskampf Theory in the Old Testament* (Winona Lake: Eisenbrauns, 2005).

Turner, M., 'Holy Spirit', in T. D. Alexander and B. S. Rosner (eds.), *New Dictionary of Biblical Theology* (Leicester: Inter-Varsity Press, 2000), pp. 551–558.

———, *Power from on High: The Spirit in Israel's Restoration and Witness in Luke–Acts*, Journal of Pentecostal Theology Supplement Series 9 (Sheffield: Sheffield Academic, 1996).

Twelftree, G. H., *Jesus the Exorcist: A Contribution to the Study of the Historical Jesus* (Eugene: Wipf & Stock, 2010).

———, 'Jesus the Exorcist and Ancient Magic', in M. Labahn and L. J. Lietaert Peerbolte (eds.), *A Kind of Magic: Understanding Magic in the New Testament and Its Religious Environment*, Library of New Testament Studies 306 (London: T&T Clark, 2007), pp. 57–86.

Utzschneider, H., and W. Oswald, *Exodus 1 – 15*, tr. P. Sumpter, IECOT (Stuttgart: Kohlhammer, 2015).

Vannoy, J. R., *1 – 2 Samuel*, Cornerstone Biblical Commentary 4a (Carol Stream: Tyndale House, 2009).

———, 'Joshua: Theology of', *NIDOTTE* 4:810–819.

Walsh, J. T., *1 Kings*, Berit Olam (Collegeville: Liturgical Press, 1996).

Waltke, B. K., and C. J. Fredricks, *Genesis: A Commentary* (Grand Rapids: Zondervan, 2001).

Walton, J. H., 'The Four Kingdoms of Daniel', *JETS* 29 (1986), pp. 25–36.

Watts, J. D. W., 'The Song of the Sea – Ex. xv', *Vetus Testamentum* 7 (1957), pp. 371–380.

Watts, J. W., ''ōlāh: The Rhetoric of Burnt Offerings', *Vetus Testamentum* 56 (2006), pp. 125–137.

Webb, B. G., *The Book of the Judges: An Integrated Reading*, JSOTSup 46 (Sheffield: JSOT Press, 1987).

——, *The Message of Isaiah: On Eagles' Wings*, The Bible Speaks Today (Leicester: Inter-Varsity Press, 1996).

——, 'Zion in Transformation: A Literary Approach to Isaiah', in D. J. A. Clines et al. (eds.), *The Bible in Three Dimensions*, JSOTSup 87 (Sheffield: JSOT Press, 1990), pp. 65–84.

Wenham, G. J., *Rethinking Genesis 1 – 11: Gateway to the Bible; The Didsbury Lectures 2013*, Didsbury Lecture Series (Eugene: Cascade, 2015).

——, *Story as Torah: Reading the Old Testament Ethically*, OTS (Edinburgh: T&T Clark, 2000).

Williams, J. F., 'Is Mark's Gospel an Apology for the Cross?', *Bulletin for Biblical Research* 12 (2002), pp. 97–122.

Williams, S. N., 'Could God Have Commanded the Slaughter of the Canaanites?', *Tyndale Bulletin* 63 (2012), pp. 161–178.

Williamson, P. R., *Abraham, Israel and the Nations: The Patriarchal Promise and Its Covenantal Development in Genesis*, JSOTSup 315 (Sheffield: Sheffield Academic, 2000).

——, *Death and the Afterlife: Biblical Perspectives on Ultimate Questions*, New Studies in Biblical Theology 44 (London: Apollos, 2017).

——, 'Promises with Strings Attached: Covenant and Law in Exodus 19 – 24', in B. S. Rosner and P. R. Williamson (eds.), *Exploring Exodus: Literary, Theological and Contemporary Approaches* (Nottingham: Inter-Varsity Press, 2008), pp. 89–122.

——, *Sealed with an Oath: Covenant in God's Unfolding Purpose*, New Studies in Biblical Theology 23 (Leicester: Apollos, 2007).

——, 'Snakes and Dragons: A Neglected Theologial Trajectory of Genesis 3:15 in Scripture?', in P. R. Williamson and R. F. Cefalu (eds.), *The Seed of Promise: The Sufferings and Glory of the Messiah; Essays in Honor of T. Desmond Alexander*, GlossaHouse Festschrift Series 3 (Wilmore: GlossaHouse, 2020), pp. 332–352.

Wilson, G. H., 'נוה', *NIDOTTE* 3:54–56.

——, 'The Structure of the Psalter', in P. Johnston and D. G. Firth (eds.), *Interpreting the Psalms: Issues and Approaches* (Leicester: Apollos, 2005), pp. 229–246.

Wiseman, D. J., *1 and 2 Kings: An Introduction and Commentary*, Tyndale Old Testament Commentaries 9 (Leicester: Inter-Varsity Press, 1993).

Wright, C. J. H., 'אב (*'ab*)', *NIDOTTE* 1:219–223.

Wright, N. T., *How God Became King: The Forgotten Story of the Gospels* (New York: HarperOne, 2012).

Zehnder, M., 'The Enigmatic Figure of the "Servant of the Lord": Observations on the Relationship between the "Servant of the Lord" in Isaiah 40 – 55 and Other Salvific Figures in the Hebrew Bible', in M. Zehnder (ed.), *New Studies in the Book of Isaiah*, Perspectives on Hebrew Scriptures and Its Contexts 21 (Piscataway: Gorgias Press, 2014), pp. 231–282.

Introduction

No series of books on the major themes of the Bible would be complete without a volume on the kingdom of God. In the field of Biblical Studies, few topics have been discussed more fully. Despite the importance of this topic, the eminent New Testament scholar N. T. Wright has recently stated that the theme of God becoming king on earth is a truth that 'the past 200 years of European and American culture have been desperately trying to stifle'.[1] According to Wright, there is an urgent need for the Christian church to rediscover the significance and relevance of the kingdom of God, especially given its centrality in the teaching of Jesus Christ as reflected in the four Gospels.

Wright intentionally concentrates his discussion on the Gospels, but this study ranges across both Old and New Testaments for we cannot fully understand the kingdom of God without considering what the whole Bible has to say. Before we begin this biblical survey, which of necessity is selective and makes no claim to be comprehensive, this introductory chapter offers a brief orientation to what follows.

When Jesus offered his disciples guidance on how to pray, they could hardly have imagined that his answer would produce some of the most frequently used words of Scripture in all of history. Unfortunately, we have become so familiar with what we now call the Lord's Prayer that we have possibly lost sight of its revolutionary nature. Jesus told his disciples:

This, then, is how you should pray:

    'Our Father in heaven,
    hallowed be your name,

---

[1] N. T. Wright, *How God Became King: The Forgotten Story of the Gospels* (New York: HarperOne, 2012), p. 162.

> your kingdom come,
> your will be done,
>   on earth as it is in heaven.
> Give us today our daily bread.
> And forgive us our debts,
>   as we also have forgiven our debtors.
> And lead us not into temptation,
>   but deliver us from the evil one.'[2]

Jesus offers his disciples a series of short petitions that they should make to God. Topping the list is the request that God's kingdom should come. By its very nature, this is evidently a petition for something that does not presently exist. God's kingdom, as envisaged by Jesus, is not a reality on the earth. If it were, there would be no reason to pray for it.

By teaching his followers to pray for the coming of God's kingdom, Jesus underlines that this is something that God himself desires. As we shall see, from the creation of this world it was God's intention that his kingdom would be established on earth. Importantly, however, underlying this request is an acknowledgment that the world is not as it should be. God's kingdom is not present on earth. Later, we shall explore why this is the case.

Without going into detail, other petitions in the Lord's prayer implicitly recognize the absence of God's reign in the world. Interpersonal relationships are flawed. The disciples are to seek forgiveness from God for their own shortcomings and they are, in turn, to offer forgiveness to others for offences committed. While Jesus does not expand upon the nature of the offences that people commit towards God and others, he recognizes the seriousness of these and the importance of both receiving and giving forgiveness.

As his short list of petitions sweeps in an arc from positive to negative, Jesus moves from requests that focus on God as the Holy One to requests that centre on the need to be delivered from evil, or perhaps more tellingly, the evil one.

As the Lord's Prayer reminds us, despite all that is truly amazing about it, this world has a stench of evil that permeates every crevice. Dictators

---

[2] Matt. 6:9–13. Luke 11:2–4 preserves a similar, but shorter, version of this prayer. As an itinerant teacher Jesus may have varied the wording of the prayer on different occasions.

use their overwhelming governmental and military power to crush their opponents. Paedophiles exploit the innocence and vulnerability of children. Perpetrators of domestic violence prey on the helplessness and weakness of those dependent upon them. Unscrupulous employers exploit labourers struggling to survive on minimal wages. Criminal gangs take advantage of refugees escaping from extreme violence desperately in search of a better life. The list could go on. At all levels of society, and in every social context, the impact of evil is never far away. Each of us has our own stories to tell by way of illustration and all of us have reasons to feel guilty due to our own malevolent actions or callous indifference to the fate of those around us. The unwelcome odour of evil is not simply a personal problem that only others need to address.

Jesus has a realistic understanding of human nature. In a culture that was heavily influenced by the dangers of ritual defilement, Jesus pointed to the real cause of human defilement:

> What comes out of a person is what defiles them. For it is from within, out of a person's heart, that evil thoughts come – sexual immorality, theft, murder, adultery, greed, malice, deceit, lewdness, envy, slander, arrogance and folly. All these evils come from inside and defile a person.[3]

When Jesus tells us to pray to our Heavenly Father 'Your kingdom come', what does he have in view? What should we expect? Ultimately, we are asking for a time when everything that happens on earth will conform to what God desires. When this occurs, God will reign unopposed as king over this world, enjoying the praise and adoration of those who acknowledge his sovereignty. Evil and everything associated with it will be banished from the world as people flourish together in a utopian paradise.

Something of this future reality is reflected in the vision that the apostle John has of New Jerusalem in Revelation 21 – 22. John sees an extraordinary city in which God comes to dwell with those who have been redeemed from the control and influence of evil powers. He briefly captures something of this transformed environment when he writes, ' "He [God] will wipe every tear from their eyes. There will be no more death" or mourning or crying or pain, for the old order of things has passed away.'[4]

---

3 Mark 7:20–23.
4 Rev. 21:4.

When Jesus encouraged his earliest followers to pray for the coming of God's kingdom on earth, he shone a bright light of hope into a dark world. As he spoke to ordinary people, struggling to survive from day to day in a social environment where they were living under foreign occupation, he created an expectation of a better life to come. In the Beatitudes that introduce some of his teaching on the kingdom, he speaks of those who mourn being comforted, of the meek inheriting the earth, of those who hunger and thirst after justice being satisfied, of the merciful receiving mercy, of the pure in heart seeing God and of peacemakers being called children of God (see Matt. 5:3–10). These expectations point to a radically different world, the new creation of Old Testament prophetic hopes and New Testament apostolic visions.

In a society where most people faced the daily challenge of putting food on their tables, where medical facilities were virtually non-existent, where people were taxed severely and social inequality was prevalent, where many women were treated as second-class citizens, where racial and class tensions separated people, Jesus brought a message that offered life-transforming prospects to those who could barely survive. His vision of the kingdom of God offered hope, not through a sudden change of circumstances – like the winning of the national lottery – but through the expectation of a future life that would be radically different regardless of present trials and tribulations. He was not a politician peddling false promises looking to gain popular support that would sweep him to power. Nor was he a charlatan seeking to enrich himself by selling the secret to a prosperous life, a health-and-wealth gospel. Those who followed him were not enticed to do so by the promise of a comfortable, secure life in the short term. Quite the contrary. Jesus points to a cosmic transformation that has personal and social consequences.

In my early career as a university lecturer, I recall well a young female student who battled day after day with cystic fibrosis. While medical treatment for this horrendous condition has advanced considerably in recent years, at that time few sufferers were expected to live beyond their early twenties. Cystic fibrosis was a disease for which there was no cure and life expectancy was very limited, so much so that the local unit for treating patients was based in the children's hospital. Margaret was not only an outstanding student, who gained a first-class honours degree despite missing numerous classes due to illness, but she was a committed follower of Jesus. Her faith radiated from her, for in the darkest of personal circumstances, she tenaciously looked forward with confidence to a better life to come. When the time of parting came, her family was devastated at losing her, yet this was not the end. She had a kingdom hope, an expectation that God's kingdom would be established in all its glory on a new earth and that she would participate fully within it.

On the last page of the final volume of his *Chronicles of Narnia*, C. S. Lewis captures something of this Christian hope. After Peter, Susan and Lucy die in a train wreck, they encounter Aslan. Describing their afterlife encounter, Lewis comments,

> All their life in this world and all their adventures in Narnia had only been the cover and the title page: now at last they were beginning Chapter One of the Great Story, which no one on earth has read: which goes on for ever: in which every chapter is better than the one before.[5]

With the skill of a master narrator, Lewis invites our imaginations to contemplate what life might be like beyond the Shadowlands. This is to experience the kingdom of God in all its glory. This is to know this world as God intended it to be.

But we are running far ahead of ourselves. We need to start the story at the beginning.

---

[5] C. S. Lewis, *The Last Battle* (London: The Bodley Head, 1956), p. 173.

Part 1
The scene is set

Genesis 1:1 – 2:3

1. The creator king

Familiarity can dull our senses to what is extraordinary. The opening words of Genesis are well known: *In the beginning God created the heavens and the earth.* We take for granted too easily how these opening words introduce us to the creator of the world in which we live.

When these words were first penned, they presented a concept that was radically different from how others in antiquity perceived the creation of the world. As Gordon Wenham observes, 'Here we meet just one all-powerful God, who speaks and what he commands comes to pass, not a multitude of competing gods and goddesses, each with his or her own sphere of influence.'[1] And in contrast to how Ancient Near Eastern creation accounts portray humanity as being formed as an afterthought to cater for the needs of gods and goddesses, Genesis 1 introduces humans as the pinnacle of divine creative activity, commissioned to serve God in a unique way.

If the account of Genesis 1 was unique in the ancient world, it continues to proclaim a distinctive message in our modern world. Genesis 1 counters the ubiquitous claims of those who believe that all creation is merely the product of chance. It challenges the belief that everything in existence came into being by accident. Genesis 1 boldly proclaims that there is a God who has created this universe.

Even the most ardent of atheists are sometimes persuaded to reconsider their stance. Such was the case with the philosopher Anthony Flew, a

---

[1] G. J. Wenham, *Rethinking Genesis 1 – 11: Gateway to the Bible; The Didsbury Lectures 2013*, Didsbury Lecture Series (Eugene: Cascade, 2015), p. 17.

leading proponent of atheism in the twentieth century. In his book *There Is a God: How the World's Most Notorious Atheist Changed His Mind,* Flew writes,

> I now believe that the universe was brought into existence by an infinite Intelligence. I believe that this universe's intricate laws manifest what scientists have called the Mind of God. I believe that life and reproduction originate in a divine Source.
>
> Why do I believe this, given that I expounded and defended atheism for more than a half century? The short answer is this: this is the world picture, as I see it, that has emerged from modern science. Science spotlights three dimensions of nature that point to God. The first is the fact that nature obeys laws. The second is the dimension of life, of intelligently organized and purpose-driven beings, which arose from matter. The third is the very existence of nature.[2]

Writing from a different perspective, the social commentator Neil Postman highlights the shortcomings of a worldview that rests on the premise that there is no creator God:

> But in the end, science does not provide the answers most of us require. Its story of our origins and of our end is, to say the least, unsatisfactory. To the question, 'How did it all begin?', science answers, 'Probably by an accident.' To the question, 'How will it all end?', science answers, 'Probably by an accident.' And to many people, the accidental life is not worth living.[3]

Postman's analysis prompts many questions. Are you and I merely the product of an exceptionally long process that began by chance? Is it by accident that we are able to think logically, to communicate, to see, smell, taste and touch? Is it by chance that we have an aesthetic appreciation of beauty both visually and aurally, that we have creative imaginations? Is it a consequence of an unplanned event that we experience a plethora of emotions, and have a moral sense of right and wrong? Is our desire to love and be loved, to enjoy relationships, simply the result of an accidental

---

[2] A. Flew and R. A. Varghese, *There Is a God: How the World's Most Notorious Atheist Changed His Mind* (New York: HarperOne, 2007), pp. 88–89.

[3] N. Postman, 'Science and the Story That We Need', *First Things* (1997), p. 31.

occurrence that happened billions of years ago? Is this planet with all its amazing variety of creatures simply here by a quirk of chance? Did some enormous accident, a Big Bang, produce a universe that can be explored scientifically because it is governed by principles that are consistent?

To believe that you and I as sentient creatures came about by chance requires, to my mind, not less faith, but more faith than believing in the reality of a creator God who purposefully designed all that exists. There are compelling grounds for accepting as true the opening words of Genesis: *In the beginning God created the heavens and the earth.*

1. An overview of creation

As a very concise description of the origin of everything Genesis 1:1 – 2:3 sets the scene for what follows. Not only is it a remarkable opening to the book of Genesis, but more importantly it is a prologue to the story of how God is working to establish his kingdom on earth. This is the start of His Story, and we are part of the script.

Against the prevailing cultures of the ancient world in which it was composed, Genesis 1:1 – 2:3 provides a uniquely monotheistic account of creation. Other Ancient Near Eastern creation stories are pervasively polytheistic, mentioning different gods, greater and lesser. In the Babylonian story entitled *Enuma Elish*, the earth is created when the god Marduk splits in half the body of Tiamat, a goddess whom he defeats in a duel. From her corpse Marduk creates the earth and sky. Later, humans are made from the blood of another god, who sided with the defeated Tiamat. Genesis 1 unequivocally rejects a polytheistic worldview.

With elegant literary skill, the author of Genesis pens an account that conveys in majestic tone the ease with which God alone creates all that exists. As Michael Fishbane remarks, 'The text shifts rhythmically between actions and results which utilize the same words ("separate") . . . "call" . . . "see" . . . "make") and sequences. Its economy of vocabulary and technique produces a dictum of controlled energy and force.'[4] The description of God's activity emphasizes the power of his commands to bring into being all that exists. The repetitive style of the narrative communicates a sense of order and purpose.

---

4 M. A. Fishbane, *Text and Texture: Close Readings of Selected Biblical Texts* (New York: Schocken Books, 1979), p. 8.

In Genesis 1 we encounter an all-powerful creator who transcends all that he makes. Underlining the importance of God's transcendent existence, Norman Habel comments, 'God appears as a being who stands outside of his cosmos and controls it with his mighty word.'[5] God oversees and controls all that happens, but is unambiguously located outside everything that is created.

This exalted portrait of God sets him apart from his creation. Yet, without detracting from this picture of a transcendent deity, Genesis 2 complements what is said by highlighting God's nearness, what theologians refer to as 'immanence'. In developing the panoramic view of the first chapter, Genesis 2 portrays God as being intimately involved in the creation of humans. Importantly, the opening chapters of Genesis reveal two aspects of God's nature that are equally significant and always need to be held in balance. God's transcendence should stop us from domesticating him by believing that he exists solely for our benefit, and his immanence should encourage us to believe that he is not a distant deity but one who is interested in our lives.

2. Setting the scene (1:1–2)

The interpretation of the opening three verses of Genesis has provoked considerable discussion. From an overview of the chapter, there are grounds to believe that verse 3 marks the beginning of Day 1. In verses 3–5, a distinctive pattern is established for Day 1 that is largely repeated in Days 2–6. Each day begins with the statement *And God said . . .* (3, 6, 9, 14, 20, 24). With this structure in view, verses 1–2 stand apart, forming an introduction to the whole chapter.

Despite the simplicity of what appears to be recorded, there is a complexity to the opening verses of Genesis 1. To begin, there are two possible ways of reading verse 1. On the one hand, it can be read as a statement of initial creation, with God making the entire cosmos.[6] This describes the beginning of God's creative activity. From verse 2 onwards we follow what

---

[5] N. C. Habel, *Literary Criticism of the Old Testament* (Philadelphia: Fortress, 1971), p. 24. A similar point is made by Fishbane, *Text and Texture*, p. 8: 'The formality of its sequences, the repetition of its key words, and the serialization of its contents combine to produce several theological meanings: that Elohim, alone, "at the beginning", created a good, ordered world; that He "separated" and hierarchically ordered the primordial mass into a "good" pattern; that the created world of nature is, as a result, a harmony; and that Elohim is Omnipotent and without rival.'

[6] The expression *the heavens and the earth* is most likely an example of merism.

happens next. On the other hand, it is possible to read verse 1 as a temporal clause, stating, 'In the beginning when God created the heavens and the earth . . .' Read in this way, verse 1 functions more like a title or summary of what follows. With this interpretation, verse 3 records God's first creative act.

Regardless of how verse 1 is understood, the syntax of verse 2 suggests that it is not part of a sequence of events. Rather, it describes a state of affairs. As such, it gives prominence to several concepts. First, it portrays the initial state of the earth as *formless and empty*. The Hebrew expression *tōhû wābōhû* is probably best understood as conveying the idea that the earth was 'a desolate and empty place, "an unproductive and uninhabited place"'.[7] By highlighting the earth's lack of structure and its emptiness, the expression *tōhû wābōhû* anticipates what follows. Days 1–3 focus on how God gives form to the earth. Building on this, Days 4–6 describe how God fills what has been formed. As many readers have recognized, there is a striking correspondence between Days 1–3 and 4–6 (see Table 1).

Table 1 The structure of the six days

Habitat		Inhabitants	
Day 1	Light (day and night)	Day 4	Luminaries
Day 2	Waters and sky	Day 5	Fish and birds
Day 3	Dry land	Day 6	Animals and humans

After describing the earth as *formless and empty*, verse 2 refers to *the deep* and *the waters*. Over the deep is darkness and over the waters is *the Spirit of God*.[8] Whereas the darkness appears to be static in nature, the *Spirit of God* hovers over the waters like a bird. This creates an expectation that God is about to act. Against this background Days 1 and 2–3 address the darkness and the waters respectively. In Day 1 darkness is separated by the introduction of a period of light to create *day* and *night*. In Day 2 the waters are divided to create the sky that separates the waters below from the waters above. A further separation of the waters under the sky occurs on Day 3 when dry land is created. In the light of these developments, verse 2 sets the scene, enabling the reader to make sense

---

[7] D. T. Tsumura, *Creation and Destruction: A Reappraisal of the Chaoskampf Theory in the Old Testament* (Winona Lake: Eisenbrauns, 2005), p. 35.

[8] The expression *rûaḥ 'ĕlōhîm* could possibly also be translated 'spirit of God' or 'wind of God'.

of God's actions in Days 1–3. The *darkness* and the *deep/waters* are the components from which everything else is formed. Allowing for the brevity of what is said, there is no reason to believe that the *darkness* and *deep/waters* existed prior to the beginning of God's creative activity (cf. Ps. 148:4–5; Isa. 45:7). Nor is there reason to think, as is sometimes claimed, that verse 2 describes a state of chaos.[9]

3. Day 1 (1:3–5)

The report of God's actions on Day 1 gives us cause to think carefully about the nature of what is being described. The author draws attention not to the creation of light as an electromagnetic force, but to the creation of light as it relates to time. Day 1 is about the separation of darkness by a period of light. Consequently, God names the light *day* and the darkness *night*. The concluding statement in verse 5 that *there was evening, and there was morning* draws attention to the transitions between day and night.[10] Day 1 is about God's ordering of time. As we shall see, Day 4, which corresponds with Day 1, focuses on how God establishes the greater and lesser lights to govern time, not only as regards day and night, but also in terms of sacred times[11] and years.

The unexpected introduction of days prior to the creation of the sun and moon has an important bearing on how Genesis 1 should be interpreted. We should be slow to jump to the conclusion that the author is describing events that took place in a week consisting of seven days, each of twenty-four hours. There is a sophistication to what is narrated in Genesis 1 that belies its apparent simplicity.[12] It is, in the words of Bruce Waltke and Cathi Fredricks, 'an artistic, literary representation of creation'.[13]

---

[9] Tsumura, *Creation and Destruction*, offers a detailed refutation of the idea that Genesis 1 presupposes a state of chaos.

[10] In the Pentateuch the day is reckoned as beginning with sunrise; see D. Miano, *Shadow on the Steps: Time Measurement in Ancient Israel*, RBS 64 (Atlanta: Society of Biblical Literature, 2010), pp. 8–13. Due to Babylonian influence after the fall of Jerusalem in 586 BC, the day was understood as beginning with sunset.

[11] Such times were determined by lunar months. Each month begins with a new moon.

[12] For a discussion of these issues, see J. D. Charles (ed.), *Reading Genesis 1 – 2: An Evangelical Conversation* (Peabody: Hendrickson, 2013); V. S. Poythress, *Christian Interpretations of Genesis 1*, Christian Answers to Hard Questions (Philadelphia: P&R, 2013).

[13] B. K. Waltke and C. J. Fredricks, *Genesis: A Commentary* (Grand Rapids: Zondervan, 2001), p. 78. In arriving at this assessment, they draw on H. Blocher, *In the Beginning: The Opening Chapters of Genesis* (Leicester: Inter-Varsity Press, 1984), pp. 50–59.

4. Day 2 (1:6–8)

Whereas Day 1 involves the *darkness* mentioned in verse 2, Day 2 centres on the *waters*. Like the darkness, the waters are separated. By doing this, God forms a vault or expanse, which he names *sky*, with waters located both above and below. In due course, this expanse will be populated with *lights* (14–19) and *birds* (20).

5. Day 3 (1:9–13)

On Day 3 God's attention turns to the waters under the sky. By gathering these together, dry land is created. In a break from the pattern of Days 1–2, God issues a second instruction on Day 3. He commands the earth to produce vegetation (11–12). By the end of Day 3, God has created three distinctive spaces – land, sea and sky – and has provided the resources necessary for them to sustain the mobile creatures with which they will begin to be populated on Days 4–6. The importance of these three regions is underlined by the fact that, apart from *day* and *night*, these are the only objects named by God in Genesis 1.

6. Day 4 (1:14–19)

Having responded to the formlessness (*tōhû*) of the earth mentioned in verse 2, God proceeds in Days 4–6 to address its emptiness (*bōhû*) by filling the various regions already created. Day 4 focuses on the creation of the sun, moon and stars that are placed in the sky/heavens. To underscore the connection between Days 1 and 4, the sun and moon are referred to as the greater and lesser lights. The designation *lights* (*mě'ōrōt*; plural of *mā'ôr*) recalls the creation of *light* (*'ôr*) on Day 1.[14]

Although God forms *day* and *night* on Day 1, he delegates the task of governing them to the greater and lesser lights. While the existence of day and night prior to the creation of the sun and moon is baffling from a scientific perspective, the order in Genesis 1 underlines that God is ultimately responsible for the ordering of time, not the sun and moon. They merely regulate time at his command. To view the sun and moon as deities, as

---

14 Some scholars suggest that the designations *greater light* and *lesser light* are an intentional polemic against those who viewed the sun and moon as deities. It is more likely, however, that these designations are intended to highlight the correspondence between Days 1 and 4.

some did in the Ancient Near East, is misguided and wrong. God alone is the one to be worshipped. Importantly, the concept of delegated authority will reappear when God instructs humans to rule over the earth.

7. Day 5 (1:20–23)

On Day 5 God begins the process of filling the two regions created on Day 2: the waters under the sky and the vault of the sky. God says, *Let the water teem with living creatures, and let birds fly above the earth across the vault of the sky* (20). The mention of *the great creatures of the sea and every living thing with which the water teems and that moves about in it* (21) points towards the variety of creatures associated with the waters. Blessed by God, the sea creatures are to fill the seas by being fruitful and increasing in number. God will express similar expectations as regards humans filling the earth.

8. Day 6 (1:24–31)

Day 6 reveals in two stages God's plans for the filling of the dry land. Before focusing on humans, God commands the earth to produce living creatures. The earth has a role to play, but under God's authority. Three categories of land animals are mentioned: *the livestock, the creatures that move along the ground, and the wild animals* (24). While most scholars suggest that the final two categories denote small and large animals respectively, such a distinction could have been explained more clearly. Adopting a different approach, Iain Provan suggests that the expression *wild animals* refers to predators, whereas the Hebrew term *remeś*, which NIV translates *creatures that move along the ground*, refers to non-predatory animals.[15] If a distinction involving carnivores and non-carnivores is being made, it has important implications, for it challenges the often made suggestion that all creatures had vegetarian diets prior to Adam and Eve's disobedience in the garden of Eden.

After instructing the earth to bring forth land animals, God announces his intention to create humans. Corresponding with Day 3, God gives a second command. Surprisingly, he says, *Let us make mankind in our*

---

[15] I. W. Provan, *Discovering Genesis: Content, Interpretation, Reception*, Discovering Biblical Texts (London: SPCK, 2015), pp. 123–124.

image, in our likeness (26). God's words are unexpected, for until this point in the narrative he alone has been the sole subject of all that has happened. No mention has been made of anyone accompanying him.

What does God mean when he says *us* and *our*? Various proposals have been offered to explain this peculiar feature.[16] Some scholars suggest that God is addressing the members of his heavenly court. Others propose that he is addressing himself in the form of a self-deliberation or self-summons. However, a better explanation is possible, drawing on what is said in verse 27. Unfortunately, the NIV translation obscures an important feature of the Hebrew text. A more literal rendering of verse 27 would read,

> And God created the human[17] [*hā'ādām*] in his own image,
> in the image of God he created him;
> male and female he created them.

Observing how 'he created him' parallels 'he created them', Thomas Keiser contends that the references to God and humankind as both singular and plural establish a correspondence between them. He suggests that 'the text's presentation of the plurality of humanity in terms of sexual diversity in some manner reflects something of the unity in the plurality of God'.[18] In Genesis 2 considerable attention is given to demonstrating the reality of a close bond between 'man' and 'woman', with them becoming 'one flesh'.[19] As an example of unity and plurality, the husband–wife relationship provides an insight into a relational dimension of God's nature. While this brief signal of unity and plurality in God's nature lacks the detail that will emerge later in the New Testament, God's use of *us* and *our* is consistent with the concept of a God who is Three in One.

What does it mean for humans to be made in the image of God (*imago Dei*)? The NIV, unlike some translations, helpfully notes the link that exists

---

16 For helpful summaries, see D. J. A. Clines, 'The Image of God in Man', *Tyndale Bulletin* (1968), pp. 63–69; G. F. Hasel, 'Meaning of "Let Us" in Gn 1:26', *AUSS* 13 (1975), pp. 58–66.

17 R. Alter, *Genesis* (New York: W. W. Norton, 1996), p. 5, makes a strong case for translating *hā'ādām* as 'the human' in this context. For a discussion of the translation of *'ādām* in the opening chapters of Genesis, see R. S. Hess, 'Splitting the Adam: The Usage of *'ādām* in Genesis I – v', in J. A. Emerton (ed.), *Studies in the Pentateuch*, VTSup 41 (Leiden: Brill, 1990), pp. 1–15.

18 T. A. Keiser, 'The Divine Plural: A Literary-Contextual Argument of Plurality in the Godhead', *JSOT* 34 (2009), p. 137.

19 Gen. 2:24. The closeness of the relationship between the man and the woman is also reflected in what the man says: 'This is now bone of my bones and flesh of my flesh; she shall be called "woman", for she was taken out of man' (2:23).

between humans being made in God's image and their ruling over *the fish in the sea and the birds in the sky, over the livestock and all the wild animals, and over all the creatures that move along the ground* (26).[20] This provides an important clue for understanding the concept of *imago Dei*. To be made in the image of God is to be given royal status as God's vicegerents. By making humans in his image, God delegates to them the role of governing on his behalf all other earthly creatures. As Ian Hart comments, 'Exercising royal dominion over the earth as God's representative is the basic purpose for which God created man.'[21] By commissioning humans to function as his vicegerents, God indicates that they will be responsible for establishing his kingdom on the earth.[22] To achieve this goal, they must fill the earth. God's rule over the earth will come through an ever-expanding human population. They will be his kingdom builders.

Support for linking the concept of *imago Dei* to humanity's vicegerent status comes from a consideration of how the expression 'image of god' was used in other Ancient Near Eastern cultures. In both Egypt and Mesopotamia, kings were commonly viewed as being made in the image or likeness of a deity. In a text associated with the Egyptian king Ramesses II (1290–1224 BC) we read,

> Utterance of the divine king, Lord of the Two Lands, lord of the form of Khepri, in whose limbs is Re, who came forth from Re, whom Ptah-Tatenen begat, King Ramses II, given life; to his father, from whom he came forth, Tatenen, father of the gods: 'I am thy son whom thou hast placed upon thy throne. Thou hast assigned to me thy kingdom, thou hast fashioned me in thy likeness and thy form, which thou hast assigned to me and hast created.'[23]

---

[20] B. Ollenburger, 'Creation and Peace: Creator and Creature in Genesis 1 – 11', in J. M. Isaak (ed.), *The Old Testament in the Life of God's People: Essays in Honor of Elmer A. Martens* (Winona Lake: Eisenbrauns, 2009), p. 146, states, 'Humanity's creation in (or as) the image of God and on the model of God's likeness has as its purpose the designated responsibility for human beings to rule or to exercise governance over or among the other creatures.'

[21] I. Hart, 'Genesis 1:1 – 2:3 as a Prologue to the Book of Genesis', *Tyndale Bulletin* 46 (1995), p. 322.

[22] S. Grindheim, *Living in the Kingdom of God: A Biblical Theology for the Life of the Church* (Grand Rapids: Baker Academic, 2018), p. 6, writes, 'To be a bearer of God's image means to be God's vice-regent; it means to govern on God's behalf.'

[23] J. H. Breasted, *Ancient Records of Egypt: The Nineteenth Dynasty*, 4 vols. (Chicago: University of Chicago Press, 1906), 3:181. For further examples, see J. R. Middleton, *The Liberating Image: The Imago Dei in Genesis 1* (Grand Rapids: Brazos, 2005), pp. 108–122.

Ramesses/Ramses speaks of his kingship in terms of being fashioned in the likeness of the god Re (also known as Ra). While other cultures restricted the concept of being made in the image of a deity to individual kings, Genesis 1 is revolutionary in stating that all humans are made in God's image. This democratization of royalty is an important counter-cultural statement that sets Genesis apart from other worldviews in antiquity.

By creating humans to rule over the earth, God expects them to rule on his behalf, exercising dominion in his name and governing as he would. They are to manage the natural world for the benefit of all its inhabitants.[24] As Iain Provan comments, 'Properly exercised royal power in the OT is not absolute and unfettered power that can be deployed just in any way that the king desires.'[25] In commissioning humans to govern the world as his image bearers, God expects them to act as he would act. They are not at liberty to exercise power autonomously. At all times they remain answerable to God as his appointed representatives.

By delegating authority to humans God privileges them above other creatures. Unfortunately, the continuing story in Genesis reveals that people fail to rule as God's representatives. This failure comes to the fore in Genesis 3 when the human couple believe the seditious insinuations of the serpent and eat from the tree of the knowledge of good and evil. By obeying a creature, over which they are expected to rule, they betray the trust that their creator God had placed in them. Their actions contradict their status as God's vicegerents. No longer can they legitimately claim to rule the earth on God's behalf. As we shall see in our next chapter, the events of Genesis 3 have important consequences for the establishment of God's kingdom on the earth.

While God intends that humanity's government of the earth should resemble his oversight of all creation, the use of the verb *kbš* 'subdue' in verse 28 possibly indicates that there may be resistance to humanity's rule. Karl Möller suggests that 'the human task envisaged here may involve some kind of struggle'.[26] The use of 'subdue' possibly anticipates the

---

24 Hart, 'Genesis 1:1 – 2:3', p. 323, writes, 'The command to "have dominion" (רדה, vv. 26, 28) is not merely a declaration that man will enjoy kingly rank; it is the apportioning of a task, an ongoing task which would be well translated by the more modern word "manage".'

25 Provan, *Discovering Genesis*, p. 66.

26 K. Möller, 'Images of God and Creation in Genesis 1 – 2', in J. A. Grant et al. (eds.), *A God of Faithfulness: Essays in Honour of J. Gordon McConville on His 60th Birthday*, LHB/OTS 538 (New York: T&T Clark, 2011), p. 23. Provan, *Discovering Genesis*, p. 64, comments that 'there are already forces in God's good world that *require* being ruled and subdued' (italics in original).

existence of creatures who will oppose God's rule on the earth. No explanation is given in Genesis 2 – 3 as to why the serpent tempts Adam and Eve to rebel against God. The serpent is merely introduced as being 'more crafty than any of the wild animals the LORD God had made' (3:1).

9. Day 7 (2:1–3)

Having instructed humans to establish his kingdom on the earth by ruling as his vicegerents, God rests from his creative activity. Reflecting this, the pattern of Days 1–6 is no longer repeated. By way of signalling the importance of God's resting *from all his work*, God blesses the seventh day and makes it holy. Completion of work is linked to rest and holiness. Implicit in this is the idea that the goal of human activity in establishing God's kingdom on the earth will also be rest and holiness. As readers of Genesis, we wait to see the outcome. We know, however, from our present experience of life that humanity's rule over the earth falls far short of creating a harmonious world in which all of creation is blessed by God. We long for the time of rest and holiness (cf. Heb. 4:1–11).

10. Conclusion

With amazing succinctness, the opening chapter of Genesis sets the scene for all that is subsequently narrated. While God is never directly referred to as a king, we witness the creative activity of a transcendent, all-powerful deity, who has the authority to entrust to others the duty of governing different aspects of his creation. Importantly, God graciously creates humans to be his vicegerents, privileging them above all other earthly creatures. They are to be his kingdom builders on the earth. By instructing them to fill the earth, God expects humans over time to establish God's kingdom throughout the earth. While everything that God does is *very good* (1:31), there is perhaps the smallest of hints that all is not quite perfect. It remains to be seen if humans will fulfil their divine calling to subdue the earth and rule over *the fish in the sea and the birds in the sky and over every living creature that moves on the ground* (1:28). How will they govern as God's vicegerents? How will God's kingdom be established on the earth?

Genesis 3:1–24

2. A royal betrayal

Disappointments and hurts come in many forms. We live in a world where people can be exceptionally cruel to others. When enemies attack us, we are rarely surprised. We may anticipate it and brace ourselves for it. Exceedingly more painful, however, are the wounds of betrayal, when we are unexpectedly stabbed in the back by those we lovingly trusted. Tragically, as we shall see, this is how Adam and Eve behave towards God.

Genesis opens with a panoramic view of creation that climaxes with God commissioning humanity to rule over the earth on his behalf. As Sigurd Grindheim observes, 'God's plan was for his kingly rule to be executed by humans.'[1] With this expectation in view, Genesis 2:4–25 offers a complementary perspective on how God creates the first human couple. This fuller account expands in a focused way on what is recorded concerning Day 6 in Genesis 1, highlighting especially God's intimate involvement in forming first Adam and then Eve.

1. God's generous care

Whereas Genesis 1 portrays God as transcendent, existing outside of creation, Genesis 2 presents a picture of God as immanent, undertaking specific tasks that are earthbound. Like a sculptor, he forms the man from the dust of the ground, breathing into his nostrils the breath of life (7). God plants a garden, where he settles the man (8, 15). God addresses the

---

[1] S. Grindheim, *Living in the Kingdom of God: A Biblical Theology for the Life of the Church* (Grand Rapids: Baker Academic, 2018), p. 6.

man, giving instructions that are to be obeyed (16–17). He brings animals and birds to the man that he might name them (19–20). Like a surgeon, God operates on the man to create from him a woman (21–22). In all these ways, Genesis 2 underlines God's close relationship with the human couple living in the garden of Eden. They are of special interest to him, in keeping with how Genesis 1 portrays humans as God's vicegerents, made in his image.

Adding to this sense of humanity's exclusive status in relation to God, Genesis 2 highlights how the man and woman are privileged by God to enjoy a unique environment located at the heart of the earth. The central setting of the garden of Eden is implied by the inclusion of details about a river that waters the garden and then separates into *four headwaters* (10). Everything points to the garden enjoying an elevated and central location. This is no ordinary setting.

Favoured above other creatures, the couple reside in a divinely constructed garden that is filled with *all kinds of trees* that are *pleasing to the eye and good for food* (9). Strikingly, this garden is distinguished from the field, the region outside the garden that has its own plants and animals.[2] This distinction between garden and field sets the former apart as a special location. Craig Bartholomew captures something of this when he writes,

> Rather than Gen 2 presenting an image of primitivism, it would appear to portray an area bounded, probably by walls, which is carefully landscaped and intensively cultivated with orchards and the like. It may well have included buildings – its urban connotations in the ancient Near East are particularly interesting in the light of the tendency to portray Eden as a form of primitivism. Thus God, as King, a central image of God in Gen 1, plants a garden, and as the under-kings, Adam and Eve dwell in the garden, which is a royal residence.[3]

God's special interest in the man, whom he has personally formed, is evident from the measures that he takes to provide for him. To care for his

---

[2] Unfortunately, the NIV translation omits to translate the term 'field' in 2:5 but does so in 3:18. Other English translations read 'plant of the field' (e.g. CSB; ESV) or something similar in 2:5. 'Field' also comes in 2:19–20 and 3:1, with reference to animals. The NIV renders the Hebrew text 'wild animals', whereas ESV adopts the more literal rendering 'beast[s] of the field'.

[3] C. G. Bartholomew, 'The Theology of Place in Genesis 1 – 3', in J. G. McConville and K. Möller (eds.), *Reading the Law: Studies in Honour of Gordon J. Wenham*, LHB/OTS 461 (Edinburgh: T&T Clark, 2007), p. 187.

physical needs, God creates a well-irrigated garden that abounds with all kinds of trees bearing fruit for food. Recognizing that something is still missing for the man's well-being (see 2:18), God creates a companion, who is, in the man's words, *bone of my bones and flesh of my flesh* (23). Designed to complement each other, the man and his wife form a unique union, becoming *one flesh* (24).

Set alongside the panoramic view of creation, Genesis 2:4–25 enhances the initial picture of humans as God's vicegerents. Their special role on earth is reinforced by their privileged location. God ensures that they have every opportunity to flourish, placing only one restriction on them: they are not to eat from the fruit of the tree of the knowledge of good and evil (17).

2. An unwelcome visitor

The harmony of the garden is disrupted by the unexpected arrival of a serpent that is described, somewhat ominously, as the craftiest of all the wild animals (3:1). Few details are provided. The history of the mysterious talking serpent is not disclosed. However, it quickly becomes apparent that this creature is no innocent onlooker. As the serpent is associated with the 'field',[4] there is good reason to think that the garden is not the serpent's natural habitat. There is something suspicious about its unexpected presence. This sense is reinforced when the serpent speaks, alluding to what God has told the man, but misrepresenting God's words: *Did God really say, 'You must not eat from any tree in the garden'?* (1).

The picture of this talking serpent, misrepresenting God, strongly suggests that it is no ordinary creature. While the serpent's identity is not disclosed fully by the author of Genesis, later biblical traditions associate the 'ancient snake' with 'the devil, or Satan, who leads the whole world astray'.[5] Capturing the serpent's true nature, James McKeown writes, 'Its devious arguments and malicious intention are enough to make it clear that this snake symbolizes evil – not the belligerent, aggressive kind of evil, but the subtle and seductive kind.'[6]

---

[4] The NIV translation *wild animals* in 3:1 could be rendered more literally 'beasts of the field' (cf. ESV).

[5] Rev. 12:9; cf. John 8:44; 1 John 3:8; Rev. 20:2. For a fuller discussion, see P. R. Williamson, 'Snakes and Dragons: A Neglected Theologial Trajectory of Genesis 3:15 in Scripture?', in P. R. Williamson and R. F. Cefalu (eds.), *The Seed of Promise: The Sufferings and Glory of the Messiah; Essays in Honor of T. Desmond Alexander*, GlossaHouse Festschrift Series 3 (Wilmore: GlossaHouse, 2020), pp. 332–352.

[6] J. McKeown, *Genesis*, Two Horizons Old Testament Commentary 1 (Grand Rapids: Eerdmans, 2008), pp. 34–35.

The serpent's words cleverly engage the woman. It speaks of *God*, avoiding his personal name Yahweh, which is translated 'LORD' in most English Bible versions. The serpent distances itself from the Lord God. Questioning the woman, the serpent implies that God is far from generous: *Did God really say, 'You must not eat from any tree in the garden'?* Yet in 2:16–17 God had told the man, 'You are free to eat from any tree in the garden; but you must not eat from the tree of the knowledge of good and evil, for when you eat from it you will certainly die.'

Replying to the serpent, the woman says,

> *We may eat fruit from the trees in the garden, but God did say, 'You must not eat fruit from the tree that is in the middle of the garden, and you must not touch it, or you will die.'*
> (2–3)

In her attempt to correct the serpent, the woman fails to report accurately God's earlier instructions. She may have been misinformed by her husband, or she may have forgotten exactly what was said. Either way, she alters God's words. She makes his command more restrictive by stating that they must not touch the tree, and she weakens the emphasis that God places on the certainty of punishment. These subtle changes suggest that the woman has not taken to heart God's instructions.

The serpent, a master of half-lies, possibly senses that the woman is amenable to disobeying God's command. Seizing the opportunity, the serpent contradicts God's warning by suggesting that God wants to prevent the humans from becoming like him, *knowing good and evil* (5). The serpent tells the woman, *You will not certainly die . . . For God knows that when you eat from it your eyes will be opened, and you will be like God, knowing good and evil* (4–5).

In the face of the serpent's seditious promptings, the couple should have exercised their God-given authority as vicegerents, wholeheartedly and unreservedly siding with God. However, they desire to be more than vicegerents. Betraying their Creator and benefactor, they yield to the serpent's temptation. In doing so, the humans elevate the serpent over God. Their actions reveal that the serpent's word carries greater authority than that of God.

Not only do the human couple directly disobey God's command, but in doing so they abandon their duty as his vicegerents. Disregarding God's instructions (1:26, 28), they fail to rule over a wild animal.[7] In their treachery they reject God's ordering of creation. Rather than governing the serpent, they heed its advice. And with the human couple under its control, the serpent can claim lordship over the earth. The authority entrusted to them by God passes to the serpent. It becomes the de facto ruler of this world (see John 12:31; 14:30; 16:11). In their desire to become like God, knowing good and evil, the human couple become the agents of evil as they betray the trust placed in them by God.

In the light of all that God has done, giving them authority to govern the whole earth, the disobedience of the human couple is a betrayal of the greatest magnitude. They turn against the one who has generously given them everything that they need to enjoy life to the full. We should not underestimate the seriousness of their betrayal of God. Their blatant disregard of God's instruction is unspeakably heinous for they have been created to be God's vicegerents and privileged above all other earthly creatures.

Against the background of Adam and Eve's betrayal of God, it is worth recalling how Jesus Christ responds when tempted by the devil. The Gospel writer Matthew records what happened:

> Again, the devil took him to a very high mountain and showed him all the kingdoms of the world and their splendour. 'All this I will give you,' he said, 'if you will bow down and worship me.'
> Jesus said to him, 'Away from me, Satan! For it is written: "Worship the Lord your God, and serve him only."'[8]

Astoundingly, the devil offers Jesus 'all the kingdoms of the world and their splendour'. This is no idle offer. This would be a meaningless temptation if they were not his to give. As the ruler of this world, the devil controls its kingdoms. The timing of his intervention is also significant. He makes his offer as Jesus Christ is about to launch his ministry of preaching and healing, with the intention of establishing God's kingdom on the earth (see Matt. 4:17, 23). As the serpent thwarted the rule of Adam and Eve, God's first vicegerents, the devil attempts to thwart the actions of Jesus Christ, God's perfect vicegerent. The outcomes, however, are very different.

---

[7] Gen. 1:26 specifically mentions wild animals as one of the categories to be governed by humans.

[8] Matt. 4:8–10; cf. Luke 4:5–7.

Adam and Eve's actions have an immediate impact on them. They acquire knowledge that they did not have before. They become aware of their nakedness and develop a sense of shame that causes them to hide from God. They now have a personal knowledge of evil that makes them fearful of God. Consequently, when God confronts them for eating from the tree of the knowledge of good and evil, they look to shift culpability to someone else. The man blames the woman; the woman blames the serpent. All, however, are guilty. Consequently, God addresses each of them in turn, announcing their punishment.

3. God's response to the serpent

Appropriately, God begins with the serpent, declaring,

> Because you have done this,
> Cursed are you above all livestock
>   and all wild animals!
> You will crawl on your belly
>   and you will eat dust
>   all the days of your life.
> And I will put enmity
>   between you and the woman,
>   and between your offspring and hers;
> he will crush your head,
>   and you will strike his heel.
> (14–15)

God curses the serpent, setting it apart from all other wild animals and livestock. In humiliation, it will be forced to crawl on its belly and eat dust. There is an element of poetic justice in the punishment; because it deceived the woman, the serpent will be punished by the woman's offspring.

Ancient tradition, stretching back to at least the second century BC, has understood the woman's offspring to be an individual. This is how the earliest Greek translation of Genesis interpreted the Hebrew text. Later, within the nascent Christian church, this reference to the defeat of the serpent was understood as alluding to Jesus Christ's overthrow of the devil. For this reason, verse 15 became known as the Protevangelium, the first announcement of the gospel or good news.

This interpretation remains important, although it has encountered considerable resistance in the past hundred years as some scholars have contended that the serpent will be defeated by the woman's offspring in general, and not by a single offspring. This alternative interpretation centres on the Hebrew term translated *offspring*. While most Hebrew nouns have distinctive singular and plural forms, the noun *zeraʿ* 'offspring' remains the same regardless of number. It resembles words like 'sheep' or 'fish' in English. A plural reading of 'offspring' creates the possibility that all of Eve's descendants will be responsible for defeating the serpent and not merely a single descendant.

Although this alternative approach has enjoyed much support, even from some conservative scholars,[9] it should be firmly rejected. First, the syntax of the sentence strongly favours a single offspring. The final part of verse 15 uses a singular verb and pronoun to refer to the woman's offspring. Had God intended to speak of offspring in the plural, he could have expressed this unambiguously by saying, 'They will crush your head, and you will strike their heels.'

Second, the continuing story in Genesis does not promote a plural interpretation of 'offspring'. There is nothing in the rest of Genesis to suggest that humanity in general will overcome the serpent. On the contrary, as the flood narrative reveals, almost all of the human race continues to side with the serpent against God. Noah alone stands apart (6:5–8). To suggest that the serpent, later identified as the devil, will be defeated by all of humanity, as a plural interpretation of offspring would suggest, runs counter to later Christian teaching that ascribes the defeat of the devil to Jesus Christ alone.

This latter observation draws attention to another important feature of the book of Genesis. From beginning to end, the Genesis story is centred around a unique patriline (that is, the line of descent traced only through males) that highlights one individual in each generation. As we shall see in our next chapter, this patriline, which is carefully demarcated throughout Genesis, anticipates the coming of a perfect vicegerent who will bring God's blessing to all the nations of the earth. There is every reason to think that this future individual will defeat the serpent.

---

9 See, for example, A. T. Abernethy and G. Goswell, *God's Messiah in the Old Testament: Expectations of a Coming King* (Grand Rapids: Baker Academic, 2020), p. 13, who write, 'It seems most natural, then, to interpret Gen. 3:15 as referring more generally to the continual enmity between evil and the sons and daughters of Eve in general.'

4. God's response to Adam and Eve

While the serpent bears much of the responsibility for cunningly encouraging Adam and Eve to betray God, the human couple are not blameless. For disregarding God's instructions and siding with the serpent, they also are punished. Addressing the woman, God says,

> *I will make your pains in childbearing very severe;*
> *with painful labour you will give birth to children.*
> *Your desire will be for your husband,*
> *and he will rule over you.*
>
> (16)

The NIV translation assumes that Eve's punishment mainly involves childbearing. God's words, however, may be interpreted more broadly as referring to both 'toil' and 'progeny'. The Hebrew expression translated *pains in childbearing* is *'iṣṣĕbônēk wĕhērōnēk*, which may be rendered more literally 'your painful toil and your pregnancy'. While many scholars assume that this expression is an example of hendiadys, with the two nouns together denoting one item, Carol Meyers has presented a good case for interpreting the nouns separately. She understands God to be saying, 'I will greatly increase your work and your pregnancies; (Along) with toil you shall give birth to children.'[10] According to Meyers, Eve's punishment will involve 'painful labour' which is not necessarily linked to childbearing. This reference to her productive work corresponds to the *painful toil* that the man must undertake to cultivate food (17).[11] While the woman will suffer pain, she will also give birth to children, reassurance that she will produce an offspring to overcome the serpent.

The interpretation of the second half of God's remark to Eve has prompted much discussion, with scholars differing over the precise meaning of the pronouncement. God says, *Your desire will be for your husband, and he will rule over you*. A somewhat similar statement occurs in 4:7, when God warns Cain that sin desires to control him, but he must

---

[10] C. L. Meyers, 'Gender Roles and Genesis 3:16 Revisited', in C. L. Meyers and K. M. O'Connor (eds.), *The Word of the Lord Shall Go Forth: Essays in Honor of David Noel Freedman* (Winona Lake: Eisenbrauns, 1983), p. 344. Cf. R. S. Hess, 'The Roles of the Woman and the Man in Genesis 3', *Themelios* 18 (1993), p. 17. Meyers assumes that God will increase the number of pregnancies, but it is possible that this refers to the length of the pregnancy. The Hebrew term *hērōnēk* 'your pregnancy' is singular.

[11] The Hebrew term *'iṣṣābôn*, which is linked to the woman's punishment, comes also in v. 17 with reference to the man's punishment.

rule over it. In this context 'desire' signifies control, and this is probably how it is best understood in 3:16. When it comes to interpreting the second half of verse 16, much depends upon how the husband–wife relationship is viewed prior to the act of betrayal. For those who believe that at creation God affirmed male headship over the woman, God's words to Eve in verse 16b may indicate that, despite the woman's desire to control her husband, God expects the man to exercise leadership. Alternatively, God may be instructing the woman to submit to her husband in order to be blessed in line with God's expectations when they were created. For those who contend that Adam and Eve enjoyed an egalitarian relationship before they disobeyed God, verse 16b possibly indicates that, contrary to God's design, women will find themselves being controlled by men as part of their punishment. Alternatively, God may be instructing the woman, as a concession to human sinfulness, to live in submission to her husband.

Bearing in mind the various interpretations of verse 16b, we should be wary of relying too much on this single verse for endorsing a particular stance on the relationship between husbands and wives. We can, however, be certain that because of their actions in betraying God, the human couple will no longer experience the harmonious relationship that they enjoyed previously. Tensions will exist, creating what today we might term the battle of the sexes. The woman will desire to control her husband, but he will want to rule over her.

Turning to the man, God says,

Because you listened to your wife and ate fruit from the tree about
*   which I commanded you, 'You must not eat from it,'*
Cursed is the ground because of you;
*   through painful toil you will eat food from it*
*   all the days of your life.*
It will produce thorns and thistles for you,
*   and you will eat the plants of the field.*
By the sweat of your brow
*   you will eat your food*
until you return to the ground,
*   since from it you were taken;*
for dust you are
*   and to dust you will return.*
(17–19)

God's punishment of the man centres on his special relationship with the ground. Apart from the fact that the Hebrew nouns for man ('ādām) and ground ('ădāmâ) reflect their close connection, the man ('ādām) is created to cultivate the ground ('ădāmâ) (implied in 2:5), and God fashions him from the dust of the ground (2:7). Like 'art' and 'artist', the man and the ground are meant to go together.[12] This unique relationship, however, is now disrupted. Due to the man's disregard for God's instruction, the ground is cursed. From now on the task of cultivation will involve *painful toil* and the ground will produce *thorns and thistles*. God's judgment also implies that the man will no longer enjoy the fruit of the numerous trees growing in the garden of Eden. His diet will consist of the *plants of the field*, which he will cultivate by the sweat of his brow. By emphasizing *the field*, God's words anticipate the expulsion of the man and the woman from the garden (see verses 23–24). No longer will they enjoy the bountiful provision of fruit from the trees of the garden. Finally, recalling how man was formed from the dust of the ground, God announces that he will return to dust. While physical death will not come immediately, the human couple will be denied the opportunity to live for ever. This outcome is reinforced when God expels them from the garden and prevents them from accessing the tree of life (22–24).

5. Alienated from God

God's judgments on the serpent, the woman and the man reflect the seriousness of what has happened in the garden. By heeding the serpent, the human couple have elevated it above the Lord God. They have put a creature before the Creator. Their action reverses the order of creation. Despite their own elevated status as his vicegerents, they reject God's intended hierarchy. By disobeying God, the human couple can no longer claim to govern the earth on his behalf.

Reflecting the changed status of the human couple, God clothes Adam and Eve with *garments of skin*. Originally set apart to rule over all other earthly creatures, their new clothing signals that they now resemble these creatures. They are no longer vicegerents. While it is frequently suggested that God's clothing of Adam and Eve recalls the description of the priestly garments worn by Aaron the high priest and hints at some form of animal

---

[12] The terms 'earth' and 'earthling' capture something of this connection.

sacrifice,[13] there is little evidence to support this claim. If there is some connection with the clothing of the high priest, the symbolism indicates that Adam and Eve are being distanced from God. Those nearest to God wear clothing made from plants (i.e. linen); materials associated with the death of animals are avoided in the manufacture of priestly garments. The same is true for the coverings over the frame of the portable sanctuary. The innermost layer is made of linen, then comes a layer woven from goat hair, and finally there are two layers of animal skins (Exod. 26:1–14). Adam and Eve's clothing conveys negative connotations in keeping with their expulsion from the garden.

As God hinted in his judgment upon the man, Adam and Eve are driven out of the garden. Previously, they had been put in the garden 'to work [ʿābad] . . . and take care of [šāmar]' the ground (2:15). God now instructs them *to work the ground* outside the garden. However, reflecting their expulsion from the garden, God entrusts to *cherubim* and *a flaming sword* the task of guarding (šāmar) *the way to the tree of life.*

With their departure from the garden, life will be very different for Adam and Eve and their descendants. As Michael Morales observes,

> The path of exile through Eden's gates was, therefore, a path from life to death, from light to darkness, from harmony to dysfunction and strife, from health to sickness, from security to violence, from compassion to inhumanity, from wholeness to brokenness, from peace with God to enmity – from a life of friendship with God to alienation.[14]

From the outset of creation, God's plan was to establish his kingdom on the earth, where he would be loved and worshipped by those he had created. Yet this was a plan full of risk. As Sigmund Grindheim writes,

> It was a plan that shows us the magnitude of God's investment in the people he had formed. He had no interest in making robots with no will of their own, robots who blindly did what he had programmed them to

---

[13] See, for example, K. A. Mathews, *Genesis 1 – 11:26*, NAC 1A (Nashville: Broadman & Holman, 1995), pp. 254–255, who speaks of 'an oblique reference to animal sacrifice'. B. K. Waltke and C. J. Fredricks, *Genesis: A Commentary* (Grand Rapids: Zondervan, 2001), p. 95, refer to 'the "sacrifice" of an animal'. They write, 'Through his [God's] sacrifice, he restores the alienated couple to fellowship with him and one another.' There is, however, no indication in Genesis 3 that Adam and Eve are restored to fellowship with God and one another.

[14] L. M. Morales, *Exodus Old and New: A Biblical Theology of Redemption*, Essential Studies in Biblical Theology (Downers Grove: IVP Academic, 2020), p. 9.

do. God wanted his people to be his coworkers, and he loved them so much that he was willing to risk everything on one grand gesture of love. He left his entire creation in their care.[15]

To be loved without coercion opens the door for rejection. Unfortunately, Adam and Eve walk through this doorway, deceived into believing that they could be more than God's vicegerents. Tragically, they become less than God intended, for they now become subservient to the mysterious serpent and are alienated from the true source of life. They immediately experience spiritual death and their lives on earth will now be lived with the knowledge that they will experience physical death.

6. Conclusion

The consequences of Adam and Eve's betrayal of God are far-reaching and devastating. As Genesis 6 reveals, the increasing human population fills the earth with violence to such an extent that God decides to wipe out the whole of humanity. Only Noah and his closest relatives are saved from destruction. And after the flood, human nature is unchanged. People aspire to create kingdoms that stand in opposition to God. Despite these bleak developments, all is not lost. God offers hope that the serpent will be defeated through an offspring of the woman. And as we shall see in our next chapter, the continuing story of Genesis reveals in a much fuller way that the woman's offspring will bring divine blessing to all the nations of the earth. God's kingdom will eventually be established on the earth through a future divinely appointed vicegerent.

---

[15] Grindheim, *Living in the Kingdom of God*, p. 6.

Genesis 17:1–27

3. A saviour king is promised

For some people, knowing their family history is very important. It gives them a sense of identity, a sense of belonging. But tracing family histories can be very complicated. My grandmother's first husband died when she was quite young, leaving her with several children. She subsequently remarried and had more children, including my father. To complicate matters, her second husband was the brother of her sister's husband. For me as a young boy this all made for a complicated picture of uncles and aunts and great-uncles and great-aunts. In some ways, reading Genesis presents a similar challenge.

The book of Genesis derives its name from the Greek term *genesis*, which means 'genealogy'. The entire book traces a unique genealogical line, a patriline, that is vital to God's plan of salvation. As one of the central figures in this patriline, the patriarch Abraham plays a vital role in the fulfilment of God's redemptive plan for humanity and the world. The account of his life occupies an important place in the Genesis story. He is first named in 11:26 at the end of a linear genealogy that traces the patriline of Noah's eldest son, Shem, over ten generations. An earlier linear genealogy in Genesis 5 provides details of the patriline that runs from Adam to Noah. Taken together the genealogies in chapters 5 and 11 place Abraham in the unique lineage that traces the offspring of Eve. As possibly the most important human participant in Genesis Abraham's interaction with God is highly significant, anticipating a vicegerent who will overcome the serpent, as promised by God in 3:15. This future human king will play a central role in establishing God's kingdom on the earth.

The story of Abraham's life draws attention to how he is especially blessed by God. The theme of blessing is first introduced when God summons Abraham to leave his homeland and relocate to the land of Canaan. In 12:1–3 the Lord says to Abraham:

> Leave your country, your people, and your father's household and go to the land I will show you, so that I may make you into a great nation and bless you and make your name great. Be a blessing, so that I may bless those who bless you, and curse the one who disdains you, and so that all the families of the ground may be blessed through you.[1]

God promises to bless Abraham and through him bless others. We see evidence of these promises being fulfilled when Abraham, towards the end of his life, commissions his most senior servant to find a wife for his son Isaac. Trekking from Canaan to Paddan Aram, the servant is providentially led to a well where he encounters Isaac's future wife Rebekah. On finding Rebekah he subsequently describes how the Lord has blessed Abraham. He declares, 'I am Abraham's servant. The LORD has blessed my master abundantly, and he has become wealthy. He has given him sheep and cattle, silver and gold, male and female servants, and camels and donkeys.'[2] While in this instance Abraham's servant focuses on his master's material prosperity, this is but one aspect of how Abraham's special relationship with God has resulted in blessing. In the light of the divine curses recorded in Genesis 3 – 11, the theme of blessing takes on special significance, signalling hope for humanity.

1. God's covenant with Abraham (17:1–2)

Within the literary context of Genesis, Abraham is especially privileged by the fact that God speaks to him on various occasions. God's speech in Genesis 17 is especially noteworthy, forming the longest divine speech in the entire book. Importantly, this speech centres on the establishment of an eternal covenant between God and Abraham that has major implications for the establishment of God's kingdom in the world.

This covenant is exceptionally important, but frequently misunderstood. Its significance is recognized in the New Testament by the apostle

---

[1] Author's translation.
[2] Gen. 24:34–35.

Paul who perceptively observes that the promises contained within this covenant find their fulfilment in Jesus Christ. Paul writes to the churches in Galatia:

> Brothers and sisters, let me take an example from everyday life. Just as no one can set aside or add to a human covenant that has been duly established, so it is in this case. The promises were spoken to Abraham and to his seed. Scripture does not say 'and to seeds', meaning many people, but 'and to your seed', meaning one person, who is Christ. What I mean is this: the law, introduced 430 years later, does not set aside the covenant previously established by God and thus do away with the promise. For if the inheritance depends on the law, then it no longer depends on the promise; but God in his grace gave it to Abraham through a promise.[3]

In Paul's thinking, the Sinai covenant, which focuses on a special relationship between God and the nation of Israel, does not annul God's earlier covenant with Abraham. For Paul, the two covenants are very different in nature and content. While the Sinai covenant focuses on the creation of Israel as God's special nation, the Abrahamic covenant has important implications for the inclusion of Gentiles within the people of God.

a. Abraham's special calling

To appreciate the significance of the covenant that God establishes with Abraham in Genesis 17, we must understand the context in which it is given. This is not the first occasion on which God speaks to Abraham. Several decades previously the Lord had challenged Abraham, at that stage called Abram, to leave his homeland to establish a new life in a new country. Within the book of Genesis God's summons to Abraham is set against the background of the construction of the city of Babel/Babylon, with its high tower, in southern Mesopotamia.[4] As a consequence of the city builders' hubristic actions, God intervenes, confusing 'their language so they will not understand each other'. In addition, he scatters the people

---

[3] Gal. 3:15–18.
[4] The city is called Babel in most English translations. This is a transliteration of the Hebrew name *bābel*. However, in other passages in the Old Testament the name *bābel* is almost always translated 'Babylon'. For a fuller discussion, see T. D. Alexander, *The City of God and the Goal of Creation*, Short Studies in Biblical Theology (Wheaton: Crossway, 2018), pp. 33–29.

'over the face of the whole earth'.[5] The impact of God's intervention is anticipated in Genesis 10 which describes how the descendants of Noah form different nations that 'spread out over the earth after the flood'.[6] Against the background of different nations being formed God calls Abraham, promising that he will become 'a great nation'. More importantly, alongside this promise of nationhood, the Lord tells Abraham, 'All peoples on earth will be blessed through you.'[7]

Responding positively to God's invitation, Abraham leaves his family in Harran, having travelled there from southern Mesopotamia (11:31), and moves to the land of Canaan where he embraces a semi-nomadic lifestyle. Sometime after Abraham's arrival in Canaan, God recognizes Abraham's trust in him by making a unilateral covenant guaranteeing to Abraham that his descendants will take possession of the 'land, from the Wadi of Egypt to the great river, the Euphrates – the land of the Kenites, Kenizzites, Kadmonites, Hittites, Perizzites, Rephaites, Amorites, Canaanites, Girgashites and Jebusites'.[8] God makes this unconditional commitment to Abraham in response to Abraham's confidence or faith in him.

At this stage in his life, Abraham has no son. His wife Sarah is unable to bear children (11:30). When Abraham questions God regarding his lack of children (15:3), God promises him a son who will be his 'own flesh and blood'. By way of confirming this promise, God invites Abraham to count the stars, and tells him, 'So shall your offspring be.' Picking up on Abraham's trust in what God promises, the narrator of Genesis writes in 15:4–6, 'Abram believed the LORD, and he credited it to him as righteousness.' This statement is exceptionally important. At the heart of it is a vital biblical truth. Righteousness comes to an individual through faith in God, that is, trusting what God says, and not through a person's own efforts to live righteously. The idea of righteousness through faith runs through the unfolding story of the biblical gospel.

b. The birth of Ishmael

The events recorded in Genesis 15 focus in part on how God promises Abraham that he will have a son who will be his own flesh and blood.

---

[5] Gen. 11:7, 9.

[6] Gen. 10:32. Gen. 10:8–10 draws attention to how Nimrod establishes a kingdom that includes Babel/Babylon. Gen. 10:25 links the name Peleg, meaning 'division', with the earth being divided, a reference to the scattering of 11:9.

[7] Gen. 12:2–3.

[8] Gen. 15:18–21.

Sometime later, as recorded in Genesis 16, Abraham's wife, Sarah, persuades him to take her Egyptian maidservant as a concubine or second wife in the hope that she will bear Abraham a son on Sarah's behalf. By their actions, Sarah and Abraham attempt to provide a human solution to their lack of a son. However, when Hagar becomes pregnant, her relationship with her mistress Sarah degenerates. With Abraham's tacit approval, Sarah mistreats her pregnant maidservant, causing Hagar to run away from Abraham's household. As Hagar journeys towards Egypt, God intervenes and instructs her to return to her 'mistress and submit to her'.[9] Reassured by God that her son will be a free man, Hagar goes back to Abraham's household and bears him a son, who is named Ishmael, which means 'God hears'. As Abraham's subsequent actions reveal, he views Ishmael as the son promised by God. However, this turns out not to be the case.

Thirteen years after the birth of Ishmael, God appears to Abraham to establish an everlasting covenant with him. Abraham is *ninety-nine years old* (17:1) and Sarah is ten years younger. He and Sarah have been living in the land of Canaan for almost twenty-five years and both are past the normal age for having children. In addressing Abraham, God states that Sarah herself will bear him a son. This promise, as we shall see, is an important element in the covenant that God will establish with Abraham.

c. In step with God

With a minimum of descriptive detail, the narrator records that the Lord appeared to Abraham. God introduces himself with the title *God Almighty* (1). This is one of several names that appear in incidents involving Abraham. Each name captures an aspect of God's nature. Melchizedek refers to him as 'God Most High'. The divine name 'the Eternal God' occurs in the context of Abraham making a friendship treaty with Abimelek, king of Gerar.[10] In Genesis 17, the designation *God Almighty* draws attention to God's omnipotence, his power to perform amazing actions. In this instance, God will enable Sarah, who has been unable to conceive, to bear a son at the age of ninety.

Before introducing the substance of the covenant that he is about to establish with Abraham, God instructs Abraham: *walk before me*

---

9 Gen. 16:9.
10 Gen. 14:19; 21:33.

faithfully and be blameless (1). These commands recall what is said earlier in Genesis 6:9 concerning Noah: 'Noah was a righteous man, blameless among the people of his time, and he walked faithfully with God.'[11] This connection with Noah is noteworthy, because God established an eternal covenant with Noah and his descendants (9:9–17).

The concept of walking before God implies obedience. We might think of this as walking in step with God. It implies a continuing relationship in which Abraham is expected to live in harmony with God. This understanding is reinforced by the command to *be blameless*. Elsewhere in the Old Testament the Hebrew term *tāmîm*, translated *blameless*, is used to describe offerings made to God that are expected to be flawless, lacking imperfections (e.g. Exod. 12:5; Lev. 1:3, 10; 3:1). God has high expectations regarding Abraham's moral behaviour.[12]

While God has already reckoned Abraham to be righteous on the basis of his faith (15:6), there is an expectation that Abraham will demonstrate this righteousness in his daily life. As the apostle James observes, drawing on the example of Abraham, 'faith without deeds is useless'. James writes,

> Was not our father Abraham considered righteous for what he did when he offered his son Isaac on the altar? You see that his faith and his actions were working together, and his faith was made complete by what he did. And the scripture was fulfilled that says, 'Abraham believed God, and it was credited to him as righteousness,' and he was called God's friend. You see that a person is considered righteous by what they do and not by faith alone.[13]

In the light of James's remarks, God's command that Abraham should be blameless complements his righteousness by faith.

God's instructions to Abraham are a precondition for the covenant that is about to be established. This is conveyed clearly in the ESV translation of 17:1–2: 'I am God Almighty; walk before me, and be blameless, that I may make my covenant between me and you, and may multiply you greatly.' God will later test Abraham's obedience by asking him to sacrifice

---

[11] The concept of walking before God is also mentioned in connection with Enoch, who stands apart from all those listed in Gen. 5. Because Enoch walked faithfully with God, God took him away (5:24). Remarkably, Enoch does not die, unlike everyone else mentioned in the genealogy.

[12] Jesus presents a similar challenge to his followers when he tells them: 'Be perfect, therefore, as your heavenly Father is perfect' (Matt. 5:48).

[13] Jas 2:20–24.

his son Isaac (22:2). When Abraham demonstrates his willingness to obey, God intervenes and prevents Isaac from being killed. Importantly, after this God swears an oath that encapsulates and guarantees unconditionally the divine promises made to Abraham. God says,

> By myself I have sworn, declares the LORD, because you have done this and have not withheld your son, your only son, I will surely bless you, and I will surely multiply your offspring as the stars of heaven and as the sand that is on the seashore. And your offspring shall possess the gate of his enemies, and in your offspring shall all the nations of the earth be blessed, because you have obeyed my voice.[14]

This oath builds on the covenant introduced in Genesis 17 and possibly completes the process by which it is established.[15]

2. Abraham, the father of many nations (17:3–8)

Many scholars assume that the covenant of Genesis 17 is merely a reiteration of the covenant in chapter 15, with some minor additions. John Currid writes, 'Whereas Genesis 15 describes the inauguration of the Abrahamic covenant, Genesis 17 declares the institution of the covenant seal, one that Abraham and his posterity would wear on their very flesh.'[16] William Dumbrell views Genesis 17 'as a consolidation of the Abrahamic covenant and as an extension of its detail'.[17] Peter Gentry and Stephen Wellum view Genesis 15 and 17 as describing the making and confirming respectively of the same covenant.[18] Rejecting the idea of two separate covenants, they write, 'Instead, it is better to think of one covenant and to view Genesis 17 as a confirmation of God's covenant

---

[14] Gen. 22:16–18, ESV.

[15] See T. D. Alexander, 'Genesis 22 and the Covenant of Circumcision', *JSOT* 25 (1983), pp. 17–22; P. R. Williamson, *Abraham, Israel and the Nations: The Patriarchal Promise and Its Covenantal Development in Genesis*, JSOTSup 315 (Sheffield: Sheffield Academic, 2000), pp. 234–259.

[16] J. D. Currid, 'Genesis', in M. V. Van Pelt (ed.), *A Biblical-Theological Introduction to the Old Testament: The Gospel Promised* (Wheaton: Crossway, 2016), p. 59. For a fuller discussion of the relationship between chs. 15 and 17, see P. R. Williamson, *Sealed with an Oath: Covenant in God's Unfolding Purpose*, New Studies in Biblical Theology 23 (Leicester: Apollos, 2007), pp. 84–91. It is best to see the covenant of ch. 15 as being subsumed into the covenant of circumcision.

[17] W. J. Dumbrell, *Covenant and Creation: An Old Testament Covenantal Theology* (Exeter: Paternoster, 1984), p. 74.

[18] P. J. Gentry and S. J. Wellum, *Kingdom through Covenant: A Biblical-Theological Understanding of the Covenants* (Wheaton: Crossway, 2012), p. 277.

with Abraham initiated in Genesis 15, tied back to the promises of Genesis 12.'[19]

While these suggestions are understandable, given the presence of a covenant in chapter 15, the differences between chapter 17 and chapter 15 go far beyond minor additions. The covenant in Genesis 17 is fundamentally different, although, as we shall see, it subsumes the covenant of chapter 15.

In announcing the covenant to Abraham in Genesis 17, God declares,

As for me, this is my covenant with you: you will be the father of many nations. No longer will you be called Abram; your name will be Abraham, for I have made you a father of many nations. I will make you very fruitful; I will make nations of you, and kings will come from you.
(4–6)

At the core of this covenant is the concept of Abraham being *the father of many nations.* This fundamental idea is emphasized through repetition of the phrase *father of many nations* in verses 4 and 5. Confirming the importance of this concept, God changes Abram's name to the more familiar Abraham, which means 'father of a multitude'. The concept of Abraham being *the father of many nations* goes well beyond the covenant made in Genesis 15. On this previous occasion, the focus is simply on Abraham being the father of one nation, which will consist of his biological descendants who will dwell in the land of Canaan. Something radically different is in view in Genesis 17, but remarkably it subsumes the earlier covenant, which guarantees that Abraham will be the father of a single nation. In 17:4–6 God speaks emphatically of Abraham being *the father of many nations.* How is this best understood?

A brief survey of the Old Testament quickly reveals that the reference to *many nations* cannot be interpreted purely in terms of Abraham's biological descendants. Few nations can claim Abraham as their genetic father. This suggests that it is preferable to adopt a metaphorical interpretation of Abraham's multinational fatherhood. Commenting on the Hebrew term for 'father', J. B. Payne writes,

'ab may designate any man who occupies a position or receives recognition similar to that of a father: the 'father' of a servant is his

---

[19] Ibid., p. 634.

master (2Kings 2:12); 'a father to the poor' (Job 29:16) is their protector; 'a father to the inhabitants of Jerusalem' (Isa 22:21) is their governor; and 'a father to Pharaoh' (Gen 45:8) is his advisor. The title 'Father' is thus used for one in authority (2Kings 2:12), whether prophet (2Kings 6:21), priest (Jud 18:19), or king (1Sam 24:11 [H 12]), or even – as a personification – the grave, 'Thou art my father' (Job 17:14).[20]

Adopting a metaphorical understanding of *father* in Genesis 17, Scott Hahn draws attention to how the term 'father' is used 'for "suzerain" in international treaties'.[21] He writes, 'Numerous studies have demonstrated that international political alliances were described in kinship terms in the ANE. Specifically, vassals were "sons" and suzerains "fathers".'[22] A similar observation is made by Jason DeRouchie, who comments,

> It seems plausible, then, to understand Abraham's fatherhood over the nations primarily as a royal designation by which he and his wife Sarah, the 'princess' (17:15), are regarded as the founders of a new dynasty that will climax in a specific, royal descendant who will rule Israelites (both native-born and alien residents) and those from vassal nations.[23]

In support of this claim, it is noteworthy that God speaks of kings coming from Abraham and Sarah (6, 16).

As the father of many nations Abraham is expected to be their benefactor. In this regard, the covenant of Genesis 17 confirms what God promised Abraham when he initially called him. Before he arrived in the land of Canaan, God told Abraham: 'Be a blessing, so that I may bless those who bless you, and curse the one who disdains you, and so that all the families of the ground may be blessed through you.'[24] This expectation is repeated in Genesis 18:18 when God says, 'Abraham will surely become a great and powerful nation, and all nations on earth will be blessed through him.'

---

[20] J. B. Payne, 'אבה ('bh)', *TWOT* 1:5. See also C. J. H. Wright, 'אב ('ab)', *NIDOTTE* 1:221. Williamson, *Abraham, Israel and the Nations*, 159, supports a metaphorical reading of *father* on the basis of the syntax of the Hebrew text in verses 4 and 5.

[21] S. Hahn, *Kinship by Covenant: A Canonical Approach to the Fulfillment of God's Saving Promises*, The Anchor Yale Bible Reference Library (New Haven: Yale University Press, 2009), p. 106.

[22] Ibid., p. 106. Hahn also suggests that the 'great name' of Genesis 12:2 'corresponds to kingship, and not just to kingship but to international suzerainty (fatherhood)' (p. 107).

[23] J. S. DeRouchie, 'Counting Stars with Abraham and the Prophets: New Covenant Ecclesiology in OT Perspective', *JETS* 58 (2015), p. 459.

[24] Gen. 12:1–3, author's translation.

Importantly, as the account of Abraham's life moves towards a conclusion, the promise of blessing for the nations of the earth is linked to one of Abraham's offspring. After Abraham's obedience is tested, God swears to Abraham: 'and in your offspring shall all the nations of the earth be blessed, because you have obeyed my voice'.[25] This promise of blessing is intimately linked to the patriline that descends from Abraham, eventually leading to the Davidic dynasty. For this reason, the blessing of the nations is later associated with a future Davidic king. This is evident from Psalm 72, which speaks of a future king:

> Then all nations will be blessed through him,
>   and they will call him blessed.[26]

3. A royal dynasty (17:19–22)

The covenant in Genesis 17 is primarily about Abraham being the founder of a royal dynasty that will mediate divine blessing to the nations by establishing God's kingdom on earth. This idea is supported by the distinction that is made between Isaac and all those who are circumcised. In addressing Abraham's concern for Ishmael, God states that the covenant will be established only with Isaac:

> Then God said, 'Yes, but your wife Sarah will bear you a son, and you will call him Isaac. I will establish my covenant with him as an everlasting covenant for his descendants after him. And as for Ishmael, I have heard you: I will surely bless him; I will make him fruitful and will greatly increase his numbers. He will be the father of twelve rulers, and I will make him into a great nation. But my covenant I will establish with Isaac, whom Sarah will bear to you by this time next year.'
> (19–21)

Despite the fact that Ishmael will become a great nation, God affirms that his covenant will pass to Isaac alone. In fulfilment of this promise,

---

[25] Gen. 22:18, ESV. For a fuller discussion supporting the idea that the offspring mentioned here is singular, see T. D. Alexander, 'Further Observations of the Term "Seed" in Genesis', *Tyndale Bulletin* 48 (1997), pp. 363–367.

[26] Ps. 72:17. See T. D. Alexander, *From Paradise to the Promised Land: An Introduction to the Pentateuch*, 4th edn. (Grand Rapids: Baker Academic, 2022) pp. 48–53.

Isaac eventually inherits the promises associated with the covenant (26:2–5).

In due course the covenant established with Isaac passes to his younger son Jacob. The complex account of Jacob's turbulent relationship with his older twin brother Esau gradually discloses how Jacob becomes the recipient of the covenant promises. Prior to their birth, God reveals to Rebekah that 'the elder will serve the younger'.[27] Building on this expectation, Genesis 25:29–34 describes how a hungry Esau sells his birthright to Jacob for a bowl of red stew.[28] This brief incident reveals much about the contrasting attitudes of Isaac's sons towards the covenant promises. Esau dismisses them as largely worthless, whereas Jacob strongly desires to possess them. Later, when Isaac decides to bless Esau, Rebekah persuades Jacob to impersonate his brother in order to receive the paternal blessing that is normally given to the firstborn son. Pretending to be Esau, Jacob receives from his elderly father a blessing that recalls the covenant of Genesis 17:

> Ah, the smell of my son
> > is like the smell of a field
> > that the Lord has blessed.
> May God give you heaven's dew
> > and earth's richness –
> > an abundance of grain and new wine.
> May nations serve you
> > and peoples bow down to you.
> Be lord over your brothers,
> > and may the sons of your mother bow down to you.
> May those who curse you be cursed
> > and those who bless you be blessed.[29]

At the heart of this blessing is the theme of governing nations. The divine promises covenanted to Abraham are now linked to Jacob.

Despite Esau's initial desire to kill Jacob, the brothers are eventually reconciled after Jacob spends twenty years exiled in Paddan Aram.

---

[27] Gen. 25:23.

[28] The son with the birthright is principal heir and receives a double portion of the inheritance.

[29] Gen. 27:27–29.

Throughout this period Jacob experiences God's blessing and when he eventually returns to settle at Bethel, God appears to him, confirming the divine promises associated with the covenant of Genesis 17:

> And God said to him, 'I am God Almighty; be fruitful and increase in number. A nation and a community of nations will come from you, and kings will be among your descendants. The land I gave to Abraham and Isaac I also give to you, and I will give this land to your descendants after you.'[30]

As the patriline moves from Abraham to Isaac to Jacob, Genesis 37 introduces the expectation that Joseph will be next in line.[31] Joseph's dreams highlight this possibility. Set against the background of Genesis 17, the story of Joseph takes on special significance. Despite his brothers' desire to kill him, and his subsequent slavery in Egypt, God blesses Joseph and elevates him to a position of authority in the land of Egypt. Remarkably, in describing his status in relation to the Egyptian king, Joseph tells his brothers in 45:8: 'So then, it was not you who sent me here, but God. He made me father to Pharaoh, lord of his entire household and ruler of all Egypt.' Joseph's words recall God's promises to Abraham that he would be the father of many nations. As father to Pharaoh, during the years of famine, Joseph is a source of blessing for the populations of Egypt and its surrounding nations.

Joseph's pre-eminence as firstborn is confirmed when Jacob blesses Joseph's two sons, Manasseh and Ephraim.[32] As he blesses them, Jacob promotes Ephraim over his older brother, continuing a pattern in which the principle of primogeniture is regularly overturned as the patriline moves from Isaac to Jacob to Joseph to Ephraim.[33]

---

[30] Gen. 35:11–12. For a fuller discussion of this passage, see C.-C. Lee, 'גים [sic] in Genesis 35:11 and the Abrahamic Promise of Blessings for the Nations', *JETS* 52 (2009), pp. 467–482.

[31] See T. D. Alexander, 'The Regal Dimension of the תלדות־יעקב: Recovering the Literary Context of Genesis 37 – 50', in J. G. McConville and K. Möller (eds.), *Reading the Law: Studies in Honour of Gordon J. Wenham*, LHB/OTS 461 (Edinburgh: T&T Clark, 2007), pp. 196–212.

[32] Joseph's status as firstborn is confirmed in 1 Chr. 5:1–2, which states, 'The sons of Reuben the firstborn of Israel (he was the firstborn, but when he defiled his father's marriage bed, his rights as firstborn were given to the sons of Joseph son of Israel; so he could not be listed in the genealogical record in accordance with his birthright, and though Judah was the strongest of his brothers and a ruler came from him, the rights of the firstborn belonged to Joseph) . . .'

[33] D. C. Mitchell, *Messiah ben Joseph* (Newton Mearns: Campbell Publications, 2016), discusses how, in later Jewish traditions, there are references to a messiah who will be descended from Joseph and Ephraim. The origins of this tradition are difficult to trace, but they may well go back to what is said in the book of Genesis.

While the patriline of Genesis is traced from Adam to Ephraim, the picture is complicated by the inclusion of material that associates future kingship with the tribe of Judah. This is most apparent in the blessings that Jacob pronounces on his sons in Genesis 49. While Jacob's blessing concerning Joseph ends by mentioning how he will be a 'prince among his brothers',[34] kingship is earlier associated with Judah. In a blessing matched in length only by the one given to Joseph, Jacob declares,

Judah, your brothers will praise you;
　your hand will be on the neck of your enemies;
　your father's sons will bow down to you.
You are a lion's cub, Judah;
　you return from the prey, my son.
Like a lion he crouches and lies down,
　like a lioness – who dares to rouse him?
The sceptre will not depart from Judah,
　nor the ruler's staff from between his feet,
until he to whom it belongs shall come
　and the obedience of the nations shall be his.
He will tether his donkey to a vine,
　his colt to the choicest branch;
he will wash his garments in wine,
　his robes in the blood of grapes.
His eyes will be darker than wine,
　his teeth whiter than milk.[35]

The expectation that one of Judah's descendants will receive the obedience of the nations is highly significant. As the continuing Old Testament story reveals, leadership of Israel eventually transfers from the tribe of Ephraim to the tribe of Judah in the time of the prophet Samuel. Psalm 78:67–72 summarizes this development:

Then he rejected the tents of Joseph,
　he did not choose the tribe of Ephraim;
but he chose the tribe of Judah,
　Mount Zion, which he loved.

34　Gen. 49:26.
35　Gen. 49:8–12.

> He built his sanctuary like the heights,
>> like the earth that he established for ever.
> He chose David his servant
>> and took him from the sheepfolds;
> from tending the sheep he brought him
>> to be the shepherd of his people Jacob,
>> of Israel his inheritance.
> And David shepherded them with integrity of heart;
>> with skilful hands he led them.

This development regarding the tribe of Judah helpfully explains why the story of Joseph's journey into slavery in Egypt is interrupted by an unusual account that focuses on the continuation of Judah's firstborn line. Strikingly, Genesis 38 ends with a birth story that involves a younger twin boy breaking out in front of his older brother, whom the midwife has identified as the firstborn using a scarlet cord. As Tamar is in labour, Perez pushes Zerah aside to emerge first from his mother's womb. From the line of Perez comes the royal dynasty of David that is to play a central role in God's plan to establish his kingdom on the earth (see Ruth 4:18–22). Importantly, these future developments are a continuation of the eternal covenant that God establishes when he declares that Abraham will be the father of many nations.

4. The sign of the covenant: circumcision (17:9–14, 23–27)

Genesis reveals that one of Abraham's descendants will bring blessing to the nations by ruling over them as a beneficent 'father'. This promise of a special offspring lies at the heart of the covenant introduced in Genesis 17. Fittingly, to highlight this promise, circumcision is introduced as the sign of the covenant. By its distinctive nature circumcision draws attention to male offspring. Importantly, in Genesis 17, circumcision is not a sign of ethnic purity, marking only Abraham's biological descendants. On the contrary, as God's speech to Abraham makes clear, he is to circumcise *those born in your household or bought with money from a foreigner – those who are not your offspring* (12). Even Ishmael is circumcised, despite God's affirmation that the covenant will be established only with Isaac. The circumcision of numerous males who are not Abraham's biological children supports the multinational nature of the covenant in Genesis 17.

5. Conclusion

The significance of the eternal covenant that God makes with Abraham is not always fully appreciated. It goes far beyond affirming that Abraham's descendants will form the nation of Israel. That is the focus of the covenant in chapter 15. This earlier covenant presents Abraham as the father of one nation. Based on this covenant, Abraham's biological descendants will possess the land of Canaan after a period of opposition in another land (see 15:13–16). While this is an important development in the fulfilment of God's redemptive plan, God has a much greater purpose in view for Abraham. Through Abraham God intends to mediate blessing to all the nations of the earth. This will occur as Abraham fulfils metaphorically the role of being father to many nations. Importantly, the covenant established with Abraham passes to his son Isaac, with the expectation that one of their future descendants will govern the nations on God's behalf. As we follow this unique family lineage through Genesis, it becomes clear that a future offspring of Eve will bring blessing to the nations of the earth by ruling as God's perfect vicegerent.

Part 2

The kingdom of God in the Old Testament

Exodus 15:1–21

4. The divine redeemer king

On 5 August 2010, thirty-three miners were trapped some 3 miles from the entrance to a mine in the Atacama Desert in northern Chile. For days rescuers on the surface drilled exploratory boreholes in a desperate attempt to discover if anyone was alive. On the seventeenth day, to their amazement and great relief, the rescuers found a note taped to a drill bit: 'We are well in the shelter, the 33 of us.' They were spurred on by this message, but it was another fifty-two days before the trapped miners could be safely brought to the surface. After such a long time underground, the men's appearance at the surface was greeted with the greatest joy. Family members and everyone involved in the rescue had every reason to celebrate. In the book of Exodus, we encounter a similar celebration.

It was no ordinary song-and-dance routine. Standing by the still waters of a large lake, surrounded by others, Miriam grabbed her tambourine and started to dance. The women nearby quickly joined her. Relieved and elated, Miriam bursts into song:

> Sing to the Lord,
>   for he is highly exalted.
> Both horse and driver
>   he has hurled into the sea.
> (21)

Those around her respond in unison, singing out,

> I will sing to the Lord,
>   for he is highly exalted.

> *Both horse and driver*
> *he has hurled into the sea.*
> (1)

Inspired by their miraculous rescue from a violent death, Miriam continues to sing, composing as she goes a remarkable tribute to the Lord who has saved her and her family from the hands of battle-hardened troops who were relishing the prospect of attacking unarmed civilians. There was every reason to sing and dance.

1. Miriam's victory celebration

Miriam leads the celebration. She sings out the newly composed words, inviting others to respond by repeating them back to her. While Miriam's role is highlighted in Exodus 15:20–21, authorship of the song's lyrics in 15:1–18 is often credited to her younger brother Moses, who is named in 15:1. It seems unlikely, however, that Moses was gifted as a singer, especially given his own reservations about speaking in public. When asked by God to speak to Pharaoh, Moses responds by saying, 'I am slow of speech and tongue.' Whatever we might make of his excuse, God aids Moses by having his brother Aaron speak for him (4:10, 14–16). Although the Exodus narrative presents the words of the song in 15:1–18 before mentioning Miriam, this appears to be done for literary impact. Readers hear all the people praising God and not just one person. Their communal voice sings out in celebration. After this comes a concluding summary in 15:19–21 that ascribes to Miriam, a prophet and sister of Aaron, the honour of having composed this amazing victory song.

The words of the victory song are intentionally placed after the prose description of God's destruction of the Egyptian army. With literary acumen, the author of Exodus inserts this poetic song of praise to encourage the reader to celebrate alongside the liberated Israelites. As Alter notes, the song is not an 'independent narrative', but a 'narrative ancillary to the previously told story'.[1] It is inserted 'to "celebrate" rather than "narrate"'.[2] Much of the song looks backwards to what has just occurred, but its final stanzas look forward in anticipation to what God will

---

[1] R. Alter, *The Art of Biblical Poetry* (New York: Basic Books, 1985), p. 52.
[2] T. D. Alexander, *Exodus*, Apollos OT Commentary 2 (London: Apollos, 2017), p. 293.

yet do. In this regard, the song has a prophetic aspect, which is in keeping with Miriam's designation as a prophet (20). The song provides a natural bridge between events in Egypt and those that follow in the rest of Exodus.

The song divides into a number of distinctive sections. The opening lines emphasize a personal response to what God has done. First person singular pronouns abound in verses 1–2. Verses 3–5 offer a more detached summary of how the Lord has caused Pharaoh's charioteers to be drowned, sinking like stones into deep water. After this short summary, the people address God directly in verses 6–12. Framed by references to God's right hand (6, 12), these verses highlight God's power to destroy his enemies. Despite their boastful threats, the Egyptian soldiers cannot escape the waters that engulf them. Having lauded God's power over his enemies, the song turns from judgment to salvation, recalling in verse 13 how God has redeemed the Israelites and guided them to their current location. However, recognizing that this is not their ultimate destination, verses 14–16 promise a safe onward journey as other nations are filled with fear due to God's annihilation of the Egyptian army. With an eye to their ultimate destination, verse 17 speaks of how God will enable the Israelites to live with him on his holy mountain. Fittingly, the song ends in verse 18 by proclaiming Yahweh as the eternal king. Freed from the control of an evil dictator, the Israelites acknowledge Yahweh's sovereignty. Their future hope rests on belonging to a kingdom over which God reigns supreme for ever.

The opening stanza of the song immediately refers to the events that have just occurred. These have been described in chapter 14, and they mark the end of a long process through which God has been active in rescuing the Israelites from slavery in Egypt. This has come to a climax with the destruction of a large Egyptian chariot force.

As the Exodus story reveals, the Egyptian kings are no benevolent monarchs. The pharaoh of chapters 1–2 is a tyrannical dictator who is even prepared to have newly born baby boys thrown into the Nile. He is the epitome of evil, using his power to oppress others. With the death of this first pharaoh, a new pharaoh appears in chapters 3–15. When God intervenes, the pharaoh of chapters 3–15 is unable to prevent the Israelites from leaving Egypt. Through a series of signs and wonders that come to a climax with Passover, God convinces the Egyptian king to drive the Israelites out of his country. There is, however, a twist in the tale, which results in one more extraordinary demonstration of God's power to save. With an

Egyptian chariot force bearing down upon the Israelites, God enables them to pass safely through a body of water that then closes over, killing all of the pursing Egyptians. It is a dramatic episode that marks the end of the Israelites' enslavement in Egypt. There is every reason to celebrate.

2. Personal gratitude (15:1–5)

As Miriam invites others to join with her in praising the Lord, she is filled with personal gratitude for what God has done. In song she testifies,

> I will sing to Yahweh,
> for he has highly exalted himself.
> The horse and its driver
> he has thrown into the lake/sea.
> Yah is my strength and song; he has been my salvation.
> This is my God, and I will praise him, my father's God,
> and I will exalt him.
> (1–2, author's translation)

Miriam's words become the testimony of every Israelite whom God has rescued. From personal experience they have witnessed God's power in defending them from the advancing army. Expecting to be brutally murdered, the people have every reason to praise and exalt Yahweh as their God. God has saved them from a bloodthirsty attack.

Shifting their focus from the personal benefit that they have received, the people recall in a few lines how the Lord has destroyed *Pharaoh's chariots and his army* (4). Their short summary emphasizes the watery demise of the Egyptian army, conveying the essence of what is reported in more detail in chapter 14. They proclaim,

> Yahweh is a warrior; Yahweh is his name.
> Pharaoh's chariot army he has hurled into the lake/sea.
> The elite of his runners have sunk into the Lake of Reeds.
> Deep waters covered them; they went down into the depths like a stone.
> (3–5, author's translation)

Those singing require few details to remind them of what has just happened. Everything is still fresh in their memories. From what is recorded in the rest of Exodus, we can piece together a fuller picture. This remarkable event possibly took place in the fifteenth century BC in the north-eastern region of the Nile Delta. For several centuries prior to this, up to the middle of the sixteenth century BC, this region was controlled by people known as the Hyksos, who were not native Egyptians. Their capital was a city called Avaris, which lay on what was then a major distributary of the Nile. Later this city would be renamed Rameses, the name that is recorded in the first chapter of Exodus. Around about 1100 BC the branch of the Nile that flowed through this ancient city dried up and the city was abandoned. Many of the city's stone monuments were then moved to Tanis. Eventually, the city of Rameses disappeared, only to be rediscovered by archaeologists in the past fifty years. Farmland now covers what was once one of the great cities of the ancient world with harbours that could hold several hundred ships.[3]

In the middle of the sixteenth century BC, the Hyksos were driven out of Avaris by an Egyptian pharaoh known as Ahmose I, the founder of the 18th Dynasty of Egypt and first ruler of what is often called the New Kingdom of Egypt. Ahmose I reigned from about 1550 to 1525 BC. An ancient wall drawing reveals that Ahmose relied on chariots, a new addition to military equipment in the middle of the second millennium, to oust the Hyksos. The use of horse-drawn chariots against the fleeing Israelites is very much in keeping with this period of history.

Ahmose I may have been the pharaoh who initiated the oppression of the Israelites. If so, Moses was probably born during his reign. By the time Moses returned to lead the Israelites out of Egypt, Thutmose III (1479–1425 BC) is king. He is the pharaoh who commands his chariot force to pursue the Israelites.[4]

As regards the location of the event, we have become accustomed to thinking that it took place in the Red Sea that separates Egypt from the Sinai Peninsula. However, the Hebrew text of Exodus refers to the location as *yam-sûp*, which can mean either 'lake of reeds' or 'sea of reeds'. The Hebrew language of the Bible does not have words to distinguish a lake from a sea. Any relatively large body of water is called a *yam*. As regards the location of the *yam-sûp*, it probably lay close to the Mediterranean Sea.

---

[3] See M. Bietak, *Avaris: The Capital of the Hyksos; Recent Excavations at Tell El-Dab'a* (London: British Museum Press, 1996).

[4] The names of the Egyptian kings are not recorded in Exodus. This is probably intentional on the part of the author. By avoiding their names, the author conveys the idea that they are largely nonentities. In marked contrast, the names of the Hebrew midwives are recorded in Exodus 1.

The eminent Egyptologist James Hoffmeier has argued that we should equate the *yam-sûp* of Exodus with the el-Ballah Lakes that lay to the east of the city of Avaris.[5]

The short summary of how Pharaoh's soldiers are drowned in the Lake of Reeds (3–5) draws attention to the Lord as a *warrior*. Pharaoh's army has encountered an opponent who is more than their match. Continuing their song of celebration, the people address God directly, singing of God's power to defeat his enemies in verses 6–12.

3. God is mighty to punish (15:6–10)

With good reason God's judgment descends on the Egyptian soldiers. As the victory song of the Israelites highlights, the soldiers were revelling in the opportunity presented to them.

> *The enemy boasted,*
> > *'I will pursue, I will overtake them.*
> *I will divide the spoils;*
> > *I will gorge myself on them.*
> *I will draw my sword*
> > *and my hand will destroy them.'*
>
> (9)

The battle-hardened soldiers cruelly anticipate the opportunity to slaughter and pillage defenceless civilians. For them this will be a one-sided affair. The Israelites are an easy target. The men lack weapons; there are women and children, both young and old. Confident of victory, the Egyptian charioteers relish this assignment. But they have not reckoned on a God who is swift to save and mighty to punish. When the waters tumble upon them, the Egyptian soldiers are powerless to escape. Those who rushed to kill suffer the fate that they planned to bring upon the helpless Israelites. With the destruction of Pharaoh's chariot force, we see what happens to those who oppress others. The proud and arrogant are brought low by God.

---

[5] See J. K. Hoffmeier, *Israel in Egypt: The Evidence for the Authenticity of the Exodus Tradition* (New York: OUP, 1997), pp. 199–222; J. K. Hoffmeier, 'Out of Egypt: The Archaeological Context of the Exodus', *BAR* 33 (2007), pp. 30–41, 77. We should bear in mind that the topology of these lakes has changed over the centuries and the present boundaries of the lakes do not necessarily reflect the boundaries that existed in the fifteenth century BC.

4. God is unique in power and holiness (15:11)

God's destruction of the chariot force demonstrates his remarkable power. Here is a God who can push aside the waters of a large lake. He can control the forces of nature, enabling the Israelites to escape from their enemy. Such exceptional occurrences are not common in the Bible. God does not reveal his power like this day after day. It is a special miracle that is intended to make God's power known. Not surprisingly, the Israelites praise God with these words:

> Who is like you among the gods, Yahweh?
> Who is like you – superior in holiness, awesome, praiseworthy,
>> doing the extraordinary?
> (11, author's translation)

This is not the first miracle of the Exodus story. God has already demonstrated his power through a series of signs and wonders that come with ever-increasing intensity to make Yahweh known to both the Israelites and the Egyptians.[6] They are God's response to the Egyptian king's refusal to let the Israelites celebrate a festival to Yahweh in the wilderness (5:1).

When Moses first approaches Pharaoh with a request for the Israelites to worship Yahweh, the king's reply is noteworthy: 'Who is Yahweh that I should heed him by releasing Israel? I do not know Yahweh and moreover I will not release Israel.'[7] As far as Pharaoh is concerned, he has no knowledge of Moses' God. Yahweh is an unknown deity. Against this background, the motif of making Yahweh known occurs frequently within the account of the signs and wonders that dominate chapters 6–12.[8]

As Moses and Aaron confront Pharaoh's obstinacy, with every sign there is a growing awareness among the Egyptians of Yahweh's power to

---

[6] We have become accustomed to referring to the miraculous occurrences in 7:14 – 12:51 as the 'ten plagues'. Unfortunately, the term 'plague' does not reflect accurately how these events are presented in the Hebrew text. When the King James Version of the Bible was translated in 1610, the term 'plague' was used in 11:1 to render the Hebrew noun *nega'*. However, *nega'* means 'blow/strike'. In seventeenth-century English, the word 'plague' meant a 'blow' or 'strike', being derived from the corresponding Latin term *plaga*. The supernatural events in Egypt are associated with God's striking the Egyptians with his staff, which is carried by Moses and Aaron. Elsewhere in the Old Testament, the commonly used expression to designate the events of Exodus 7 – 12 is 'signs and wonders' (e.g. Deut. 4:34; 6:22; 7:19).

[7] Exod. 5:2, author's translation.

[8] See 6:3–7; 7:5, 17; 8:10, 22; 9:14, 16, 29; 10:1–2; 11:7.

perform miraculous events. Pharaoh's 'sorcerer-priests',[9] who can replicate a few of the miraculous signs, soon recognize Yahweh's superior power, telling Pharaoh, 'This is the finger of God.'[10] When 'festering boils' come upon the Egyptians, the sorcerer-priests are powerless to protect themselves (9:11). As the intensity of the signs grows, some of Pharaoh's officials take seriously the threats and act to avoid their impact (see 9:20–21). While those around him gradually recognize Yahweh as a powerful deity (see 10:7), Pharaoh himself refuses to acknowledge him, although at times he comes close to doing this (see 9:27–28; 10:16–17). Eventually, with the deaths of all the Egyptian firstborn males, Pharaoh is compelled to expel the Israelites from Egypt (12:31–32). However, he subsequently has second thoughts and assembles a massive chariot force to pursue the fleeing Israelites (14:5–7). In doing so, he offers Yahweh a further opportunity to make himself known to the Egyptians (see 14:4, 18).

5. God alone gives victory (15:12)

As the Israelites celebrate in song, they rightly emphasize what God has done for them in striking down their enemy. God alone has rescued them and defeated the Egyptian army. He has done what Moses said would happen, when he encouraged the people to trust in Yahweh's deliverance:

> Do not be afraid. Stand firm and you will see the deliverance the LORD will bring you today. The Egyptians you see today you will never see again. The LORD will fight for you; you need only to be still.[11]

For the Israelites the idea of being still in the face of the advancing Egyptian army would have seemed bizarre advice. Surely they ought to do something to defend themselves. Not so. This is a powerful reminder that our salvation does not depend on what we do to save ourselves, but on what God does on our behalf.

---

[9] The NIV translation 'magicians' fails to convey adequately the idea that these men were closely associated with religious practices in ancient Egypt. Hoffmeier, *Israel in Egypt*, p. 88, contends that the Hebrew noun ḥarṭummîm, 'sorcerer-priests', comes from an abbreviation of an Egyptian expression meaning 'chief lector priest'. Lector priests studied ritual and magical texts in libraries linked to temples. Religious practices in ancient Egypt sometimes involved magic.

[10] Exod. 8:19.

[11] Exod. 14:13–14.

As the Israelites praise God for delivering them from their enemy, this section of the song is framed by references to God's *right hand* (6, 12). This is not an insignificant mention given the fuller story in Exodus. Previously, when Pharaoh had vindictively increased the burden of the Israelites, God instructed Moses to say to the people:

> I am the LORD, and I will bring you out from under the yoke of the Egyptians. I will free you from being slaves to them, and I will redeem you with an outstretched arm and with mighty acts of judgment.[12]

God speaks of redeeming the people with an outstretched arm. In the signs and wonders that follow, there are frequent references to Moses and/or Aaron stretching out their hand or staff (e.g. 7:19; 8:5–6, 17; 9:22–23; 10:12–13, 21–22). These are associated with God's acts of judgment upon Pharaoh and his people. This applies also to the parting of the lake and the return of the water (14:16, 21, 26–27). When Moses and/or Aaron stretch out their hand, the staff they hold is the staff of God (4:20). Their action draws attention to God's outstretched arm as he punishes those intent on doing evil.

In this story of redemption there is a movement from death to life. On the Egyptian side of the Lake of Reeds, death looms large over the fleeing Israelites. As they pass through the waters, they move from death to life. Their situation is transformed solely by God. He is their redeemer, their saviour.

6. God is swift to save (15:13a)

If God is mighty to punish, he is also swift to save. The story that unfolds over chapters 1–15 is of God's redemption of the Israelites from the tyranny of evil. God stands on the side of the enslaved Israelites. He rescues them from their harsh treatment under the Egyptian taskmasters. He cares for the oppressed.

The opening chapters of Exodus introduce the plight of the Israelites as the Egyptian king acts to restrain their growing population. In doing so, he sets himself at odds with God and his plans for humanity. Through a careful choice of words, the author of Exodus in 1:7 portrays the

---

[12] Exod. 6:6.

Israelites as fulfilling God's creation mandate: 'but the Israelites were exceedingly fruitful; they multiplied greatly, increased in numbers and became so numerous that the land was filled with them.' This statement echoes closely Genesis 1:28: 'God blessed them and said to them, "Be fruitful and increase in number; fill the earth and subdue it."' The fruitfulness of the Israelites has every appearance of being in keeping with God's plan for humanity.[13] Against this background, Pharaoh's actions are the antithesis of what God expects. Moreover, Pharaoh conscripts the Israelites, forcing them to serve him by building store cities to enhance his own kingdom. When harsh labour fails to restrict the numerical growth of the Israelites, the Egyptian king resorts to selected genocide. He looks to kill all newly born males, eventually commanding his people to drown them in the Nile. In every way possible, Pharaoh is the embodiment of evil. As Sigurd Grindheim remarks, 'Pharaoh stands as the archetype of earthly powers that buck God's rule and refuse to submit to his will.'[14] Into a world dominated by a human king who views himself as divine, God comes to establish his authority as a powerful, benevolent redeemer.

The Israelites see themselves as those whom God has lovingly redeemed: *In your unfailing love you will lead the people you have redeemed* (13). Their reference to redemption echoes what God said to them when he declared in 6:6: 'I will free you from being slaves to them, and I will redeem you with an outstretched arm and with mighty acts of judgment.' Recognizing the injustice of their enslavement, God speaks of redeeming the Israelites through 'mighty acts of judgment'. God's actions resemble how someone might redeem a relative who has become enslaved. This process of redemption normally involves paying for that person's freedom. In this instance, however, the Israelites have been unjustly enslaved for an exceptionally long period of time. No payment is required to free them. On the contrary, God ensures that they will be compensated by the Egyptians (see 11:2–3; 12:35–36).

Pharaoh's refusal to set the Israelites free results in divine judgment. The liberation of the Israelites from an evil dictator is a necessary and vital step in the process by which they become citizens of God's kingdom.

---

[13] This is even more evident in the Hebrew text, which uses the noun *'eres*, translated 'earth' in Gen. 1:28 and 'land' in Exod. 1:7.

[14] S. Grindheim, *Living in the Kingdom of God: A Biblical Theology for the Life of the Church* (Grand Rapids: Baker Academic, 2018), p. 8.

Redemption lies at the heart of this. As Israel's redeemer, God frees them from the grip of evil. In this context, redemption speaks of liberation from an evil power.[15]

This concept of redemption reappears in the Bible as a significant theological idea. In the Old Testament, the prophet Isaiah pre-eminently speaks of God being the Redeemer of Israel. Robert Hubbard provides an excellent summary of how the concept is used by Isaiah:

> Yahweh's identity as Redeemer reassures Israel that, as a compassionate husband, he will take back his wife (Isa 54:5, 8) and that, as guardian of justice, he will come to the repentant in Zion (59:20). It also gives certainty to the prophet's taunt song about Babylon's future humiliation (47:4–5). Given Babylon's might, Yahweh's incredible rescue of Israel will even enhance his reputation as Redeemer (49:26) and result in greater glory for Israel (60:16). Part of a communal complaint (63:16) likewise appeals to Yahweh as Israel's ancient Redeemer to end their present punishment. By recalling the first Exodus in many of the above texts (e.g., 43:16–21), the prophet portrays future events as a new exodus, which frees Israel from slavery and restores them to their rightful, original owner.[16]

As the prophet Isaiah proclaims, what God has done in the past in redeeming the Israelites from slavery creates an expectation that he will do something even more marvellous in the future.

The concept of redemption from evil figures prominently in the New Testament. Two examples illustrate its presence. Jesus draws attention to it when he declares to some Jews: 'If you hold to my teaching, you are really my disciples. Then you will know the truth, and the truth will set you free.' Apparently suffering from amnesia as regards the book of Exodus, they reply, 'We are Abraham's descendants and have never been slaves of anyone. How can you say that we shall be set free?' Responding to their mistaken claim, Jesus says,

> Very truly I tell you, everyone who sins is a slave to sin. Now a slave has no permanent place in the family, but a son belongs to it for ever. So if the Son sets you free, you will be free indeed.[17]

---

[15] The Hebrew verb *gā'al* is often used to describe the actions of someone who assists a relative who is suffering hardship, sometimes unjustly.

[16] R. L. Hubbard, 'גאל (*g'l*)', *NIDOTTE* 1:792.

[17] John 8:31–36.

By emphasizing how people are enslaved to sin, Jesus highlights how he has come as a redeemer to free sin's captives.

In a similar way, the apostle Paul speaks of redemption from slavery when he writes to the churches in Galatia. Paul refers to himself and his readers as being 'in slavery under the elemental spiritual forces of the world'.[18] He later adds, 'You were slaves to those who by nature are not gods.' Drawing attention to the concept of being enslaved by evil powers, Paul highlights how Jesus Christ brings freedom. He writes,

> But when the set time had fully come, God sent his Son, born of a woman, born under the law, to redeem those under the law, that we might receive adoption to sonship. Because you are his sons, God sent the Spirit of his Son into our hearts, the Spirit who calls out, 'Abba, Father.' So you are no longer a slave, but God's child; and since you are his child, God has made you also an heir.[19]

Paul underlines the impact of being liberated by Christ. People are transformed from being slaves to being children of God. As with the Israelites in Egypt, redemption from slavery to evil leads to a new status in relation to God. Now that they have experienced freedom, Paul warns his readers against allowing themselves to be enslaved by 'those who by nature are not gods'.[20]

7. God has shepherded his people (15:13b)

Continuing to reflect on the events of the previous few days, the Israelites praise God for shepherding them on their journey out of Egypt. The NIV translation mistakenly takes verse 13 as referring to God's actions in the future. However, it is more likely that in verse 13 the people refer to what God has already done. The verbs in the Hebrew text are best understood as denoting completed activities. A better translation is as follows:

> You led in your steadfast love
> the people you have redeemed.

---

[18] Gal. 4:3. See M. S. Harmon, *Galatians*, Evangelical Biblical Theology Commentary (Bellingham: Lexham Academic Press, 2021), pp. 220–221, for a helpful assessment of the expression 'elemental spiritual forces of the world', which CSB translates 'the elements of the world'.

[19] Gal. 4:4–7.

[20] Gal. 4:8; cf. 5:1.

In your strength you guided them
to your holy resting place.
(13, author's translation)

The correct interpretation of this verse rests largely on the sense of the Hebrew expression *nĕwēh qodĕšekā* 'your holy resting place', which comes only here in the whole of the Old Testament. Some scholars assume that this is a reference to Mount Sinai, towards which the Israelites are journeying. But the noun *nāweh* is usually associated with shepherds, referring to their campsite or pasture. With this in view, it is noteworthy that the verbs 'led' and 'guided' in verse 13 are associated with shepherding. In line with the concept of shepherding, the expression *nĕwēh qodĕšekā* conveys the idea of a safe resting place on a journey. In the context of this song, verse 13 refers to the Israelite encampment set up after they have safely passed through the parted waters of the Lake of Reeds. This is their 'holy resting place'.

8. God's presence in the future (15:14–18)

Having acknowledged how God has brought them safely to their present location, the remaining lines of the song anticipate their onward trek. God's goal is for the Israelites to take possession of the land of Canaan. He declared this to Moses when he spoke to him from the burning bush in 3:8:

> So I have come down to rescue them from the hand of the Egyptians and to bring them up out of that land into a good and spacious land, a land flowing with milk and honey – the home of the Canaanites, Hittites, Amorites, Perizzites, Hivites and Jebusites.

Later, when Pharaoh rejected Moses' request to allow the people to worship Yahweh in the wilderness, God spoke once more of his determination to bring the Israelites into the land of Canaan: 'And I will bring you to the land I swore with uplifted hand to give to Abraham, to Isaac and to Jacob. I will give it to you as a possession. I am the Lord.'[21] Various nations, however, stand between the fleeing Israelites and their destination. Focusing on the

---

[21] Exod. 6:8.

inhabitants of Philistia, Edom, Moab and Canaan, the people sing of how these nations will offer no resistance when they learn of how God has destroyed Pharaoh's prized military machine. With confidence the people sing,

> By the power of your arm
>   they will be as still as a stone –
> until your people pass by, LORD,
>   until the people you bought pass by.
> (16)

God's ability to protect the Israelites from Pharaoh's army reassures them as they look ahead to settling in the Promised Land. As John Watts comments, 'These verses, as they stand, are dominated by one theme: God's power reflected in the victory at the sea will bring them to their goal.'[22]

To conclude their song of celebration, the Israelites anticipate a special future that will see them dwelling with God on his holy mountain. Addressing God, they sing,

> You will bring them in and plant them
> on the mountain of your inheritance –
> a place you made for your dwelling, Yahweh,
> a sanctuary, my Lord, your hands have put in place.
> (17, author's translation)

Importantly, the people look ahead to living with God on his holy mountain. The mountain is described as a *sanctuary*.[23] It is not merely a place of protection, which the term 'sanctuary' often implies in English (e.g. a bird sanctuary). The Hebrew term *miqdāš* denotes a place that is holy. Previously, when Moses encountered God at the burning bush, he was instructed to take off his sandals because he was standing on holy ground. God's holiness consecrated the area around the bush. In a similar fashion, when the Israelites come to Mount Sinai, God's presence makes the mountain holy.[24]

---

[22] J. D. W. Watts, 'The Song of the Sea – Ex. xv', *Vetus Testamentum* 7 (1957), p. 377.

[23] This is realized when the Israelites capture Jerusalem, and Mount Zion becomes the location where God dwells (see Ps. 48).

[24] As we shall observe in chapter 5, only those who are holy can dwell with God on his holy mountain.

The Israelites' trek to Canaan takes an unusual detour. Before they arrive at God's holy mountain in the land of Canaan, God leads them to another mountain, Mount Sinai. Previously in Exodus 3:1, it has been designated 'the mountain of God'. At this isolated location, God establishes a special relationship with the Israelites that is intended to prepare them for living in his presence in Canaan.[25] This goal reflects a partial reversal of the expulsion of Adam and Eve from the garden of Eden. People will no longer be alienated from God but will live in close proximity to him. This outcome determines much of what happens at Mount Sinai as the Israelites transition from being slaves in Egypt under a despotic tyrant to living as a holy nation in the presence of Yahweh, their mighty redeemer.

In recognition of all that God has done for them as he has displayed his sovereign power, destroying his enemies, the Israelites conclude their celebratory song by proclaiming him as king: 'Yahweh reigns for ever and ever' (18, author's translation). As they look to a future lived in God's holy presence, the people envisage God's kingdom being established on the earth.

9. Conclusion

The book of Genesis creates an expectation that the formation of God's kingdom on earth will involve a future king who will mediate God's blessing to the nations of the world. This king will be God's vicegerent, undertaking the role that God expected Adam and Eve and their descendants to fulfil in establishing God's kingdom on the earth. The book of Exodus complements the Genesis narrative by illustrating how God restores people to a harmonious relationship with himself. This involves various stages, the first of which is the redemption of people from evil powers. This is a necessary and vital step towards establishing God's rule on earth.

God's redemption of the Israelites from slavery in Egypt involves much more than the liberation of oppressed people from an evil dictator. It is not about people being set free to determine their own destiny. Importantly, it is about the restoration of a harmonious relationship with God. With this in view, the book of Exodus provides a vivid example of how

---

[25] We shall explore this development in our next chapter.

The Message of the Kingdom of God

God redeems people from the powers of evil, initiating a process that will make it possible for them to dwell in his holy presence. This reveals an essential step towards the unveiling of God's kingdom in the world.

Exodus 24:1–11

5. The divine king and his chosen people

My son and his wife have just celebrated their fifth wedding anniversary. Wedding anniversaries are special because they recall the day on which a relationship between two people was formalized and they became husband and wife. Family and friends are often present to witness and celebrate this special occasion, which marks a significant new stage in a relationship that has already existed for some time. From this point on both partners have new expectations. Their wedding brings them together into a relationship of exclusive and mutual love. They belong to each other in a new way. The wedding ceremony reminds them that the new status of husband and wife comes with all kinds of implications both social and legal. While a successful marriage requires much more than what happens on the wedding day, nevertheless the wedding itself is exceptionally important.

As the book of Exodus reveals, redemption from evil powers is a vital step towards being part of God's kingdom. However, this is only part of a more complex process that involves people making a personal commitment to serve Yahweh as their one and only God. This commitment is necessary to form an exclusive relationship that is formally established by what the Bible calls a covenant. All who are subjects of God's kingdom enter into a covenant relationship with their king.

1. A relationship made in heaven (24:1–2)

The events recorded in Exodus 24:1–11 describe a special day that in many ways resembles a wedding. Two parties come together to form a unique relationship that will have major implications for both as regards their future lifestyle. While marriage illustrates well something of what is happening, one important element is very different: the two parties to this relationship are far from equals.[1] On the one hand, there is Yahweh, the God of heaven and earth, whom the Israelites have previously described as 'majestic in holiness, awesome in glory, working wonders'.[2] On the other hand, there are the Israelites, the descendants of the patriarchs Abraham, Isaac and Jacob, who have been recently liberated from slavery in Egypt and now find themselves landless, trekking through the Sinai Peninsula. To these homeless people, God comes to create a relationship that will transform them into a holy nation.

Exodus 24 begins with instructions that will form the climax of the ceremony that establishes a unique bond between Yahweh and the Israelites. God's words in verses 1–2 come at the end of a long divine speech that starts in 20:22. These final instructions are set apart from the rest of the speech by the statement: 'And to Moses he said . . .' (author's translation). This brief report presupposes that God is the one speaking; no specific subject is mentioned in verse 1.[3] Exodus 20:22 reveals that the whole of God's speech in 20:22 – 23:33 is addressed to all of the Israelites. In Exodus 24:1–2 Yahweh now directs his comments to Moses alone, giving him and selected others instructions about ascending Mount Sinai. As we shall see, this invitation is highly significant, for prior to this time the Israelites have been strictly warned not to approach the mountain. Anyone attempting to ascend must be put to death (19:12–13).

When Yahweh finishes speaking, Moses descends from the mountain and relays to the Israelites everything God has said. The people respond unanimously, stating that they will do what Yahweh asks. Moses then records Yahweh's speech. Appropriately, this written record is called the Book of the Covenant (24:7).[4] While it consists of various distinctive sections, this document contains obligations that the Israelites are expected to fulfil in the future as a consequence of being in a covenant relationship with Yahweh.

---

[1] For this reason, many Old Testament commentators prefer to explain the covenant relationship at Mount Sinai as resembling Ancient Near Eastern suzerain treaties, in which a greater king establishes a relationship with a lesser king.

[2] Exod. 15:11.

[3] Although the NIV reads, *Then the LORD said to Moses*, the subject *the LORD* is added in the translation to remind readers that he is the one speaking. The Hebrew text simply has 'he said'.

[4] Although English translations refer to this document as a book, it did not take the form of a modern book with pages. It is more likely to have been in the form of a scroll.

2. At the mountain of God

Before we explore the obligations that are placed upon the Israelites, it may be helpful to step back in time to the start of events at Mount Sinai. As we briefly noted in our previous chapter, God's plan for the Israelites is that they should dwell with him on his holy mountain (15:17). Before this happens, God leads the people to another mountain to prepare them for what lies ahead. Everything taking place at Mount Sinai anticipates Yahweh and the Israelites living together on Mount Zion in the land of Canaan.

When the Israelites arrive at Mount Sinai, they camp at the foot of the mountain, but Moses ascends to meet with God. This recalls what God had promised Moses when he appeared to him at the burning bush (3:12). Returning to Mount Sinai, Moses retraces his steps possibly to where he first encountered God.

On the mountain Yahweh gives Moses a short but important message for the Israelites. In essence it resembles a marriage proposal. Yahweh invites the people to be his treasured possession.[5] If they agree to this proposal, they will become 'a kingdom of priests and a holy nation'.[6] However, for this to happen Yahweh asks for total compliance from the people. They must obey him fully and keep his covenant (19:5). He is to be their king and they are to be his loyal subjects. This will create a unique kingdom, one that is established by the freely given consent of the people. It is not a kingdom created by a ruler who uses force to coerce people into compliance.

The relationship proposed by God involves the making of a covenant. The Old Testament records various covenants, not all of which are similar in nature.[7] Some covenants involve only human parties. Abimelek, the king of Gerar, asks Abraham to make a covenant with him to guarantee their peaceful coexistence (Gen. 21:22–31). Laban makes a covenant with Jacob, wanting a solemn guarantee that Jacob will not abandon Laban's daughters as he returns to the land of Canaan (31:43–54). The covenant

---

[5] This reflects the following translation of 19:5–6: 'Now if you will truly obey me and will keep my covenant, and be for me a treasured possession out of all the peoples, for all the earth is mine, then you yourselves will be for me a kingdom of priests and a holy nation.' See T. D. Alexander, *Exodus*, Apollos OT Commentary 2 (London: Apollos, 2017), pp. 358–359.

[6] Exod. 19:6.

[7] For a helpful survey of biblical covenants, see P. R. Williamson, *Sealed with an Oath: Covenant in God's Unfolding Purpose*, New Studies in Biblical Theology 23 (Leicester: Apollos, 2007).

offered by God to the Israelites resembles the friendship treaty made between Abraham and Abimelek.

Yahweh's offer of a covenant relationship with the Israelites is a generous offer that does not depend upon what the Israelites have already done. It is an act of grace on the part of God. While the covenant will place important demands on the Israelites, the initiation of the special relationship precedes their fulfilment. As God's remarks to the Israelites highlight, he has already acted graciously in rescuing them 'out of Egypt, out of the land of slavery'.[8] Throughout this whole process, God takes the initiative.

While Yahweh could justifiably contend, based on all that he has already done for the Israelites, that they owe him their loyalty, he does not compel the people to obey him against their will. He issues an invitation that they may accept or reject. God generously invites them to become his special people. Unlike the king of Egypt, Yahweh does not use force to make the Israelites obey him. Had the Israelites wished, they could have walked away from this proposal.

3. A kingdom of priests and a holy nation

Although God expects exclusive and loyal obedience from the Israelites, the benefits of the covenant relationship are noteworthy. Through compliance, the Israelites will become 'a kingdom of priests and a holy nation'.[9] Remarkably, this is the only occurrence of these expressions in the whole of the Old Testament. Various interpretations have been suggested to explain the phrase 'a kingdom of priests'. The most likely meaning is that all Israelites will have both priestly and royal status. This may be expressed either as 'priestly royals' or 'royal priesthood'.[10] This is a remarkable expectation, given the Israelites' prior experience in Egypt when they were viewed with disdain and subjected to harsh treatment as slaves. God speaks of them enjoying a status that recalls in certain regards the lives of Adam and Eve prior to their expulsion from the garden of Eden.

---

[8] Exod. 20:2.

[9] Exod. 19:6. For a fuller discussion, see J. A. Davies, *A Royal Priesthood: Literary and Intertextual Perspectives on an Image of Israel in Exodus 19.6*, JSOTSup 395 (London: T&T Clark International, 2004), pp. 63–100. A shorter summary comes in Alexander, *Exodus*, pp. 367–370.

[10] Alluding to Exod. 19:5–6, 1 Pet. 2:9 states, 'But you are a chosen people, a royal priesthood, a holy nation, God's special possession, that you may declare the praises of him who called you out of darkness into his wonderful light.'

In the beginning God created humans to rule over the earth on his behalf (Gen. 1:26, 28). Relative to all other earthly creatures, Adam and Eve were royalty. God also privileged Adam and Eve by giving them access to his presence (Gen. 3:8). This resembles how priests are permitted to come closer to God than others at the sanctuary. This ability to approach God is also reflected in the expression 'holy nation'. Only those who are holy may come into God's presence.[11] Taking these factors into account, God's proposal to the Israelites suggests that he views the covenant relationship as reversing in some manner the expulsion of Adam and Eve from the garden of Eden.

In the light of all that has occurred and the possibility of being transformed from slaves into priestly royals, it is perhaps no surprise that the people respond positively to God's proposal. When Moses speaks to them, they unanimously agree to obey God (19:8). This, however, is only the first step towards the covenant being ratified. Before this happens, God will appear before the people to set out the conditions of the covenant relationship more fully. This is not a relationship to be entered into lightly. It comes with significant implications for the lifestyle of the Israelites. To be citizens of God's kingdom on earth, the people need to recognize their new responsibilities.

4. The ten principal obligations

Prior to the ratification of the covenant agreement, God comes to Mount Sinai to speak directly to the people, setting out the obligations that they are expected to keep. His arrival on the mountain is marked by dramatic events that highlight his supernatural presence: the mountain trembles and smoke billows upward (19:18). God then addresses the people directly. His initial speech sets out the principal obligations of the covenant (ch. 20). We have come to know these as the Ten Commandments.[12]

From Mount Sinai God addresses everyone individually, using the second person singular form. After briefly recalling how he has rescued them from slavery in Egypt, God lists in descending order of importance a series of principles that are to shape the Israelite community.[13] Later,

---

[11] See next chapter.

[12] Most English versions render the Hebrew expression *'ăśeret haddĕbārîm* as 'Ten Commandments', but a more literal translation is 'ten words' or 'ten statements'; cf. Exod. 34:28, JPS.

[13] For a fuller discussion, see Alexander, *Exodus*, pp. 390–432.

God's speech will be recorded on stone tablets, underlining the import-ance of these principal obligations (34:1).

When reading the Ten Commandments, it is important to appreciate that they are not formulated for use in a legal setting. No punishments are given, unlike the case laws recorded in Exodus 21:2 – 22:20. Moreover, the language used to set out these ten principles lacks the kind of precision that we would expect with legal precepts. For example, the prohibition against having other gods before Yahweh is expressed in a way that covers a whole range of activities. These are expressed elsewhere in the Old Testament in more specific ways: invoke/mention; go after; serve; worship/bow down to; speak in the name of; turn to; play the harlot after; lay hold on; make; fear; sacrifice to; burn incense to; pour out drink offerings to. Exodus 20:3 offers an umbrella prohibition that covers every-thing to do with foreign gods.

By being formulated using less specific language, the Ten Command-ments function like mission statements. They point towards the kind of behaviour that God desires. Unlike case laws they do not establish a precise boundary between legal and illegal actions, a very necessary dis-tinction if a law is to be used to acquit or condemn an individual.

This difference between broad principles and specific legislation is helpful for understanding Jesus' remarks concerning the 'antitheses' in Matthew 5:21–48. Jesus implicitly condemns those who interpret the Ten Commandments in a narrow or restrictive fashion. He, by way of contrast, sees the Commandments as enunciating broad principles. Thus, the command not to kill condemns behaviour that involves any kind of harm that an individual might inflict on another, including hating them (see Matt. 5:21–26).[14] Jesus is not replacing the Ten Commandments with stricter rules. He addresses the way in which they have been misinterpreted by his contemporaries. Jesus seeks to expound the meaning of the Commandments as originally given.

Not surprisingly, given the exclusive nature of the relationship that is being created, the general obligations in the Ten Commandments begin by emphasizing that the Israelites are to have no other gods in Yahweh's pres-ence (20:3).[15] In an ancient world dominated by polytheistic beliefs, Yahweh's

---

[14] It is worth observing that the Hebrew verb used in Exod. 20:13 presents a challenge for translators rendering it in English. The translation of *rāṣaḥ* as 'to murder' is too narrow, for the Hebrew verb is not restricted to the intentional taking of a human life. The translation 'to kill' is too general, for the Hebrew term refers to the taking of human life, not animal life.

[15] On the sense of the expression 'before me' in 20:3, see Alexander, *Exodus*, pp. 400–402.

dismissal of other gods is radically significant. Yahweh is unwilling to grant any form of recognition to other gods, even to those of a lesser nature. He demands exclusive worship from the Israelites. By prohibiting the Israelites from acknowledging the existence of other gods, Yahweh sets himself apart as the one and only true God. This monotheistic outlook is the foundation on which the whole covenant relationship rests. Although the first obligation is expressed using only a few words, it is exceptionally important.

5. The Book of the Covenant (24:3–4a)

When Yahweh finishes addressing the people from Mount Sinai, they are filled with fear. The whole experience is too much for them, and so they ask Moses to mediate with God on their behalf. This request leads to a second divine speech that is recorded in chapters 21–23, with a short introduction and conclusion coming in chapters 20 and 24 respectively. As we have already noted, Moses subsequently records this speech in a document known as the Book of the Covenant (24:7).

Whereas God's first speech lists ten main obligations, presented as broad principles, the requirements set out in the Book of the Covenant are expressed using several different literary forms and cover a variety of issues. Exodus 21:1 – 22:20 lists various case laws that are intended to provide guidance for the Israelites as regards the moral values that are to permeate their society. In general terms, by emphasizing that the punishment should reflect the severity of the offence that has occurred,[16] these case laws prioritize the value of human life over property. Unlike comparable collections of laws from the Ancient Near East, the case laws in 21:1 – 22:20 treat all citizens as equals. No distinction is drawn between different classes of people. While there is a recognition that debt slavery will exist, slaves are not viewed simply as the material property of their owners. If slaves are severely mistreated, they have the right to go free (21:26–27). There is also the expectation that Hebrew slaves must be freed, if they desire, after seven years of service (21:2–4).

Alongside sample case laws, God includes moral exhortations that are intended to create a compassionate society with a just legal system (22:21 – 23:9). These exhortations go beyond what may be enforced by law,

---

16 This is reflected in the concept of *lex talionis*, 'an eye for an eye' (see 21:23–25). The biblical statement is frequently misunderstood as having been applied literally. This, however, was not the case. See Alexander, *Exodus*, pp. 485–489.

emphasizing that the Israelites should care for the most vulnerable members of society: widows; the fatherless; migrants. The Israelites are to recall their own experience as foreign slaves in Egypt and ensure that they do not subsequently act like their Egyptian oppressors.

Somewhat uniquely, God includes obligations that highlight the importance of the Sabbath as a time of rest for everyone, including slaves and animals (23:10–12). Listed among the main obligations (20:8–11), the observance of the Sabbath as a day of rest is both a reminder of how God has delivered the people from harsh labour in Egypt and a sign of hope for the future. Sabbath rest symbolizes the opportunity to enjoy life free from the burden of the hard labour that has impacted human existence as a consequence of Adam and Eve's actions in the garden of Eden. Importantly, the Sabbath is the sign of the covenant (31:12–17).

Bringing the Book of the Covenant to a conclusion, God warns the Israelites against various dangers that will arise when they begin to take possession of the land of Canaan (23:20–33). In their interface with other people, they will come under pressure to compromise their covenant relationship with Yahweh. God warns them that they will need to address this danger in a direct and uncompromising manner.

Much more could be said about the contents of the Book of the Covenant.[17] Viewed in conjunction with the Ten Commandments, both divine speeches establish the type of kingdom community that God desires to create. As the Israelites voluntarily commit to serving Yahweh as their sole king and to maintaining the obligations of the covenant, they will form God's kingdom on earth. If they keep the covenant, they will be 'a kingdom of priests and a holy nation'.

However, as soon becomes evident, even before they leave Mount Sinai, the Israelites display a remarkable inability to adhere to the demands of the covenant. Despite prohibitions against making images to represent Yahweh (20:4–6, 23), the people en masse encourage Aaron to make an idol (32:1–6). The Israelites believe that Yahweh is present in this idol, which is fashioned in the form of a golden calf or bull.[18] This breach of the

---

[17] For a fuller discussion, see T. D. Alexander, 'Book of the Covenant', in T. D. Alexander and D. W. Baker (eds.), *Dictionary of the Old Testament: Pentateuch* (Leicester: Inter-Varsity Press, 2003), pp. 94–101; Alexander, *Exodus*, pp. 437–537.

[18] The actions of the Israelites at the foot of the mountain are full of irony. They request an idol in order to have Yahweh present in their midst. However, at the summit of the mountain, God instructs Moses concerning the manufacture of an ornate tent in which he will dwell in the midst of the Israelite camp. God desires to be present in the camp, but the people endanger this possibility through their own attempt to bring him into the camp by means of an idol.

covenant, which almost ends their special relationship with Yahweh, is an ominous sign that the Israelites will struggle to be God's kingdom on earth. Centuries later, God will establish a new covenant, mediated by Jesus Christ.

After Moses conveys the covenant obligations spoken to him by God, which are subsequently recorded in the Book of the Covenant, the Israelites once more unanimously agree to do all that Yahweh says (24:3). Importantly, as the ratification takes place, Moses reads the obligations to the people. After hearing them for a second time, the Israelites affirm once more their willingness to keep them (24:7).

6. The blood of the covenant (24:4b–11)

A brief description of the formal ratification of the covenant comes in 24:4–11. The process begins with the construction of an altar on which burnt/ascension offerings and fellowship/peace offerings will be offered up to Yahweh.[19] This part of the process recalls the instructions that God gives in 20:24–26. While there are earlier references to burnt/ascension offerings in connection with Noah and Abraham (Gen. 8:20; 22:2–3, 6, 13), fellowship/peace offerings are mentioned here for the first time in the Old Testament. Their inclusion in the ratification ceremony is probably linked to the blood that is sprinkled on the people (6, 8) and the food that is consumed on the mountain (11).

The narrator provides no explanation as to the significance of the different elements that go into the ratification of the covenant in 24:4–11. However, there is good reason to see parallels between what happens at the foot of Mount Sinai and the process by which the high priest is consecrated to serve in the portable sanctuary.[20] The ratification of the covenant involves the people being made sufficiently holy that they may now safely ascend the slope of Mount Sinai. Previously, God had instructed the people to consecrate themselves by washing their clothes (19:10, 14). This

---

[19] For a short discussion of the different types of sacrifices, see T. D. Alexander, *From Paradise to the Promised Land: An Introduction to the Pentateuch*, 4th edn (Grand Rapids: Baker Academic, 2022), pp. 156–168.

[20] P. R. Williamson, 'Promises with Strings Attached: Covenant and Law in Exodus 19 – 24', in B. S. Rosner and P. R. Williamson (eds.), *Exploring Exodus: Literary, Theological and Contemporary Approaches* (Nottingham: Inter-Varsity Press, 2008), p. 117, writes, 'Possibly what we have here is an ordination rite, similar to that described in chapter 29, when Aaron and his sons are ordained to serve Yahweh as priests. Thus understood, here all Israel is being ordained to the service of Yahweh; this is a commissioning service for Israel to be the priestly kingdom and holy nation God had spoken of back in chapter 19.'

action prepares them for the consecration ritual that involves the offering of sacrifices and the sprinkling of blood.

To sanctify the high priest, after he has washed himself and been clothed with special garments, a ram is presented to God as a burnt/ascension offering (29:15–18; Lev. 8:18–21).[21] This appears to be a payment that ransoms the high priest from death. A second ram is then presented to God as an offering (29:19–34; Lev. 8:22–36). Only selected parts of the ram are placed on the altar, a procedure that resembles a fellowship/peace offering (see Lev. 3:1–17). Interestingly, the blood from this ram is applied to the high priest in two stages, first to purify and then to consecrate. The second stage involves blood that has been made holy through contact with the altar. Finally, the high priest eats unleavened bread and meat from the second ram after it has been cooked.[22]

Comparing the ritual for the consecration of the high priest with the covenant ratification ritual, it is noteworthy that similar offerings are made. While the details are limited, it seems likely that the blood collected by Moses in bowls is sprinkled on the people to cleanse and sanctify them. Moses underlines the importance of this blood by describing it as *the blood of the covenant* (8). Centuries later, the author of Hebrews picks up on the significance of this blood when he writes, 'This is why even the first covenant was not put into effect without blood.' Observing that the Sinai covenant required blood to be ratified, he then adds,

> In the same way, he [Moses] sprinkled with the blood both the tabernacle and everything used in its ceremonies. In fact, the law requires that nearly everything be cleansed with blood, and without the shedding of blood there is no forgiveness.[23]

The author of Hebrews associates the blood of the covenant with cleansing from the defilement of sin and with forgiveness. In addition, Hebrews 10:29

---

[21] According to Exod. 29:10–14 and Lev. 8:14–17, this is preceded by a sin/purification offering involving a young bull. The blood from the bull cleanses the bronze altar that has been manufactured by the Israelites. However, in Exod. 24 there is no offering made to purify the altar. In all likelihood, by their following the instructions of Exod. 20:25, the altar has not been defiled by being made using metal tools.

[22] It is noteworthy that there are parallels with the Passover ritual, which involves the consecration of the firstborn males (see Exod. 13:2; Num. 3:12–13; 8:17). The NIV translations of Num. 3:12–13 and 8:17 fail to convey adequately the idea that at Passover the firstborn males are made holy (contrast ESV).

[23] Heb. 9:18, 21–22.

speaks of 'the blood of the covenant that sanctified them'. Elsewhere, having associated the blood of the covenant with Christ's death on the cross, the author of Hebrews remarks, 'We have been made holy through the sacrifice of the body of Jesus Christ once for all.'[24] Not only does the author of Hebrews associate the blood of the covenant with cleansing, but he also links it to sanctification.[25]

In contending that Jesus Christ is the mediator of a new covenant, the author of Hebrews supports the tradition preserved in the Synoptic Gospels and in 1 Corinthians concerning the Passover meal that Jesus celebrated with his disciples before his death (Matt. 26:26–29; Mark 14:22–24; Luke 22:17–22; 1 Cor. 11:23–26). Matthew and Mark use the expression 'This is my blood of the covenant.' Luke and Paul write, 'This cup is the new covenant in my blood.'[26] All four writers link blood with covenant. Matthew and Mark speak of Jesus' blood being 'poured out for many', with Matthew adding, 'for the forgiveness of sins'.[27] Jesus deliberately recalls the role played by blood in ratifying the Sinai covenant.

After the sacrifices have been offered and the blood has been sprinkled on the people, Moses and other prominent Israelites ascend the slope of Mount Sinai, as previously instructed by God (24:1–2, 9). They stop short of going to the summit. Those who ascend the mountain experience something that was unimaginable prior to the covenant being ratified: they see *the God of Israel*. The description that follows probably implies that they see God from a distance and from below. Attention is drawn to what is under God's feet: *Under his feet was something like a pavement made of lapis lazuli, as bright blue as the sky* (10). Whereas, previously, anyone attempting to ascend the mountain would have been put to death, Moses and those with him are not harmed. As the narrator records, *God did not raise his hand against these leaders of the Israelites; they saw God, and they ate and drank* (11). Cleansed and consecrated, those who ascend the mountain are privileged to see something of God's glory.[28]

---

[24] Heb. 10:10.

[25] According to Heb. 9:11–22, the concepts of blood and covenant are intimately connected. See T. D. Alexander, *Face to Face with God: A Biblical Theology of Christ as Priest and Mediator*, Essential Studies in Biblical Theology (Downers Grove: InterVarsity Press, 2021), pp. 117–121.

[26] Matt. 26:28; Mark 14:24; Luke 22:20; 1 Cor. 11:25.

[27] Matt. 26:28; Mark 14:24.

[28] This experience falls short of seeing God's face. Moses subsequently asks to see God's glory but is denied this possibility (33:18–23).

7. Conclusion

The events of Exodus 24 are a significant development in the process by which God comes to establish his kingdom on earth. Yet this is merely a beginning. Having redeemed the people from slavery in Egypt, God graciously invites them to embrace him as their king. By ratifying the covenant, the Israelites commit themselves to giving Yahweh their exclusive obedience. This will require them to keep the covenant stipulations that are set out in the Ten Commandments and the Book of the Covenant. God also graciously provides the people with the means to be cleansed and consecrated, without which they would lack the holiness necessary to live in proximity to their divine king.

As God begins the process of establishing his kingdom on earth, the Israelites are the first nation to enjoy a covenant relationship with him. Their privileged status will be confirmed when God comes to dwell among them. This will require the construction of a portable sanctuary, which will be God's earthly dwelling-place. The importance of this dwelling is underlined by the attention that is given to describing its construction in Exodus 25 – 31 and 35 – 40. God's presence among the Israelites marks an important new development in the establishment of his kingdom on the earth. But, as we shall see in our next chapter, with God's arrival in their midst, the Israelites will face the serious challenge of being holy as he is holy.

Leviticus 9:1 – 10:11

6. The holy king and his high priest

In a world scarred by human hostilities, intermediaries play an important role in bringing warring parties together. The signing of the Good Friday Agreement on 10 April 1998 brought a noticeable degree of peace to the people of Northern Ireland after decades of violent conflict. Crucial to the success of reaching this point was the input of a retired American senator, George Mitchell, who was appointed by President Clinton in 1995 to be the United States Special Envoy for Northern Ireland. Alongside others, Mitchell helped establish a series of principles involving disarmament that enabled paramilitary groups to engage in all-party talks. This paved the way for the Good Friday Agreement. Mitchell's role as an intermediary was important in bringing peace to a divided community.

In a very different context, God appointed an intermediary, a high priest, whose role was to facilitate a harmonious relationship between God and the Israelites. As we shall explore in this chapter, the creation of God's kingdom on earth is intimately connected to the activities of a unique high priest who serves as a mediator between the people and God.

To many it might seem that the events of Exodus 24 conclude the process by which God makes the Israelites his chosen people. Yahweh has powerfully redeemed them from subjugation to a despotic ruler, who is the epitome of evil. Having rescued them, he leads the Israelites to Mount Sinai and establishes with them a friendship treaty that anticipates the people living with God on his holy mountain in the land of Canaan. Yet, despite these positive developments, further steps are necessary to secure the special relationship between God and the Israelites. These centre on the appointment of Moses' brother, Aaron, as a high priest. In this unique role he will play a significant part in maintaining harmony between

Yahweh and the Israelites. The high priest's ministry is vital for establishing God's kingdom on earth.

After the Israelites willingly agree to live in a covenant relationship with Yahweh, God commands Moses to construct a unique portable sanctuary that will become his earthly residence among the people. The importance of this structure is underlined by the lengthy account of its construction that comes in Exodus 25 – 31 and 35 – 40. The author of Exodus records in considerable detail God's instructions for the manufacture of a special tent or tabernacle and all its furnishings. God's speech also includes instructions for the production of clothing for a high priest and his consecration. Under the guidance of two skilled craftsmen, Bezalel and Oholiab, who are specially gifted by God's Spirit, the Israelites construct the tent and its accessories. When these are eventually made in accordance with Yahweh's instructions, Moses oversees the tent's erection. Significantly, the book of Exodus concludes by recording,

> Then the cloud covered the tent of meeting, and the glory of the LORD filled the tabernacle. Moses could not enter the tent of meeting because the cloud had settled on it, and the glory of the LORD filled the tabernacle.[1]

God's arrival in the middle of the Israelite camp brings the book of Exodus to a significant climax. This is a development that will have a profound effect on the people camped around the portable sanctuary. God's presence will significantly influence their lifestyle in numerous ways. Something of this is conveyed in the book of Leviticus with its special emphasis upon holiness. A holy lifestyle will be the hallmark of those who are citizens of God's kingdom.

Importantly, the erection of the tabernacle with its altar and curtained courtyard does not complete all of God's instructions in Exodus 25 – 31. The task of consecrating the high priest remains to be undertaken. The account of this comes in Leviticus 8. As with the construction of the portable sanctuary, the report of Aaron's consecration follows closely the instructions that God gave to Moses. Through a complex ritual that includes washing, the offering of sacrifices and the application of blood, Aaron and his sons are ritually cleansed and sanctified.[2] To achieve the

---

[1] Exod. 40:34–35.

[2] For a fuller discussion, see T. D. Alexander, *Exodus*, Apollos OT Commentary 2 (London: Apollos, 2017), pp. 589–599.

degree of holiness necessary for Aaron to approach God within the tabernacle the ritual is repeated daily for seven days.

1. Moses assembles the offerings (9:1–6)

When Aaron's consecration is completed, the scene is set for the events recorded in Leviticus 9. This is the inauguration of the sacrificial system that will enable the Israelites to live in proximity to Yahweh. This chapter highlights the vital role that the high priest performs in making atonement for the people through the presentation of offerings to God. Since this will involve four different types of offerings, Moses assembles the appropriate animals and grain before the tent of meeting. Detailed instructions for all of the offerings are recorded in Leviticus 1 – 7.[3] The various animals listed in 9:2–4 are in keeping with these instructions.

Everything is assembled before the *tent of meeting* in readiness for Aaron to present them to Yahweh. Moses also gathers the people. Jay Sklar observes that the mention of the Israelites coming near and standing before the Lord 'is royal language'. He writes,

> One stands before a ruler or person in authority (1 Kgs 1:28), often to seek his favour and/or await his decision (Gen. 43:15; Num. 27:2; cf. Deut. 19:17). Similarly, the Israelites now stood before the Lord, their covenant King, to offer him sacrifice and to await his favourable response.[4]

As the Sinai covenant emphasizes, the Israelites are to give their exclusive loyalty to Yahweh as king.

Moses explains to the people why he has assembled them before the tent of meeting: *This is what the LORD has commanded you to do, so that the glory of the LORD may appear to you* (6). The appearance of Yahweh's glory before the people is undoubtedly meant to confirm his presence in their midst. This, however, is conditional upon the offerings that Aaron will present to Yahweh. These offerings are essential if the Israelites are to experience God's presence. To underline their importance, after the sacrifices have been offered Yahweh's glory appears before the people and

---

[3] Of the various offerings listed in Leviticus 1 – 7 only the reparation offering is not presented on this occasion.

[4] J. Sklar, *Leviticus: An Introduction and Commentary*, Tyndale Old Testament Commentaries 3 (Nottingham: Inter-Varsity Press, 2013), p. 150.

fire from his presence consumes items on the altar (23–24a). With this, the people rejoice and bow down in worship (24b).

The portable sanctuary is called *the tent of meeting* in verses 5 and 23. This is no random title. It is deliberately used to highlight one of the important functions of the structure that is erected in the middle of the Israelite camp. Importantly, this designation is closely tied to the activity of the high priest. This is especially evident from how occurrences of the expression 'the tent of meeting' are distributed in God's speech to Moses concerning the construction of the portable sanctuary and its accessories. Throughout Exodus 25:1 – 27:19, God consistently uses the Hebrew term *miškān* to denote the tent. This noun means 'dwelling', although it has become a tradition for most translators of the English Bible to render it 'tabernacle' (e.g. CSB, ESV, KJV, NIV, NRSV, NJPS). The consistent use of *miškān* throughout 25:1 – 27:19 highlights how the portable sanctuary will be God's residence. God will dwell in this tent as he accompanies the Israelites from Mount Sinai to the Promised Land. In line with this usage, the furnishings mentioned in Exodus 25:10–40 are those normally associated with a human residence: a chest; a table; a lampstand.

Beyond 25:1 – 27:19, in the second half of Yahweh's speech, the term *miškān* 'dwelling' is consistently replaced by the expression *'ōhel mô'ēd* 'tent of meeting'. This change in designation is deliberate and draws attention to the second major function of the tabernacle. It is the location where the high priest comes to make atonement for the Israelites and intercede on their behalf. The importance of this high-priestly activity is underlined by the detailed instructions in Exodus 28 – 30 regarding the clothing of the high priest, his consecration and the manufacture of a golden altar that is placed inside the tent in front of the curtain leading into the Most Holy Place.[5]

2. The need for atonement (9:7)

After Moses assembles all of the items to be presented to God as offerings at *the tent of meeting*, he says to Aaron: *Come to the altar and sacrifice your sin offering and your burnt offering and make atonement for yourself*

---

[5] Although the golden altar is placed inside the Holy Place alongside the table and lampstand, the instructions for its manufacture are deliberately placed after the instructions for the consecration of the high priest. This underlines that the high priest and the golden incense altar are closely linked to the sanctuary's function as a tent of meeting.

and the people; sacrifice the offering that is for the people and make atone-
ment for them, as the LORD *has commanded* (7). Moses refers twice to how
the offering of sacrifices will *make atonement* for the Israelites. The
Hebrew verb used here is *kipper*.[6] According to Jay Sklar, this verb 'refers
to "ransom-purification": that which rescues the sinful and impure from
the wrath of the Lord (ransom), and cleanses their sin and impurity
(purification)'.[7] Unfortunately, neither of these ideas is immediately
apparent in the English expression 'make atonement'.[8] However, the
concepts of 'ransom' and 'purification' figure prominently in the burnt/
ascension[9] and sin/purification[10] offerings respectively. Moreover, according to Harold Attridge,

> Sin may be conceived as an objective defilement, a form of pollution that
> infects the sinner and the people and places with which the sinner might
> come in contact . . . Alternatively, sin may be understood in more
> personal terms as an insult or offense to divine power.[11]

Since these two aspects of sin create a barrier between God and the Israelites, both need to be addressed for reconciliation to occur.

3. Aaron atones for his sin (9:8–14)

Before Aaron can do anything for the Israelites he must first atone for his
own sin. This involves two different sacrifices, a sin/purification offering
and a burnt/ascension offering. Of these the burnt/ascension offering is
the more important,[12] although it is offered after the sin/purification

---

6 A noun derived from this verb is used in the expression Yom Kippur, 'Day of Atonement'.

7 Sklar, *Leviticus*, p. 53.

8 The English word 'atonement' means 'at one-ment' or 'to be united'; it is derived from the mediaeval Latin term *adunamentum* which means 'unity'. For a fuller discussion of the topic of 'atonement' in the Pentateuch, see T. D. Alexander, 'Pentateuch', in A. Johnston (ed.), *T&T Clark Companion to Atonement* (London: Bloomsbury T&T Clark, 2017), pp. 677–684.

9 The Hebrew term *'ōlâ* is usually translated 'burnt offering' on the basis that the entire animal is consumed by fire on the altar. However, the noun *'ōlâ* is derived from the verb *'ālâ* which has the sense 'to go up/ascend'.

10 Most English translations use 'sin offering' to translate the Hebrew term *ḥaṭṭā't*, which in other contexts often denotes 'sin'. However, given the purpose of the offering, the translation 'purification offering' better conveys its function.

11 H. W. Attridge, 'Pollution, Sin, Atonement, Salvation', in S. I. Johnston (ed.), *Ancient Religions* (Cambridge, MA/London: Belknap, 2007), p. 71.

12 See J. W. Watts, ''ōlāh: The Rhetoric of Burnt Offerings', *Vetus Testamentum* 56 (2006), pp. 125–137. Watts describes it as 'the paradigmatic offering of the Hebrew Bible' (p. 125).

offering. The greater importance of the burnt/ascension offering is indicated by the fact that it is listed first in the sequence of offerings recorded in Leviticus 1 – 7. The burnt/ascension offering is the only offering in which the entire animal is consumed by fire on the altar. For all other offerings a portion is placed on the altar. As Michael Morales observes,

> The Pentateuch portrays the ascension offering as highly cherished by YHWH God, and is not averse to using anthropomorphic language to convey its prominent role (cf. also Lev. 26:31). He smells its restful aroma and his grieving heart is pacified, so that he turns away from a posture of wrath toward humanity.[13]

a. The sin/purification offering

Aaron begins the process of making atonement for himself by offering a bull calf as a sin/purification offering (8–11):

> So Aaron came to the altar and slaughtered the calf as a sin offering for himself. His sons brought the blood to him, and he dipped his finger into the blood and put it on the horns of the altar; the rest of the blood he poured out at the base of the altar. On the altar he burned the fat, the kidneys and the long lobe of the liver from the sin offering, as the LORD commanded Moses; the flesh and the hide he burned outside the camp.

The brief comment *as the LORD commanded Moses* (10) alludes to the directives given in 4:1–12. Only part of the animal is placed on the altar. Attention focuses mainly on the blood of the young bull. Aaron takes some of it and daubs the four horns of the bronze altar. This action is perceived as ritually purifying the altar from human defilement. It resembles the process by which the high priest himself is purified by having blood placed on the lobe of his right ear, the thumb of his right hand and the big toe of his right foot (Exod. 29:20; Lev. 8:23).[14] By ritually

---

[13] L. M. Morales, 'Atonement in Ancient Israel: The Whole Burnt Offering as Central to Israel's Cult', in J. C. Laansma et al. (eds.), *So Great a Salvation: A Dialogue on the Atonement in Hebrews*, Library of New Testament Studies (London: T&T Clark, 2019), p. 31.

[14] It should be noted, however, that blood from a sin/purification offering is never placed on people. It is applied only to the sacred items in the sanctuary, which have become defiled due to human sin. For the cleansing/purification of the high priest, the blood is taken from a peace/fellowship offering.

cleansing the extremities of the altar, the entire altar is perceived as having been purified. After this, the remainder of the bull calf is removed from the camp and burned (11).

The Hebrew verb for the burning that takes place outside the camp is *śārap* 'to burn'. The burning of items outside the camp is carefully distinguished from what happens on the altar inside the courtyard of the portable sanctuary. The verb *hiqṭîr* 'to turn into smoke' is used to describe the burning that occurs on the altar. Unfortunately, most English translations fail to reflect this difference in vocabulary. In connection with the altar, the Hebrew verb *hiqṭîr* denotes the transformation of something into smoke that has a pleasant smell. This recalls what is said of various offerings being 'an aroma pleasing to the LORD'.[15]

The use of the verb *hiqṭîr* 'to turn into smoke' creates a significant connection between what occurs on the large bronze altar outside the tent of meeting and what happens inside the tent when the high priest burns incense on the golden altar. The Hebrew noun for incense is *qĕṭōret*, a term related to the verb *hiqṭîr*. A deliberate link is made between the two altars, which have been manufactured to resemble each other. What happens on the bronze altar outside the tent is replicated on the golden altar inside the tent. This connection is reinforced by the fact that the high priest brings burning coals from the bronze altar to the incense altar. The correspondence between the two altars is significant for it highlights that the high priest's role in burning incense is to present to Yahweh the offerings on the bronze altar. For this reason, the golden altar is deliberately placed close to the entrance into the Most Holy Place.[16]

The image of the high priest presenting offerings to Yahweh is reinforced by the Hebrew term *qorbān* 'offering'. This noun is derived from the verb *hiqrîb* which means 'to bring near'. Offerings are items that are brought near to Yahweh. This is the one element that all of the different sacrifices listed in Leviticus 1 – 7 have in common. As we shall explore in more detail later, only the high priest is authorized to bring the offering near to God at the tabernacle.

---

[15] Lev. 1:9, 13, 17; 2:2, 9; 3:5; 4:31; 6:15, 21. The first mention of a burnt/ascension offering in the Old Testament comes when Noah emerges from the ark and offers sacrifices to God (Gen. 8:20). The narrative states: 'The LORD smelled the pleasing aroma' (8:21).

[16] Despite being in the Holy Place, the golden incense altar is viewed as belonging to the Most Holy Place in several biblical texts (e.g. Exod. 40:5; 1 Kgs 6:22; Heb. 9:3–4). It may well be that the bronze altar was also considered as belonging to the Most Holy Place. In various texts it is described as 'most holy' (Exod. 29:37; 30:29; 40:10), language that points towards the Most Holy Place.

b. The burnt/ascension offering

After the sin/purification offering has been completed, cleansing the altar from any defilement that may be due to Aaron's own sinfulness, Aaron then presents a ram as a burnt/ascension offering to God (12–14):

> Then he slaughtered the burnt offering. His sons handed him the blood, and he splashed it against the sides of the altar. They handed him the burnt offering piece by piece, including the head, and he burned them on the altar. He washed the internal organs and the legs and burned them on top of the burnt offering on the altar.

Once more Aaron's actions conform to the instructions recorded earlier in Leviticus (see 1:3–9). Aaron's sons collect the ram's blood, but it is not used to cleanse the altar. It is thrown against the sides of the altar. After being suitably prepared, the entire ram is transformed into smoke on the altar to create a pleasing aroma that goes upward.

4. Aaron atones for the Israelites (9:15–21)

After atoning for his own sin, Aaron proceeds to atone for the sins of the Israelites. He takes the goat and offers it as a sin/purification offering (15), repeating the ritual that he performed with the male calf (8–11). After the goat, he offers a calf as a burnt/ascension offering (16). He then offers a lamb as a burnt/ascension offering. The lamb is carefully distinguished from the calf; the lamb is *the morning's burnt offering*. Previously, God had instructed Moses that Aaron as high priest was to offer daily, morning and evening, a lamb as a burnt/ascension offering. These instructions are included in the directions for the consecration of the high priest in Exodus 29:38–43:

> This is what you are to offer on the altar regularly each day: two lambs a year old. Offer one in the morning and the other at twilight. With the first lamb offer a tenth of an ephah of the finest flour mixed with a quarter of a hin of oil from pressed olives, and a quarter of a hin of wine as a drink offering. Sacrifice the other lamb at twilight with the same grain offering and its drink offering as in the morning – a pleasing aroma, a food offering presented to the LORD.
>
> For the generations to come this burnt offering is to be made regularly at the entrance to the tent of meeting, before the LORD. There I will meet

you and speak to you; there also I will meet with the Israelites, and the place will be consecrated by my glory.

Leviticus 9:17 records briefly the first occasion on which this daily offering of a lamb is made along with a grain offering.[17] This will be a regular part of the high priest's duties at the tabernacle. Morning and evening he will offer a lamb as a burnt/ascension offering.

After the sin/purification and burnt/ascension offerings, Aaron presents a fellowship/peace offering. This involves an ox and a ram. With this offering only the fat portions of the ox and the ram are placed on the altar to be turned into smoke. The bulk of the animals will provide meat for a special meal that the Israelites will eat to celebrate God's gracious forgiveness. They now enjoy peace with Yahweh. While most of the meat goes to the non-priestly worshippers, the items waved by Aaron are given to the priests (cf. 7:28–36). Aaron's actions are in line with the fuller instructions recorded in Leviticus 3:1–11.

5. Aaron blesses the people (9:22–24)

After the various offerings have been placed on the bronze altar outside the entrance to the tent of meeting, Aaron blesses the people (22). He and Moses then enter the tent (23). Prior to this, Moses has been prohibited from going into the tent (Exod. 40:35). Nothing is said about what happens within the tent. These details are not necessary in the present context, because the emphasis is upon what occurs outside the tent of meeting. It seems likely, however, that on entering the tent, Aaron offers incense on the golden altar. This would fulfil the instructions that were given by God to Moses in connection with the incense altar (Exod. 30:7–9). By burning incense, Aaron replicates what is occurring on the bronze altar, and in doing so he presents the offerings to God on behalf of the Israelites. This role belongs uniquely to Aaron as high priest. As we shall observe shortly, any other person undertaking this responsibility places his life in danger.

When Moses and Aaron exit the tent, they once more bless the people. With this, *the glory of the* LORD appears to *all the people* (23), fulfilling what Moses had previously said (4, 6). Then, by way of confirming his approval of all that Aaron has done, Yahweh sends fire to consume the

---

[17] Fuller instructions regarding the grain offering come in Lev. 2:1–3.

burnt offering and the fat portions of the fellowship/peace offering that are on the bronze altar. In response, the people shout *for joy* and fall face down in worship (24).

God's appearance before the people is his stamp of approval on all that has taken place in setting up the portable sanctuary, the consecration of Aaron as high priest and the inauguration of sacrificial ritual at the tent of meeting.[18] Importantly, these developments emphasize the special status of the high priest. Aaron alone is divinely appointed to atone for the Israelites, using the sacrifices that God has directed. There is only one high priest who is sufficiently holy to present the offerings of the people to Yahweh.

6. The deaths of Nadab and Abihu (10:1–11)

Aaron's unique role as high priest is reinforced by the tragic events that immediately follow the appearance of Yahweh's glory before the people. Inexplicably, *Aaron's sons Nadab and Abihu* attempt to burn incense before the Lord (10:1). They mistakenly attempt to undertake the unique role that God has assigned to their father as high priest. Only Aaron is authorized to burn incense in God's presence. Despite being Aaron's eldest sons, and among those who had previously ascended the slope of Mount Sinai (Exod. 24:9), they are struck dead by fire that comes from the presence of the Lord. The manner of their deaths is noteworthy because it resembles what has just happened when fire consumed the burnt offering on the altar (9:24). Whereas the first was a sign of God's grace, the second is a sign of divine judgment. As Mark Rooker comments, 'The serious consequence of Nadab and Abihu's disobedience is a reminder of how resolutely important the worship of God is to be for a believer's life.'[19]

Responding to what has happened, Moses says,

This is what the LORD spoke of when he said:

'Among those who approach me
I will be proved holy;

---

[18] M. F. Rooker, *Leviticus*, NAC 3A (Nashville: Broadman & Holman, 2000), p. 154, writes, 'In Exodus 24 the glory of the Lord rests on the mountain at Sinai. In Exodus 40 the glory of the Lord fills the tabernacle, indicating that the tabernacle has become a portable Sinai. The next appearance of the glory of the Lord in Leviticus 9 in the context of the inauguration of the priesthood indicates that God has established and approved the sacrificial system.'

[19] Ibid., p. 158.

in the sight of all the people
I will be honoured.'

(3)

The deaths of Nadab and Abihu are a serious warning to all the Israelites, and especially the priests, regarding God's holiness. The presence of a holy God in the midst of the Israelite camp has weighty implications for what the people may or may not do.

The concept of holiness permeates the book of Leviticus. Words based on the Hebrew root *qādaš* (e.g. 'holy', 'holiness', 'sanctify') come 152 times in Leviticus; this is about one-fifth of all Old Testament occurrences. God tells Aaron that one of his important tasks is to *distinguish between the holy and the common* (10). In practical terms, this distinction establishes a boundary that coincides with the curtained fence around the portable sanctuary. Everything inside this area is considered *holy*. Everything outside is *common*.

In addition to this holy–common boundary, a second boundary is established by God, distinguishing *between the unclean and the clean* (10). This boundary coincides with the perimeter of the Israelite camp. Everything inside the camp, including the tabernacle, is *clean*, whereas everything outside is *unclean*. The existence of these two boundaries creates three distinctive regions: (1) The portable sanctuary at the heart of the camp is both holy and clean; (2) the camp surrounding the sanctuary is clean; (3) outside the camp is unclean.[20] By creating this tripartite structure that may for simplicity be considered as creating three regions, holy–clean–unclean, God impresses upon the Israelites the idea that only those who are holy may approach him. Those who are unclean must remain at a distance. With good reason, God tells Moses and Aaron: 'You must keep the Israelites separate from things that make them unclean, so they will not die in their uncleanness for defiling my dwelling-place, which is among them.'[21] In the face of such danger, the Israelites are divinely commanded to be holy as Yahweh is holy (11:44–45; 19:2; 20:7, 26; 21:6).

In establishing this tripartite structure of holy–clean–unclean, God conveys important ideas regarding the concept of holiness, cleanness and uncleanness. Holiness is associated with life, whereas uncleanness is

---

[20] For a fuller discussion, see T. D. Alexander, *Face to Face with God: A Biblical Theology of Christ as Priest and Mediator*, Essential Studies in Biblical Theology (Downers Grove: InterVarsity Press, 2021), pp. 40–50.
[21] Lev. 15:31.

linked to death. This is reflected in the instructions that are given regarding the removal of the corpses of Nadab and Abihu to outside the camp:

> Moses summoned Mishael and Elzaphan, sons of Aaron's uncle Uzziel, and said to them, 'Come here; carry your cousins outside the camp, away from the front of the sanctuary.' So they came and carried them, still in their tunics, outside the camp, as Moses ordered.
> (4–5)

Since corpses are associated with uncleanness, it is inappropriate for the bodies of Nadab and Abihu to remain inside the camp.

Underlining this distinction between life and death, Aaron and his two sons Eleazar and Ithamar are not permitted to display signs of mourning while they remain inside the holy area of the tabernacle complex. Later in Leviticus, fuller instructions are given regarding the contact that priests may have with corpses:

> The LORD said to Moses, 'Speak to the priests, the sons of Aaron, and say to them: "A priest must not make himself ceremonially unclean for any of his people who die, except for a close relative, such as his mother or father, his son or daughter, his brother, or an unmarried sister who is dependent on him since she has no husband – for her he may make himself unclean. He must not make himself unclean for people related to him by marriage, and so defile himself."'[22]

Only for the closest of relatives may an ordinary priest come into contact with a corpse. Stricter rules apply to the high priest:

> The high priest, the one among his brothers who has had the anointing oil poured on his head and who has been ordained to wear the priestly garments, must not let his hair become unkempt or tear his clothes. He must not enter a place where there is a dead body. He must not make himself unclean, even for his father or mother, nor leave the sanctuary of his God or desecrate it, because he has been dedicated by the anointing oil of his God. I am the LORD.[23]

---

[22] Lev. 21:1–4.
[23] Lev. 21:10–12.

The stringent rules applying to the high priest reflect the higher level of holiness that he is required to have in order to approach God.

Such is God's abhorrence of death that even the signs of mourning must not be evident in the holy area of the camp. Holiness and life go together. Those who are holy ultimately enjoy life in all its abundance. Death, associated with sin and alienation from God, has no place in God's presence.

7. Conclusion

The image of a high priest offering sacrifices and burning incense inside a tent is far removed from the experience of most Christians today. Yet these activities are highly relevant for understanding how Jesus Christ enables subjects of his kingdom to come into God's holy presence. The rituals associated with the tabernacle illustrate how this is achieved. This correspondence rests on the fact that the portable sanctuary made at Mount Sinai is deliberately patterned on the heavenly sanctuary (see Exod. 25:9, 40); it is 'a copy and shadow of what is in heaven', according to Hebrews 8:5.

Before sinful people can come into God's presence, there needs to be a process of atonement. What happens at the earthly sanctuary sheds light on how Jesus Christ makes atonement at the heavenly sanctuary. First, at both sanctuaries, atonement requires the offering of a suitable sacrifice. For this reason, New Testament writers understand Jesus Christ's death on the cross in sacrificial terms. As John the Baptist remarks, Jesus Christ is 'the Lamb of God, who takes away the sin of the world'.[24] Jesus himself tells his disciples that he has come 'to give his life as a ransom for many'.[25] Contrasting the numerous sacrifices made by the Aaronic high priest with Christ's single sacrifice, the author of Hebrews writes,

> Day after day every priest stands and performs his religious duties; again and again he offers the same sacrifices, which can never take away sins. But when this priest [Jesus Christ] had offered for all time one sacrifice for sins, he sat down at the right hand of God, and since that time he waits for his enemies to be made his footstool. For by one sacrifice he has made perfect for ever those who are being made holy.[26]

---

[24] John 1:29.
[25] Mark 10:45.
[26] Heb. 10:11–14.

Christ's sacrificial death on the cross is a vital and necessary component for reconciling people to God.

Second, as the rituals at the earthly sanctuary reveal, the atoning sacrifice has to be brought near to God. This is the role of the high priest. To this end, Jesus Christ ascends to the heavenly sanctuary in order, as our great High Priest, to present his self-offering to the Majesty in heaven. Christ's ascension is important. Without it, his self-sacrifice on the cross remains outside the heavenly sanctuary. Through his ascension, Christ presents his self-sacrifice as an atoning offering to God. In this respect, Christ's ascension is foreshadowed by the burnt/ascension offering.

Appointed by God, Jesus Christ enjoys a unique priesthood that parallels that of the Aaronic high priest. However, Jesus Christ is not related to the Aaronic priestly family genealogically. He belongs to the tribe of Judah. Drawing on Psalm 110, the author of Hebrews views Jesus as being appointed by God as a priest-king for ever (Heb. 6:20 – 7:17). Jesus does not belong to a priestly family and does not establish a priestly dynasty, but he resembles the mysterious Melchizedek who unexpectedly appears in the Genesis story (Gen. 14:18–20). Melchizedek's ancestry is unknown and there is no mention of his priesthood passing to his son. The same is true for Jesus Christ.

Observing that Abraham gives Melchizedek a tithe, the author of Hebrews argues that Melchizedek's priesthood is superior to that of the Aaronic high priest (Heb. 7:1–10). The author of Hebrews also contends that Jesus Christ's high priesthood is superior to the Aaronic high priest. This is evident from the fact that he serves in the heavenly sanctuary, of which the tabernacle is merely a 'copy and shadow'.[27] The Aaronic high priest of necessity must atone daily for his own sin, but this is not required for Jesus Christ because he is sinless. The Aaronic high priest goes in and out of the tent of meeting, standing before God when inside the tent, but Jesus Christ enters the heavenly sanctuary once and remains there, seated at the right hand of the Majesty in heaven.

Drawing on Psalm 110, the New Testament presents the ascended Jesus as a unique priest-king whom God appoints to rule over his earthly kingdom.[28] Christ's reign as king is all-important, but we should not lose sight of his role as our great High Priest, who not only has presented his

---

[27] Heb. 8:5.

[28] See M. H. Emadi, *The Royal Priest: Psalm 110 in Biblical Theology*, New Studies in Biblical Theology 60 (London: Apollos, 2022).

self-offering as an atoning sacrifice for our sins, but continues to intercede with God the Father for us because of our continuing sinfulness (see 1 John 2:1–2).

Joshua 1:1–18

7. A royal inheritance

Many people aspire to be leaders, but few become great leaders. When we think of truly outstanding leaders in recent history, we are likely to recall people such as Winston Churchill, Mahatma Gandhi, Martin Luther King Jr., Nelson Mandela and Mother Teresa. Going back in time, great leaders figure prominently in the overarching biblical story. Some are highlighted because in differing ways they display characteristics that prefigure Jesus Christ, the greatest of all human leaders. Ultimately, he will exercise authority as a king over all the earth, and through him the kingdom of God will be established.

Of the many great leaders found in the Old Testament, Moses stands apart. In the complex and compelling narrative that runs through the books of Genesis to Kings, Moses figures prominently in four of the ten books.[1] From his birth at the start of Exodus to his death at the end of Deuteronomy, Moses plays a central role in the narrative that records a series of events, from God's redemption of the Israelites from slavery in Egypt to their arrival on the eastern side of the River Jordan. He is the one who leads the people through the wilderness during their forty years of wandering. While Moses himself will die before taking the Israelites into the Promised Land, his oversight of the people, under the authority of God, is significant.

Given Moses' importance, it is no surprise that the opening sentences of the book of Joshua abound in references to him as the narrative now

---

[1] Counting 1 and 2 Samuel and 1 and 2 Kings as constituting two books, as they were originally composed.

focuses on his successor, Joshua. Appointed before Moses' death (Num. 27:18-21; Deut. 3:28; 31:7-8, 14), Joshua must continue the work undertaken by Moses. Leading the people into the Promised Land, he must oversee the transformation of the Israelites from landless clans into a nation that possesses its own territory. The responsibility placed on Joshua's shoulders is substantial. The next stage in the creation of God's kingdom on the earth depends on his successful leadership.

1. Joshua, a second Moses (1:1)

Deuteronomy concludes by recording the death and burial of Moses 'in Moab, in the valley opposite Beth Peor'.[2] For thirty days the Israelites grieve, a sign of the deep respect that the people have for Moses, their leader for forty years. With no headstone to mark the location of his burial, the book of Deuteronomy concludes with a fitting epithet in 34:10-12:

> Since then, no prophet has risen in Israel like Moses, whom the LORD knew face to face, who did all those signs and wonders the LORD sent him to do in Egypt – to Pharaoh and to all his officials and to his whole land. For no one has ever shown the mighty power or performed the awesome deeds that Moses did in the sight of all Israel.

Who could possibly fill the void created by Moses' death?

The opening words of Joshua 1 set the scene by noting *the death of Moses the servant of the LORD* (1). As a fitting tribute to the memory of Moses, he is designated *the servant of the LORD*. This description has been used once before of Moses, in Deuteronomy 34:5. It is frequently associated with Moses throughout the book of Joshua (1:1, 13, 15; 8:31, 33; 11:12; 12:6 [x2]; 13:8; 14:7; 18:7; 22:2, 4–5; 24:29), but rarely appears elsewhere in the remainder of the Old Testament (2 Kgs 18:12; 2 Chr. 1:3; 24:6). Remarkably, there are only two occurrences of the expression *the servant of the LORD* that do not refer to Moses. Both relate to Joshua. The first comes in connection with the death of Joshua (Josh. 24:29). The second occurs shortly afterwards in Judges 2:8. Given its strong association with Moses, the expression 'Joshua son of Nun, the servant of the LORD' is a significant

---

[2] Deut. 34:6.

tribute, placing Joshua on a par with Moses. This epithet fittingly reflects the manner in which Joshua is presented as a second Moses throughout the book of Joshua.

Although Joshua will eventually be viewed as resembling Moses, he is initially introduced as *Moses' assistant* (1). This title is used elsewhere of him, reflecting the fact that from his youth, Joshua assisted Moses (see Num. 11:28; cf. Exod. 24:13; 33:11).[3] Long before he was appointed as leader of the Israelites, Joshua enjoyed an exceptionally close and privileged relationship with Moses. He was with Moses on Mount Sinai when Moses received instructions for the building of the tabernacle (see Exod. 24:13; 32:17). Other passages indicate that Joshua was sometimes with Moses when God spoke to him (Exod. 33:11). This may explain why Joshua resembles Moses closely; he spent time with him and was mentored by him.

As the story unfolds, we encounter various incidents that provide striking parallels between the lives of Moses and Joshua. The crossing of the River Jordan parallels the crossing of the Lake of Reeds. On both occasions the waters part in an extraordinary way, enabling the Israelites to go over safely. Later, when Joshua encounters the commander of the Lord's army, he is told, 'Take off your sandals, for the place where you are standing is holy.'[4] The correspondence with Moses' encounter at the burning bush in Exodus 3:5 is striking.[5] In Joshua 12 Moses' victories over enemies are listed immediately before those of Joshua. Similarly, details of Moses' allocation of territory are placed immediately prior to a description of Joshua's allocation of land (Josh. 13 – 14). Finally, like Moses, Joshua makes two important speeches just prior to his death (Josh. 23 – 24). These parallels give the strong impression that Joshua is a 'second Moses'.

While Joshua is initially described as *Moses' assistant* (1), Yahweh reassures him that he will successfully enable the people to take possession of the land, as he had promised Moses (Deut. 1:38; 3:28). Soon afterwards the Transjordanian tribes acknowledge Joshua's authority when they comment, 'Just as we fully obeyed Moses, so we will obey you. Only may the LORD your God be with you as he was with Moses.'[6] Their remarks confirm Joshua's status as Moses' successor.

---

[3] Deut. 1:38 speaks of Joshua as someone 'who stands before' Moses.

[4] Josh. 5:15.

[5] It is worth observing that Joshua's encounter implies that God's presence is no longer to be associated with Mount Sinai but with the Promised Land.

[6] Josh. 1:17.

2. Joshua and the land of Canaan (1:2–6)

At the outset of the book, God sets before Joshua the challenge of leading the Israelites into the land of Canaan so that they may take possession of it:

> Moses my servant is dead. Now then, you and all these people, get ready to cross the River Jordan into the land I am about to give to them – to the Israelites. I will give you every place where you set your foot, as I promised Moses. Your territory will extend from the desert to Lebanon, and from the great river, the Euphrates – all the Hittite country – to the Mediterranean Sea in the west. No one will be able to stand against you all the days of your life. As I was with Moses, so I will be with you; I will never leave you nor forsake you. Be strong and courageous, because you will lead these people to inherit the land I swore to their ancestors to give them.
> (2–6)

The land is a gift from Yahweh. As the creator of the world, he alone has the right to allocate territory to a nation. While in this context the emphasis is on the gift of land to the Israelites, elsewhere God warns the Israelites against encroaching on the territory of other nations because he has determined the boundaries of their lands (see Deut. 2:9, 19). The gift of Canaan to the Israelites fulfils God's promise to the patriarchs, Abraham, Isaac and Jacob. God covenanted with Abraham that his descendants would inherit land 'from the Wadi of Egypt to the great river, the Euphrates – the land of the Kenites, Kenizzites, Kadmonites, Hittites, Perizzites, Rephaites, Amorites, Canaanites, Girgashites and Jebusites'.[7] The boundaries mentioned in Joshua 1:4 reflect the territory promised to the patriarchs.

In response to God's directive, Joshua instructs 'the officers of the people' to tell them: 'Get your provisions ready. Three days from now you will cross the Jordan here to go in and take possession of the land the LORD your God is giving you for your own' (10–11). The process by which the Israelites will take possession of the land is reflected in the structure of the book of Joshua. H. J. Koorevaar observes that the book of Joshua

---

7 Gen. 15:18–21; cf. Deut. 1:6–8; 11:24; 34:1–4.

is designed around the themes of 'taking' and 'dividing'.[8] Whereas 5:13 – 12:24 emphasizes Joshua's role in 'taking' the land, 13:1 – 21:45 focuses on his part in 'dividing' the land. This involves a wordplay in Hebrew: the verb for 'taking' is *lāqaḥ* and the verb for 'dividing' is *ḥālaq*. Furthermore, Koorevaar observes that the two remaining sections of Joshua, 1:1 – 5:12 and 22:1 – 24:33, are linked by wordplay involving the concepts of 'going over' (Hebrew *'ābar*) and 'worshipping/serving' (*'ābad*). These observations provide a helpful summary of the four phases through which Joshua courageously and wisely guides the people. Put simply, under Joshua's leadership the Israelites go over the Jordan and take the land. Thereafter Joshua divides the land and encourages the people to worship and serve only the Lord.

Despite popular perceptions of a violent conquest, the taking of the land is largely a process of gradual occupation as the Canaanite inhabitants lose control of the territory. While some biblical texts are perceived as stating that the inhabitants of the land are to be annihilated in a process of ethnic cleansing, this is a misconception that is even evident in the book of Joshua itself.[9] While the Israelite assault on Jericho gives its inhabitants ample time to vacate the city, even with the divine destruction of the walls, Rahab and her family survive (2:1–24; 6:22–25). Her rescue stands in marked contrast to the death of Achan, an Israelite, who disregards God's instructions regarding the taking of booty from the city (7:1–26). The subsequent account of the Gibeonites establishing a peace treaty with the Israelites reinforces the idea that not all Canaanites are put to death by the Israelites (9:1–27).[10]

Throughout the book of Joshua, the successful invasion of the land of Canaan is associated with divine activity. The success of the whole venture is summarized in these words:

So the LORD gave Israel all the land he had sworn to give their ancestors, and they took possession of it and settled there. The LORD gave them rest

---

[8] Drawing on H. J. Koorevaar, 'De Opbouw van het Boek Jozua' (PhD diss., University of Brussels, 1990). See J. G. McConville, *Grace in the End* (Carlisle: Paternoster, 1993), pp. 101–102; J. R. Vannoy, 'Joshua: Theology of', *NIDOTTE* 4:811–814.

[9] W. A. Ford, '"Dispossessing" the Canaanites in Deuteronomy', in M. Spalione and H. Paynter (eds.), *Map or Compass? The Bible on Violence*, Bible in the Modern World 79 (Sheffield: Sheffield Phoenix, 2022), pp. 56–71. See also P. Copan, *Is God a Moral Monster? Making Sense of the Old Testament God* (Grand Rapids: Baker, 2011); P. Copan and M. Flannagan, *Did God Really Command Genocide? Coming to Terms with the Justice of God* (Grand Rapids: Baker, 2014).

[10] See D. G. Firth, *Including the Stranger: Foreigners in the Former Prophets*, New Studies in Biblical Theology 50 (Nottingham: Apollos, 2019), pp. 27–33.

on every side, just as he had sworn to their ancestors. Not one of their enemies withstood them; the LORD gave all their enemies into their hands. Not one of all the LORD's good promises to Israel failed; every one was fulfilled.[11]

While this passage appears to suggest that by the end of Joshua's life the Israelites have taken possession of the entire land of Canaan, a more nuanced reading of this summary in the light of all that is said in the rest of Joshua reveals that this is not the case.[12] This passage most likely alludes to Exodus 23:20–33, where a subtle distinction is drawn between the extent of the initial stage of settlement and what is finally achieved.[13]

This distinction between an initial occupation that involves only part of the land of Canaan and a later broader occupation of all the land is reflected in Joshua 14 – 19 regarding the allocation of territory to the tribes. Whereas the tribes of Judah, Ephraim and the half-tribe of Manasseh are portrayed as having already taken possession of territory (Josh. 14 – 17), the land yet to be possessed is allocated by lot to the tribes of Benjamin, Simeon, Zebulun, Issachar, Asher, Naphtali and Dan (Josh. 18 – 19). This distinction between territory that is already under Israelite control and that which has still to be taken should inform our reading of Joshua 21:43–45.[14] Moreover, it is noteworthy that in the larger narrative, the settlement of Canaan only concludes when David takes the Jebusite city of Jerusalem (2 Sam. 5).[15] In the light of this gradual process of settlement, Joshua's warning to the Israelites in 23:12–13 makes good sense:

> But if you turn away and ally yourselves with the survivors of these nations that remain among you and if you intermarry with them and associate with them, then you may be sure that the LORD your God will no longer drive out these nations before you. Instead, they will become snares and

---

[11] Josh. 21:43–45; cf. 10:40–43; 11:16–23.

[12] For a fuller discussion, see T. A. Clarke, 'Complete v. Incomplete Conquest: A Re-Examination of Three Passages in Joshua', *Tyndale Bulletin* 61 (2010), pp. 89–104.

[13] Clarke, 'Complete v. Incomplete Conquest', p. 101, writes, 'An examination of Exodus 23:20–33, which records the first promise of the land to the generation coming out of Egypt, shows that the Lord had indeed promised to bring Israel into the land of the Amorites, Hittites, Perizzites, Canaanites, Hivites and Jebusites (cf. v. 23). The Lord goes on to say that he would give the land to Israel in stages. In the first stage, he would drive out the Hivites, Canaanites and Hittites, but the Amorites, Perizzites and Jebusites would apparently remain at the end of the first phase of the conquest.'

[14] We should also recall God's words to Joshua in 13:1–7.

[15] Reflecting this, the Jebusites are always mentioned last in the lists of people who will be dispossessed (see Gen. 15:21; Exod. 3:8, 17; 13:5; 23:23; 33:2; 34:11; Deut. 7:1; 20:17; Josh. 3:10; 9:1; 11:3; 12:8; 24:11).

traps for you, whips on your backs and thorns in your eyes, until you perish from this good land, which the LORD your God has given you.

The establishment of God's kingdom in the land of Canaan not only depends upon the expulsion of those who refuse to recognize God's authority (i.e. the Canaanites), but it requires the exclusive loyalty of the Israelites. As the continuing story reveals, this latter requirement will be a constant challenge for the people, eventually leading to their temporary expulsion from the land during the period of the Babylonian exile.

3. Joshua and the Book of the Law (1:7–11)

As Moses' successor, Joshua faces a great challenge in leading the Israelites into the Promised Land. Aware of this, Moses exhorts Joshua to be courageous when he appoints him as leader:

> Be strong and courageous, for you must go with this people into the land that the LORD swore to their ancestors to give them, and you must divide it among them as their inheritance. The LORD himself goes before you and will be with you; he will never leave you nor forsake you. Do not be afraid; do not be discouraged.[16]

Strikingly, God's speech to Joshua echoes what Moses had said: *Be strong and very courageous . . . Have I not commanded you? Be strong and courageous. Do not be afraid; do not be discouraged, for the LORD your God will be with you wherever you go* (7a, 9).

Building on these words of encouragement, God reminds Joshua that his success as a leader will depend upon his diligence in obeying God. The Lord reminds Joshua of the importance of keeping his instructions:

> *Be careful to obey all the law my servant Moses gave you; do not turn from it to the right or to the left, that you may be successful wherever you go. Keep this Book of the Law always on your lips; meditate on it day and night, so that you may be careful to do everything written in it. Then you will be prosperous and successful.*
> (7–8)

---

16 Deut. 31:7–8.

What is the *Book of the Law*? This is an important question for it is often assumed that this title refers to the books of Genesis–Deuteronomy. In Jewish tradition, the Hebrew Bible consists of three main sections, which are designated the Law, Prophets and Writings. The Law refers to the first five books of the Bible, what is known as the Pentateuch in Christian tradition. The Hebrew noun translated *Law* is *tôrâ*. The term Torah is generally taken to denote all of Genesis to Deuteronomy. However, when Yahweh refers to the *Book of the Law* in Joshua 1:8, he is not thinking of the five books that constitute the Pentateuch. He has something more specific in view. This becomes evident when we consider how the expression 'Book of the Law' is used in the final chapters of Deuteronomy. It comes in Deuteronomy 28:61, 29:21 and 31:26. From these passages it is apparent that the Book of the Law contains the instructions and laws that Moses gave the Israelites when they were camped on the eastern side of the River Jordan. Deuteronomy 31:24 records how Moses wrote 'in a book the words of this law from beginning to end'. This reflects what God says when he tells Joshua, *Be careful to obey all the law my servant Moses gave you* (7). In the light of these observations, the *Book of the Law* in Joshua 1:8 is probably all of the material in Deuteronomy 5:1 to 26:19, including possibly also chapters 27 – 28 which record instructions for inscribing the law on plastered stones and a list of curses and blessings.[17]

In Deuteronomy the importance of the Book of the Law is underlined through various instructions that Moses gives to the people. First, Moses instructs them to have the Book of the Law inscribed on plaster-coated stones on Mount Ebal (Deut. 27:1–8), with a further copy being placed beside the ark of the covenant (31:24–26). Second, Moses commands the priests and elders to read the law to the people every seventh year (31:9–13). In these ways, the contents of the Book of the Law are to be placed at the centre of the nation's public life. To reinforce the importance of the law, a list of curses, which are to be recited by the Levites, ends by stating, 'Cursed is anyone who does not uphold the words of this law by carrying them out.'[18]

---

[17] R. S. Hess, *Joshua*, Tyndale Old Testament Commentaries (Leicester: Inter-Varsity Press, 1996), pp. 79–80, comments, 'Given the close parallels with Deuteronomy already noted, the reference is probably to Deuteronomic law. This is supported by the warning not to turn to the right or to the left, which also occurs throughout Deuteronomy (2:27; 5:29 [5:32]; 17:11, 20; 28:14).' The expression 'law of the Lord' comes in Ps. 1:2. Here too it probably denotes the bulk of Deuteronomy rather than the books of Genesis to Deuteronomy.

[18] Deut. 27:26.

Although there is a long-standing tradition that the Hebrew word *tôrâ* should be translated 'law', this is unfortunate. A better translation is 'instruction' (see the CSB rendering of Josh. 1:7) or 'teaching' (cf. NJPS translation of Josh. 1:7).[19] This not only conveys more accurately the meaning of the noun *tôrâ* but better reflects the nature of the material that is included in Deuteronomy 5 – 28, much of which is not strictly speaking 'law'.

Turning to the book of Joshua, obedience to the *Book of the Law* undoubtedly accounts for the successful invasion of the land of Canaan. Joshua acknowledges the importance of keeping all that is recorded in the Book of the Law, and his obedience to God is exemplary. Among the various ways in which this is evident is his desire to circumcise the people and keep the Passover (Josh. 5:1–12). Soon after this, in keeping with the instructions of Deuteronomy 27, Joshua renews the covenant at Mount Ebal (8:30–35). Joshua's commitment to the Book of the Law is evident towards the end of his life when he addresses the Israelites: 'Be very strong; be careful to obey all that is written in the Book of the Law of Moses, without turning aside to the right or to the left.'[20] By way of reinforcing this request, Joshua, like Moses before him, arranges for God's decrees and laws to be inscribed on a large stone that is set up at Shechem (24:25–26).

Merely possessing the Book of the Law is not sufficient to guarantee success for Joshua. God commands him to *meditate on it day and night* (8).[21] Kenneth A. Mathews helpfully observes, '"Meditate" (*hagah*) does not refer to a repetition of mystic words (mantra) or to reaching a height-ened level of spiritual awareness. It describes contemplation for the purpose of understanding and obedience.'[22] As a practice offering success for living, meditating on the Book of the Law involves a process of careful reflection. As David Firth remarks,

> Meditation involves more than simply memorizing Torah in order to carry out certain actions at definite points in time. Rather than a set of commandments designating specific actions, the Torah is better

---

[19] T. D. Alexander, *From Paradise to the Promised Land: An Introduction to the Pentateuch*, 4th edn (Grand Rapids: Baker Academic, 2022), p. 201.

[20] Josh. 23:6.

[21] Similar advice comes at the start of the book of Psalms (1:2).

[22] K. A. Mathews, *Joshua*, Teach the Text Commentary (Grand Rapids: Baker, 2016), p. 14.

understood as a form of structured wisdom, something that gives shape to life and demonstrates the patterns of order God desires.[23]

As we shall see, the task of meditation on the Book of the Law is closely tied to Joshua's calling to be the people's leader.

Joshua's commitment to obey the Book of the Law leads naturally to another important aspect of how he is portrayed. In all but title, Joshua is presented as a king. Joshua's wholehearted obedience to the Book of the Law is very much in keeping with what is expected of a king. According to Deuteronomy 17:18–20, the king is to centre his life on the Book of the Law:

> When he takes the throne of his kingdom, he is to write for himself on a scroll a copy of this law, taken from that of the Levitical priests. It is to be with him, and he is to read it all the days of his life so that he may learn to revere the LORD his God and follow carefully all the words of this law and these decrees and not consider himself better than his fellow Israelites and turn from the law to the right or to the left. Then he and his descendants will reign a long time over his kingdom in Israel.

Joshua's commitment to the Book of the Law has 'royal' overtones. This is not unexpected when we recall how the book of Genesis associates future kingship with Joseph's younger son Ephraim.[24] Joshua belongs to the tribe of Ephraim and displays leadership qualities. He commands the armed unit that defeats the Amalekites when they attack the Israelites (Exod. 17:8–16). Joshua is selected to represent the tribe of Ephraim when twelve spies are sent to reconnoitre the land of Canaan (Num. 13:1 – 14:45). Like the judges and kings of Israel, he is empowered by God's Spirit (Num. 27:18).

While Joshua is never designated a monarch, he leads the Israelites to victory against various coalitions of kings. Under Joshua's leadership, the Israelites defeat so many kings that an entire chapter is given over to listing them (Josh. 12:1–24). Furthermore, when victory is achieved Joshua establishes Shiloh in the territory allocated to the tribe of Ephraim as the

---

[23] D. G. Firth, *Joshua*, Evangelical Biblical Theology Commentary (Bellingham: Lexham Academic, 2021), p. 35. Recognizing how the Book of the Law is designed to function, Firth remarks, 'This would require seeing the instruction as guidance for situations that would be faced rather than as a comprehensive set of rules that could simply be applied. Joshua would need a deep knowledge of God's instruction, which meant both knowing its content and reflecting on how it could be applied' (p. 73).

[24] See chapter 3.

location for the ark of the covenant, the footstool of God's throne. This event underlines the importance of Ephraim as the tribe from which the divinely promised king will come. However, as the books of Judges and Samuel reveal, the tribe of Ephraim becomes morally and spiritually corrupt. When God eventually rejects the tribe of Ephraim, kingship passes to the tribe of Judah (see Ps. 78:56–72).[25]

Joshua's style of leadership prefigures that of Jesus Christ. Linked to the royal house of David, Christ is deeply committed to obeying the Book of the Law. Deuteronomy's influence pervades Jesus' teaching. When asked by 'an expert in the law', 'Which is the greatest commandment in the Law?', Jesus responds by quoting Deuteronomy 6:5: 'Love the Lord your God with all your heart and with all your soul and with all your mind.'[26] Elsewhere his commitment to the agenda set by the Book of the Law is clearly seen in the parallel accounts of his temptation (Matt. 4:1–11; Luke 4:1–13). On each of the three occasions when he is tested by the devil Jesus replies by quoting from Deuteronomy.[27] In doing so he highlights one of the principal tenants of the book: 'Worship the Lord your God, and serve him only.'[28]

While the leadership provided by Joshua provides a model for future Israelite kings to follow, and is fully exemplified in Jesus Christ, Joshua's faithful obedience to God is not maintained by his own descendants, as revealed in the book of Judges.

4. Joshua and rest (1:12–15)

Behind the establishment of God's kingdom in the land of Canaan is the goal of creating an environment where God's people may flourish, secure from all harm and danger. This hope is encapsulated by the mention of *rest* in the statement *The LORD your God will give you rest by giving you this land* (13; cf. verse 15). The connection between *rest* and *land* is important. For the landless Israelites, rest can be achieved only when they

---

[25] For a fuller discussion, see T. D. Alexander, 'The Regal Dimension of the תלדות־יעקב: Recovering the Literary Context of Genesis 37 – 50', in J. G. McConville and K. Möller (eds.), *Reading the Law: Studies in Honour of Gordon J. Wenham*, LHB/OTS 461 (Edinburgh: T&T Clark, 2007), pp. 196–212; S. Dalrymple, 'Ephraim or Judah: Divine Sovereignty and the Potential for Kingship in Joshua–Judges', in P. R. Williamson and R. F. Cefalu (eds.), *The Seed of Promise: The Sufferings and Glory of the Messiah; Essays in Honor of T. Desmond Alexander*, GlossaHouse Festschrift Series 3 (Wilmore: GlossaHouse, 2020), pp. 50–73.

[26] Matt. 22:35–37. Parallel accounts come in Mark 12:28–34 and Luke 10:25–28.

[27] See Deut. 6:13, 16; 8:3.

[28] Deut. 6:13 as quoted in Matt. 4:10 and Luke 4:8.

have a place to settle permanently. This will require enemies to be subdued and land to be allocated. As David Firth observes,

> Rest in Joshua can thus be summed up as something that emerges in stages. Settlement is a key goal, but to achieve it Israel first needed the absence of war. Only then could they have rest as a settled life, yet this settled life could be enjoyed only through continued faithfulness.[29]

Importantly, the source of true rest is God himself, as highlighted in 21:43–44:

> So the LORD gave Israel all the land he had sworn to give their ancestors, and they took possession of it and settled there. The LORD gave them rest on every side, just as he had sworn to their ancestors. Not one of their enemies withstood them; the LORD gave all their enemies into their hands.

The divine gift of rest, linked to the gift of land, is a significant factor in the establishment of God's kingdom on the earth. Highlighting this theme, Richard Hess writes,

> The 'rest' from their enemies that Joshua's generation first enjoyed (Josh. 21:44; 22:4; 23:1) forms the model for the rest given to Israel in later generations (1 Kgs 5:4; 1 Chr. 22:9, 18; 23:25; 2 Chr. 14:6–7; 15:15; 20:30), for the prophetic expectation of a future time of peace (Isa. 2:2–4; Mic. 4:1–4) and for the New Testament promise of a coming rest for those redeemed by Christ (Heb. 4).[30]

The climax of God's redemptive activity is the creation of a new earth, where his resurrected people will experience life in all its fullness, safe and secure in God's presence (see Isa. 65:17–25; Rev. 21:1 – 22:5).[31] As Jesus proclaimed in Matthew 5:5, 'Blessed are the meek, for they will inherit the earth.'

---

29 Firth, *Joshua*, p. 60.

30 Hess, *Joshua*, p. 85.

31 For a sample of recent studies that explore the creation of a new earth, see J. R. Middleton, *A New Heaven and a New Earth: Reclaiming Biblical Eschatology* (Grand Rapids: Baker, 2014); C. W. Morgan and R. A. Peterson (eds.), *Heaven*, Theology in Community (Wheaton: Crossway, 2014); T. D. Alexander, *The City of God and the Goal of Creation*, Short Studies in Biblical Theology (Wheaton: Crossway, 2018); D. W. H. Thomas, *Heaven on Earth: What the Bible Teaches about Life to Come* (Fearn: Christian Focus, 2018).

5. Conclusion

From the outset of creation, humanity and the earth/ground are intimately connected. With their expulsion from the garden of Eden, Adam and Eve forfeited the idyllic environment of a unique location where they could prosper and flourish, enjoying a harmonious relationship with God their Creator. As God's redemptive plan unfolds, his rescue of the Israelites from slavery in Egypt marks an important development towards the establishment of God's kingdom on earth. This process will include the acquisition of territory as God gives the land of Canaan to the Israelites. The Canaanites' loss of land is a solemn reminder that only those who express exclusive loyalty to God may ultimately dwell in his holy presence. The beneficiaries of the gift of God's rest must disassociate themselves from human kingdoms that deny the supremacy of God's authority.

Joshua's leadership, shaped by his meditation on the Book of the Law, prefigures Jesus Christ's role in overcoming enemies in order to establish God's kingdom throughout the whole world. As in the book of Joshua, kingdom membership is not determined by ethnicity or nationality. As David Firth remarks: 'We see foreigners integrated into Israel, but we also see Israelites excluded . . . The people of God are not identified on the basis of ethnicity but rather on the basis of a relationship with God.'[32] Those who might outwardly proclaim allegiance to Jesus Christ will be judged not by the vociferousness of their claims of loyalty, but by the fruit of their actions (Matt. 7:21–23).

---

[32] Firth, *Joshua*, pp. 38–39.

Judges 2:6–23

8. Conflicting loyalties

Loyalty and obedience are fundamental to the establishment of God's kingdom on the earth. The covenant mediated by Moses at Mount Sinai demands exclusive obedience to Yahweh. The Israelites are prohibited from serving, even partially, other deities. Under Moses' guidance, the covenant first made at Mount Sinai is renewed by the next generation of Israelites prior to crossing the River Jordan (see Deut. 29:1 – 30:20). Affirming this unique relationship, obedience to God is the formula for Joshua's success in taking possession of some of the land of Canaan. This is illustrated positively in the book of Joshua, but, in marked contrast, the book of Judges portrays the consequences of disobedience as the Israelites turn to other deities, disregarding their covenant obligations to Yahweh.

The opening chapter of Judges echoes something of the success story of Joshua. However, there are signs that the Israelites' settlement of the land is beginning to falter. Judges 1 reveals that the Israelites are unable to dislodge some of the inhabitants of Canaan. What starts as a relatively minor failing leads to a cycle of stories in chapters 3–16 that eventually climaxes in chapters 17–21 with a picture of gross moral and spiritual apostasy within the nation of Israel accompanied by intertribal conflict. By the end of Judges, the glorious days of Joshua are a distant memory and the once all-conquering Israel now appears to be in danger of self-destruction. Whereas the book of Joshua emphasizes the success of the Israelite campaign in Canaan, Judges portrays the Israelites as losing ground to their enemies, as well as engaging in internecine warfare.

To comprehend the book of Judges we need to look beyond the inspiring accounts of Gideon's defeating thousands of Midianites with only three hundred men and Samson's overcoming single-handedly hordes of Philistines. The overall message of Judges is not about the amazing feats of Israel's Spirit-empowered leaders. Rather, it is a story about God's people deserting him and going their own way. The end result is far from wholesome, as is evident in the rape and murder of a woman from Bethlehem by men from the tribe of Benjamin and in her husband's callous response to this horrendous crime (19:1–30).

1. Two generations (2:6–10)

The events recorded in the book of Judges contrast strikingly with those found in the book of Joshua. This contrast is introduced in 2:6–10 as the narrator notes the passing of Joshua's generation and the rise of the next generation. The brief summary of Joshua's generation is positive:

> After Joshua had dismissed the Israelites, they went to take possession of the land, each to their own inheritance. The people served the LORD throughout the lifetime of Joshua and of the elders who outlived him and who had seen all the great things the LORD had done for Israel.
> Joshua son of Nun, the servant of the LORD, died at the age of a hundred and ten. And they buried him in the land of his inheritance, at Timnath Heres in the hill country of Ephraim, north of Mount Gaash.
> (6–9)

Joshua's special standing is encapsulated in the designation the servant of the LORD (8). As we saw in the previous chapter, this is a title of honour, a title that is used consistently in the book of Joshua of Moses to portray his life of obedience to God. The title linked to Moses is given to Joshua at the end of his life (Josh. 24:29). Joshua's devotion to Yahweh is replicated throughout the nation of Israel as the people served the LORD throughout the lifetime of Joshua (7).

With the passing of Joshua's generation, a different situation arises. There is a new generation that knows neither the LORD nor what he had done for Israel (10). A significant generational gap develops. This new generation abandons the beliefs and values of its parents. They lack knowledge in two distinctive but related ways. First, most tellingly, they have no personal knowledge of Yahweh. This is not simply a case of not knowing about him, although that is a contributing factor. More importantly, they lack a personal relationship with him. It is one thing to say that you know about someone; it is entirely different to claim that you know someone personally. The lack of a personal relationship between the new generation of Israelites and God will prove to be disastrous for their well-being as a nation. Second, the next generation has no knowledge of what Yahweh has done for Israel. Lacking the personal experiences of their parents, this new generation is ignorant of all that Yahweh has done for their parents and their ancestors. This lapse of memory may explain their failure to have a personal knowledge of Yahweh. Such memories are important for they provide roots that nourish the creation of a stable community. Regrettably, the new generation of Israelites abandons the faith of its parents in favour of the deities worshipped by the inhabitants of Canaan.

2. Apostasy (2:11–15)

By failing to drive out the inhabitants of Canaan, the Israelites expose themselves to being influenced by the customs and practices of other nations. This point is made explicit at the start of Judges 2 when God announces to the Israelites that these nations shall become thorns in their side (see 2:1–3). This becomes a reality as the post-Joshua generation abandons Yahweh in favour of other gods. Their actions are summarized in verses 11–13:

> Then the Israelites did evil in the eyes of the LORD and served the Baals. They forsook the LORD, the God of their ancestors, who had brought them out of Egypt. They followed and worshipped various gods of the peoples around them. They aroused the LORD's anger because they forsook him and served Baal and the Ashtoreths.

As Daniel Block observes, the chiastic structure[1] of these verses highlights through repetition how the next generation forsakes Yahweh in order to serve Baal[2] and Astarte (the Ashtoreths):[3]

---

[1] D. I. Block, *Judges, Ruth*, NAC 6 (Nashville: Broadman & Holman, 1999), p. 124.

[2] According to Block, *Judges, Ruth*, p. 125, 'When the plural form *ba'ălîm* occurs, the reference is not to a multiplicity of gods but to numerous manifestations of the one weather god, on whose blessing the fertility of the land was thought to depend.'

[3] Block, *Judges, Ruth*, p. 125, writes, 'Like *ba'ălîm*, the present plural form refers to the local manifestations of the deity.'

A   They served the Baals (11b)

    B   They abandoned Yahweh (12a)

        C   They pursued other gods (12b)

        C' They worshiped them (12c)

    B' They abandoned Yahweh (13a)

A' They served the Baals and the Astartes (13b)

Noting how these gods are associated with fertility, Block remarks,

> In the fertility cult of Canaan, Baal was represented by an upright stone
> (maṣṣēbâ); Astarte was portrayed by carved female figurines, with
> exaggerated breasts and prominent genitals. Together these two gods
> formed a powerful force in ancient Near Eastern spirituality. Israel's
> abandonment of Yahweh may be attributable to an inability to conceive
> of Yahweh as the God of this land where Baal and Astarte ruled with
> apparent effectiveness.[4]

By abandoning their covenant relationship with Yahweh, the Israelites
arouse *the LORD's anger* (13). Consequently, Yahweh removes his protection
of and support for the Israelites. As the author of Judges records,

> *In his anger against Israel the LORD gave them into the hands of raiders*
> *who plundered them. He sold them into the hands of their enemies all*
> *around, whom they were no longer able to resist. Whenever Israel went*
> *out to fight, the hand of the LORD was against them to defeat them, just*
> *as he had sworn to them. They were in great distress.*
> (14–15)

Without Yahweh's intervention, the Israelites are helpless when attacked by
their enemies. No longer do they experience the success enjoyed by Joshua's
generation.

3. God's merciful intervention (2:16–19)

Yet God does not abandon the Israelites completely to their enemies. As
Judges 2:16, 18 states,

---

[4] Ibid., p. 125.

Then the LORD raised up judges, who saved them out of the hands of these raiders . . . Whenever the LORD raised up a judge for them, he was with the judge and saved them out of the hands of their enemies as long as the judge lived; for the LORD relented because of their groaning under those who oppressed and afflicted them.

The Hebrew term *šōpēṭ*, translated 'judge' in these verses, is often associated with the implementation of justice. However, in ancient Israel this task was not undertaken by professional lawyers but by civic leaders, sometimes the elders of the community. In this context, however, the task associated with the 'judge' suggests that the term *šōpēṭ* might be better translated 'governor'. Importantly, as Judges 2:18 reveals, God is responsible for empowering these leaders and, while they may fulfil a judicial role within the community, their significant contribution is soteriological: they rescue their fellow Israelites from the control of hostile enemies.

The individuals designated as 'judges' are civil rulers who command considerable respect, being able to muster an armed force from the local population. They are not viewed as kings, although Gideon's son Abimelek may have hoped to exploit his father's status as a deliverer when he sought to become king over Israel (9:1–57). The name Abimelek means 'my father is king'.

From descriptions of these God-appointed leaders, it becomes apparent that they are empowered by God's Spirit to fulfil their role. As such, they succeed in bringing relief to the Israelites. However, this is time-limited due to the propensity of the Israelites to abandon Yahweh for other deities. Consequently, Judges 2:10–19 describes a pattern that consists of the following elements:

- disobedience and rebellion by the Israelites (10–13)
- punishment at the hands of their enemies (14–15)
- God raising up a Spirit-empowered leader/judge to rescue the people (16, 18)
- the people reverting to their old ways when the leader/judge dies (17, 19)

Expressed more concisely, we have here the pattern sin–punishment–deliverance–sin. This pattern is cyclical, but Judges 2:19 makes the point that each time it occurred *the people returned to ways even more corrupt than those of their ancestors.* What we have here is not simply circular motion, as on a stadium racetrack, but rather a downward motion, like descending a spiral staircase. As Barry Webb remarks, 'Israel is depicted as spiralling downwards into worse and worse apostasy.'[5] It is important to observe this pattern, for the whole of Judges portrays Israel as spiralling out of control, ending in what can only be described as a state of sordid moral and social anarchy. They are far from being the kingdom of God.

After informing the reader in the prologue of Judges about the circular pattern of Israelite history after the time of Joshua, the central part of the book (chs. 3–16) narrates in detail six cycles of decline. In each cycle the reader is introduced to a 'judge' who is empowered by God to deliver the Israelites from their oppressors. These cycles focus on the following leaders: Othniel; Ehud; Deborah; Gideon; Jephthah; Samson. While these are the most prominent deliverers mentioned, there are brief references to other leaders (i.e. Shamgar of Anath [3:31]; Tola from Issachar [10:1–2]; Jair from Gilead [10:3–5]; Ibzan of Judah [12:8–10]; Elon of Zebulun [12:11–12]; Abdon of Ephraim [12:13–15]). Although other leaders/judges existed, the author of Judges deliberately focuses attention on six of them. In doing so he provides a framework designed to help the reader compare and contrast the actions of these judges. This framework is reasonably consistent, but as we progress from one deliverer to the next we encounter a worsening moral situation among the Israelites.

At the outset we are introduced to Othniel. Relatively little is said about him (five verses in all), but he is presented as a faultless deliverer/judge (3:7–11).[6] He becomes the standard by which other deliverers may be evaluated. The next judge is the left-handed Ehud. Judges records only the account of his somewhat surprising assassination of Eglon, the overweight king of Moab (3:12–30).

The third main judge is Deborah, a woman. According to Judges 4:4–5, Deborah 'was leading Israel at that time. She held court under the Palm of Deborah between Ramah and Bethel in the hill country of Ephraim, and the Israelites went up to her to have their disputes decided.' As a prophetess,

---

[5] B. G. Webb, *The Book of the Judges: An Integrated Reading*, JSOTSup 46 (Sheffield: JSOT Press, 1987), p. 112.

[6] See G. J. Wenham, *Story as Torah: Reading the Old Testament Ethically*, OTS (Edinburgh: T&T Clark, 2000), pp. 60–61; S. Dalrymple, 'Ephraim or Judah: Divine Sovereignty and the Potential for Kingship in Joshua–Judges', in P. R. Williamson and R. F. Cefalu (eds.), *The Seed of Promise: The Sufferings and Glory of the Messiah; Essays in Honor of T. Desmond Alexander*, GlossaHouse Festschrift Series 3 (Wilmore: GlossaHouse, 2020), pp. 66–68.

Deborah conveys God's message to Barak son of Abinoam from Kedesh in Naphtali, instructing him to lead an army of ten thousand men against Sisera, the commander of a Canaanite army linked to the city of Hazor.

In contrast to Othniel and Ehud, Barak is reluctant to obey the call of God, even when reminded of God's command by Deborah. He says to her: 'If you go with me, I will go; but if you don't go with me, I won't go.'[7] This is a strange request from the man who is supposed to lead the Israelites against their enemies. These are hardly the words of a strong and courageous leader.[8] Agreeing to his request, Deborah says to him: 'Certainly I will go with you . . . But because of the course you are taking, the honour will not be yours, for the LORD will deliver Sisera into the hands of a woman.'[9] Later, Deborah's prediction is fulfilled when Jael, an ordinary woman, strikes Sisera dead using a tent peg and a hammer. Barak may be the military commander, but Jael is remembered and honoured as the one who struck the fatal blow.

While it is important to recognize the achievements of these two women and the honour given to them, we should not lose sight of the fact that their success is ultimately due to God's empowering. Drawing attention to God as the source of salvation, Daniel Block remarks, 'He is the chief Operator, pulling the strings, raising generals, deploying armies, dictating strategy, and effecting victory. In the end both narrative and song celebrate the saving work of Yahweh.'[10]

Gideon, the next deliverer, is even more reluctant and fearful than Barak. Before he will accept the Lord's commission, he places certain demands before God (6:17, 36, 39). Gideon's use of a fleece reflects his inability to trust God's word alone. When subsequently asked by God to destroy an altar to Baal and an Asherah pole, Gideon does so at night 'because he was afraid of his family and the townspeople'.[11] Later, having sent home twenty-two thousand men who were afraid to fight the Midianites, Gideon himself is shown to be fearful when he goes down with Purah to hear what is being said in the Midianite camp (7:9–11).

Alongside Gideon's reluctance and fear, the narrator draws attention to other shortcomings. Gideon is the first deliverer to attack fellow Israelites,

---

[7] Judg. 4:8
[8] Joshua is instructed by God to be strong and courageous (Josh. 1:7, 9; cf. 1:18).
[9] Judg. 4:9.
[10] Block, *Judges, Ruth*, p. 186.
[11] Judg. 6:27.

killing some of them. When the men of Sukkoth and Peniel refuse to feed Gideon's three hundred men, out of fear that the Midianites will attack them, Gideon takes revenge (8:4–17). Although Gideon initially destroys an altar made by his father to Baal and an Asherah pole beside it (6:25–32), he later makes a golden ephod that the Israelites adopt as an object of false worship (8:22–27).[12] Adding to Gideon's failings, he marries a Canaanite, who gives birth to Abimelek. Later, wanting to establish himself as the first king of Israel, Abimelek kills seventy of his relatives (see 9:24, 56). Given Gideon's various shortcomings, Robert O'Connell makes the interesting observation that 'Gideon, like Barak, is a microcosm of Israel's reluctance to follow YHWH wholeheartedly . . . A deliverer who acts like Israel can hardly be expected to save Israel from the inclinations that lead them to return to evil.'[13]

Jephthah, the fifth main deliverer, is portrayed in an even more negative light. After making an ill-conceived and unnecessary vow, Jephthah finds himself compelled to sacrifice his only child, a daughter (11:34–40). When challenged by the Ephraimites, Jephthah's response results in forty-two thousand of them being killed by other Israelites (12:1–6). A similar crisis had occurred in the time of Gideon, but he successfully defused the situation, avoiding intertribal warfare (8:1–3).

Samson is the last in the series of deliverers. According to Gordon Wenham, 'his miraculous conception by a barren couple and his life-long Naziriteship make him unique among the judges'.[14] Despite being set apart to follow the consecrated life of a Nazirite, he craves foreign women, a recurring motif in the Samson story. Samson's desire for foreign females mirrors the Israelites' yearning after other gods. In the end, the judge who was appointed to rescue Israel from its enemies is imprisoned in a Philistine jail and dies in a pagan temple.

As with other judges, Samson's life reflects that of the nation. Stephen Dempster captures something of this when he writes,

> Samson, the supernaturally born Israelite, was set apart as a Nazirite with a distinctive vocation. He constantly breaks his religious vows, is enamoured of Philistine women, loses his identity and physical strength

---

[12] Wenham, *Story as Torah*, pp. 122–123, notes that the use of golden earrings taken from the defeated Midianites is reminiscent of how golden earrings are used to manufacture the golden calf in Exod. 32:1–6.

[13] R. H. O'Connell, *The Rhetoric of the Book of Judges*, VTSup 63 (Leiden: E. J. Brill, 1995), p. 163.

[14] Wenham, *Story as Torah*, p. 64.

through these encounters, becomes a slave and has his eyes gouged out by the enemy. He represents his own people, who had a supernatural origin, were set apart from among the nations with a distinctive vocation, broke their vows and were enamoured of foreign idols, until finally they lost their identity and spiritual power and became the blind slaves of their oppressors in exile.[15]

From these observations we see that Judges highlights the deteriorating situation regarding the safety of the Israelites within the land of Canaan. This is underlined by the fact that some of the deliverers are described as bringing rest to the land; this occurs with Othniel (3:11), Ehud (3:30), Deborah (5:31) and Gideon (8:28). After Gideon, however, there is little evidence that the activities of either Jephthah or Samson enable the Israelites to enjoy peace in the land. In the case of Samson, it is merely stated that 'he shall begin to save Israel from the hand of the Philistines'.[16]

By way of confirming the moral and spiritual decline of the Israelites, the book of Judges concludes with an extended epilogue that consists of two longer narratives, the first of which focuses on a Levite from Bethlehem (17:1 – 18:31) and the second on a Levite whose concubine was a Bethlehemite (19:1 – 21:25). The epilogue is marked off from the rest of the book of Judges by the refrain 'In those days there was no king in Israel. Everyone did what was right in his own eyes',[17] the first part of this statement being repeated in 18:1 and 19:1. Commenting on this refrain, Lawson Stone remarks, 'The characters in chs 17–21 all worship Yahweh, but their insistence on determining their own behavior spawns arguably worse disasters than those that befell Israel for its apostasy.'[18]

Stone possibly overstates the case. Those highlighted in the epilogue give the appearance of worshipping Yahweh, but their actions speak otherwise. They have broken the covenant by disregarding its obligations. Micah's actions are a testimony to how the post-Joshua generation has abandoned the covenant commitments that had shaped the beliefs and behaviour of their parents. While they retain some residual elements

---

[15] S. G. Dempster, *Dominion and Dynasty: A Biblical Theology of the Hebrew Bible*, New Studies in Biblical Theology 15 (Leicester: Apollos, 2003), p. 132.

[16] Judg. 13:5, ESV.

[17] Judg. 17:6; 21:25, ESV.

[18] J. Coleson, L. G. Stone and J. Driesbach, *Joshua, Judges, Ruth*, Cornerstone Biblical Commentary (Carol Stream: Tyndale House, 2012), p. 430.

of those beliefs, these have become corrupted beyond recognition. We see this manifested in the shrine that Micah constructs and his hiring of a young Levite as his priest. Ironically, this Levite, who subsequently establishes a priestly dynasty in the city of Dan, is a grandson of Moses (18:30).

4. God's testing of Israel (2:20–23)

While much of Judges 2 focuses on highlighting the cyclical pattern of sin–punishment–deliverance–sin, the chapter also reveals that God intentionally does not expel all of the nations living in the land of Canaan during the time of Joshua's leadership. As witnessed in Judges 1, after Joshua's death the Israelites are unable to take possession of all the territory. Importantly, Judges 2:20–23 observes that the presence of the nations in the land of Canaan was purposely designed by God to test the obedience of the Israelites:

> Therefore the LORD was very angry with Israel and said, 'Because this nation has violated the covenant I ordained for their ancestors and has not listened to me, I will no longer drive out before them any of the nations Joshua left when he died. I will use them to test Israel and see whether they will keep the way of the LORD and walk in it as their ancestors did.'
> (20–22)

While it may seem strange that God deliberately allows some of the Canaanite nations to remain in the land, he is well aware that the faithful commitment of one generation does not automatically pass to the next. To this end, God comes to test the Israelites to see if they will *keep the way of the LORD and walk in it as their ancestors did.* Had all the nations been removed swiftly from Canaan, there would have been little need for the next generation of Israelites to trust God. As Daniel Block comments, 'Subsequent generations would not simply inherit the blessings, the rewards of a previous generation's faith. They needed to demonstrate their commitment to Yahweh themselves.'[19]

We encounter here an interesting insight into how God may test the genuineness of an individual's faith. In the New Testament, the apostle

---

[19] Block, *Judges, Ruth*, p. 134.

James highlights this idea when he writes to 'the twelve tribes scattered among the nations'. He begins his letter with these words:

> Consider it pure joy, my brothers and sisters, whenever you face trials of many kinds, because you know that the testing of your faith produces perseverance. Let perseverance finish its work so that you may be mature and complete, not lacking anything.[20]

In a similar vein, the apostle Peter directs his readers' attention to the inheritance that is 'kept in heaven' for them, 'an inheritance that can never perish, spoil or fade'. Reminding his readers that they 'are shielded by God's power', he nevertheless speaks of how they now 'for a little while' 'may have had to suffer grief in all kinds of trials'. Recognizing these hardships, he continues, 'These have come so that the proven genuineness of your faith – of greater worth than gold, which perishes even though refined by fire – may result in praise, glory and honour when Jesus Christ is revealed.'[21] As with the Israelites, God tests us to see the genuineness of our faith.

5. Conclusion

Israel's failure to possess the 'Promised Land' after Joshua's death is clearly not a reflection of Yahweh's inability to defeat the nations already resident there. Despite the overall gloomy picture, Judges contains a variety of episodes that emphasize the power of God to overcome Israel's enemies. Israel's failure results from the disobedience of the people themselves. The book of Judges is a vivid reminder of the Deuteronomic idea that obedience to God brings blessing, but disobedience curses (see Deut. 27:15 – 28:68). As Gordon Wenham observes, Judges is 'a tale of repeated conflicts which show the nation becoming ever more negligent of its covenant obligations and hence becoming totally frustrated as it is unable to escape the consequences of its own incorrigibility'.[22] Yet remarkably, despite the apostasy of the Israelites, God graciously intervenes to raise up deliverers for them. His intervention on behalf of the Israelites who have turned away from him is reminiscent of what the apostle Paul writes to the followers of Jesus at Rome:

---

[20] Jas 1:1–4.

[21] 1 Pet. 1:4–7.

[22] Wenham, *Story as Torah*, p. 58.

You see, at just the right time, when we were still powerless, Christ died for the ungodly. Very rarely will anyone die for a righteous person, though for a good person someone might possibly dare to die. But God demonstrates his own love for us in this: while we were still sinners, Christ died for us.

Since we have now been justified by his blood, how much more shall we be saved from God's wrath through him! For if, while we were God's enemies, we were reconciled to him through the death of his Son, how much more, having been reconciled, shall we be saved through his life![23]

Although the Israelites are unfaithful to the covenant inaugurated at Mount Sinai, Yahweh remains firmly committed to them. This is stressed when the angel of the Lord comments, 'I will never break my covenant with you.'[24] The six narrative cycles in chapters 3–16 reveal God's patience in the face of the apostasy of the Israelites. While God commissions Spirit-empowered individuals to 'save' the Israelites from their enemies, these deliverers reflect the failings of the people. In the light of this, the refrain of the concluding chapters of Judges, 'in those days Israel had no king',[25] seems to imply that the situation can be changed only through the establishment of a monarchy in Israel. In the light of this expectation, the books of Ruth and Samuel record the divine appointment of the Davidic dynasty in Jerusalem. This will reverse the spiral of downward moral and spiritual decline in Israel and will have positive outcomes for the creation of God's kingdom. Importantly, the provision of a king to rescue the Israelites from their enemies anticipates the coming of a greater king, Jesus Christ, whose primary mission will be to establish God's kingdom throughout the whole world.

---

[23] Rom. 5:6–10.
[24] Judg. 2:1.
[25] Judg. 17:6; 18:1; 19:1; 21:25.

Part 3
Anticipating the saviour king

1 Samuel 2:1–10

9. The divine king who raises up and brings down

Strange as it may seem in our self-fixated Western world, in recent decades psychologists have recognized the importance of humility, especially for those aspiring to be leaders. In contrast to having an inflated sense of our own importance and ability, humility in leaders encourages trust, better strategic thinking and increased performance.[1] The virtue of humility, which modern psychologists are now acknowledging to be an important moral quality, lies at the very heart of God's choice of the king who will establish and rule over God's kingdom.

As we have already observed, the story of redemptive history begins in Genesis with the expectation that there will be a human vicegerent who will establish God's rule on earth, a future king who belongs to the patriline of Abraham, Isaac and Jacob. To prepare for his coming, God establishes the Israelites as a nation by redeeming them from slavery in Egypt. This marks the first stage towards God's rule being extended throughout all the world. While the covenant at Mount Sinai privileges the Israelites over other nations, the benefits of the covenant are experienced only by those who keep its obligations. Tragically, the Israelites fail to give exclusive obedience to God. Despite this failure, God graciously intervenes and raises up a king whose dynasty will be established for ever. As we shall see, the books of Samuel shed important light on how God appoints this king.

---

[1] See the article by A. K. Schaffner, 'What Is Humility & Why Is It Important?', PositivePsychology.com, 27 August 2020, <https://positivepsychology.com/humility/>.

In the sweeping story that is told throughout the closely connected books of Genesis to Kings, it is striking that the books of Samuel begin by focusing on the plight of a childless woman (1 Sam. 1:1–20). To compound her disappointment at not being able to conceive, her husband has another wife who bears him sons and daughters. Within this dysfunctional family, Hannah is mocked because of her childlessness. Yet Hannah will play a vital part in the outworking of God's purposes as the biblical story moves towards the establishment of a royal dynasty that will bring to fulfilment God's promises to Abraham. This dynasty will ultimately lead to Jesus Christ, the 'son of David'.

1. Anticipating a king (2:10)

When God graciously reverses Hannah's childlessness, she responds by composing a theologically rich song of thanksgiving. Importantly, her carefully crafted prayer introduces themes that will recur throughout the books of Samuel. Her words are applicable to her own situation, but they move beyond this in a remarkable way. As Stephen Dempster writes,

> This thanksgiving poem is a masterpiece of early Hebrew poetry but it was not chosen as an introduction to this historical work primarily because of its literary beauty; it was selected for its hermeneutical value, to provide the fundamental key to understanding the historical events for which it provides a framework.[2]

Hannah's song is given pride of place at the start of the books of Samuel. By incorporating it into his narrative, the author of Samuel draws attention to various important themes, the outworking of which will be vividly illustrated in the rest of the book. This is especially so as regards the portrayals of Saul and David. While Hannah's prayer is spoken prior to the establishment of any monarchy in Israel, her concluding words focus on God's support for his king:

He will give strength to his king
and exalt the horn of his anointed.
(10)

---

[2] S. G. Dempster, 'Hannah's Song, a New World Order and the Right Side of History', in M. A. G. Haykin, D. G. Barker and B. H. Howson (eds.), *Ecclesia Semper Reformanda Est – The Church Is Always Reforming: A Festschrift on Ecclesiology in Honour of Stanley K. Fowler* (Dundas: Joshua Press, 2016), p. 4.

The prayer's conclusion is unexpected, for there is no Israelite king. This will change, however, when Hannah's son, Samuel, under instruction from God, anoints Saul and then David to be king over Israel.

The poetic parallelism of Hannah's prayer confirms that *his king* and *his anointed* refer to the same person. The king is 'the LORD's anointed', a concept that takes on special significance as the narrative later records the tense relationship that develops between Saul and David. Repeatedly, David refuses to kill Saul, for Saul, as king, is 'the LORD's anointed'.[3] Importantly, the Hebrew word for 'anointed one' is *māšîaḥ*, from which we derive the English term 'messiah'. The anointings of Saul and David, which indicate their divine appointment as kings, are important for appreciating the royal connotations underlying the terms *māšîaḥ* 'messiah' and its Greek equivalent *christos* 'Christ' when applied to Jesus of Nazareth.[4]

2. The incomparable God (2:1–2)

Through Hannah's experience, we encounter another example of divine grace transforming a broken life. With God's intervention, Hannah bears a son, Samuel, who enjoys a close relationship with God, as a prophet and judge. The solution to Hannah's crisis does not mean that God responds in the same way to the cry of every childless woman, but it does reveal that he may choose to intervene meaningfully in the lives of those who face personal disappointment and opposition from others. Hannah's own experience shapes her understanding of God's actions in the world. She gives voice to this in a prayer that encapsulates in poetry the nature of God's activity in the world.

From the outset, Hannah's thoughts are focused on God. 'The object of Hannah's delight is neither herself – that she has overcome the disgrace of barrenness – nor her son; instead it is the Lord, who is the source of both her son and her happy circumstance.'[5] Hannah proclaims exuberantly:

> My heart rejoices in the LORD;
> in the LORD my horn is lifted high.

---

[3] 1 Sam. 24:6, 10; 26:9, 11, 16, 23; cf. 2 Sam. 1:14, 16.

[4] While Jesus refrained from using the title Anointed One/Christ/Messiah of himself, his followers consistently used this title for him after his resurrection and ascension to heaven.

[5] R. D. Bergen, *1, 2 Samuel* (Nashville: Broadman & Holman, 1996), p. 75.

> *My mouth boasts over my enemies,*
> *for I delight in your deliverance.*
> (1)

Yahweh has transformed Hannah's life through the gift of her son, Samuel. Her prayers have been answered and she rejoices. To express her sense of elation, she speaks of her *horn* being *lifted high*. This metaphor conveys a sense of victory. As Philips Long remarks, 'Horns served as "weapons" and lent a regal appearance to animals sporting them. The image of the raised horn evokes a majestic picture of an animal victorious over its foe or prey.'[6]

In the eyes of Hannah, 'Israel's God is beyond compare'.[7] In three lines that are closely bound together by the repetition of the Hebrew word *'ên*, translated *There is no . . .* , Hannah highlights God's incomparable nature:

> *There is no one holy like the LORD;*
> *there is no one besides you;*
> *there is no Rock like our God.*
> (2)

In the words of Robert Vannoy, God 'is one who is absolutely holy, completely unique . . . and supremely strong'.[8]

3. God exalts the lowly (2:4–8)

While Hannah's prayer ends by speaking of a king, she alludes to the idea that God raises up the poor and the needy to seat them with princes (8). This comes as part of a longer passage that focuses on how God intervenes in human affairs. Through various contrasts, Hannah describes how God's actions may affect people in opposite ways:

> *The bows of the warriors are broken,*
> *but those who stumbled are armed with strength.*

---

[6] V. P. Long, *1 and 2 Samuel: An Introduction and Commentary*, Tyndale Old Testament Commentaries (London: Inter-Varsity Press, 2020), p. 47.

[7] J. G. Baldwin, *1 and 2 Samuel: An Introduction and Commentary*, Tyndale Old Testament Commentaries 8 (Leicester: Inter-Varsity Press, 1988), p. 61.

[8] J. R. Vannoy, *1 – 2 Samuel*, Cornerstone Biblical Commentary 4a (Carol Stream: Tyndale House, 2009), p. 54.

Those who were full hire themselves out for food,
  but those who were hungry are hungry no more.
She who was barren has borne seven children,
  but she who has had many sons pines away.
The LORD brings death and makes alive;
  he brings down to the grave and raises up.
The LORD sends poverty and wealth;
  he humbles and he exalts.
He raises the poor from the dust
  and lifts the needy from the ash heap;
he seats them with princes
  and makes them inherit a throne of honour.

(4–8)

In this series of contrasts, Hannah conveys an important principle regarding God's actions in the world. As Robert Vannoy observes,

> Hannah saw her own experience of God's deliverance (2:1–3) as an example of how God works in the larger world of people and nations (2:4–9). In both realms God's justice is often visible in his lifting up the weak and humble and in his bringing down the strong and arrogant. Hannah used a series of seven contrasts (mighty and weak [2:4], well fed and starving [2:5a], barren and fertile [2:5b], death and life [2:6a], sickness and health [2:6b], poor and rich [2:7], common and noble [2:8]) to depict the reversals of status that God sovereignly brings about in the affairs of individuals and nations.[9]

God restores life or brings death; he gives food or brings hunger; he provides wealth or sends poverty. In the light of such actions, Hannah expresses powerfully the principle that God exalts the poor and needy to royal heights.

a. Example 1: Saul

In the light of this expectation, the lowly origins of Saul and David receive special mention in the story of their being chosen as kings. When Samuel

---

[9] Ibid., pp. 54–55. Capturing this series of reversals, Bergen, *1, 2 Samuel*, p. 76, writes: 'The Lord's actions can be extremely positive: he "makes alive" (v. 6), "raises . . . from the dust" (v. 8), "lifts . . . from the ash heap" (v. 8), "exalts" (v. 7), causes people to "inherit a throne" (v. 8), "seats" people "with princes" (v. 8), "sends . . . wealth" (v. 7), "will guard" (v. 9), "will give strength" (v. 10), and "raises up" from "the grave" (v. 6). In contrast, the Lord also "sends poverty" (v. 7), "humbles" (v. 7), "will thunder" (v. 10), "will judge" (v. 10), "brings death" (v. 6), and "brings down to the grave" (v. 6).

is instructed by God to anoint Saul as king (1 Sam. 9:16), Saul stresses the insignificance of his own family: 'But am I not a Benjaminite, from the smallest tribe of Israel, and is not my clan the least of all the clans of the tribe of Benjamin?'[10] His remarks recall how the tribe of Benjamin is reduced to only six hundred men after a punitive attack by the other tribes (Judg. 20:1–48). Despite being anointed by Samuel, Saul does not disclose this fact to his uncle when he returns home (1 Sam. 10:16). Saul does not boast of becoming king. Whereas 1 Samuel 9:1 – 10:16 records Saul's private anointing by Samuel, 1 Samuel 10:17–27 records the public selection of Saul as king from among all the men of Israel. When Samuel draws lots in front of all the people to identify God's choice of king, Saul hides among the baggage (10:22–23). He displays little desire to be king over Israel. Saul's dramatic appointment as king reflects Hannah's affirmation that God exalts the poor and needy who trust in him. Unfortunately for Saul, the reverse is also true. His reign begins well, but his rise to power has a negative impact upon his character. Pride gradually takes over and eventually he is brought down to the grave.

b. Example 2: David

Saul's rise from obscurity to become king is paralleled by how God exalts David from lowly origins. When Samuel visits Jesse to anoint one of his sons as king, David's father does not consider him a suitable candidate. As the youngest of his eight sons, David is sent off to tend the flock. In his father's eyes, one of David's older brothers is a more fitting candidate to be king. Yet, as Samuel remarks in 16:7: 'The LORD does not look at the things people look at. People look at the outward appearance, but the LORD looks at the heart.'

David's lowly origins are again evident when later King Saul offers him the opportunity to marry his eldest daughter Merab. Declining Saul's invitation, David responds, 'Who am I, and what is my family or my clan in Israel, that I should become the king's son-in-law?' When Saul renews this invitation, David replies, 'Do you think it is a small matter to become the king's son-in-law? I'm only a poor man and little known.'[11] His remarks are full of irony, for as the narrator notes shortly afterwards, David's success in battle against the Philistines results in him becoming well

---

[10] 1 Sam. 9:21.
[11] 1 Sam. 18:18, 23.

known (18:30). Still later, when Saul pursues David to kill him, David refers to himself as a 'dead dog' and a 'flea'.[12] Why should Saul be concerned about someone who is of no significance?

Further evidence of David's identification with those of lowly status comes when, as the newly appointed king, he arranges for the ark of the covenant to be transported to Jerusalem. Celebrating the arrival of the ark in Jerusalem, David strips off his royal garments and dances in public. After witnessing his actions from a distance, his wife Michal, one of Saul's daughters, arrogantly rebukes David: 'How the king of Israel has distinguished himself today, going around half-naked in full view of the slave girls of his servants as any vulgar fellow would!'[13] She views David's actions as unbefitting a king; in her eyes he has demeaned himself before others. As a former princess and now queen, Michal is offended by her husband's actions; she is far superior to the servant girls before whom David dances. In response David remarks,

> It was before the LORD, who chose me rather than your father or anyone
> from his house when he appointed me ruler over the LORD's people
> Israel – I will celebrate before the LORD. I will become even more
> undignified than this, and I will be humiliated in my own eyes. But
> by these slave girls you spoke of, I will be held in honour.[14]

For David, it is a virtue to be humble in God's presence. Ironically, because of her arrogant attitude, Michal is childless for the rest of her life (2 Sam. 6:23). Due to her pride, her experience is the reverse of Hannah's.

4. Relying on God (2:3, 9–10)

Hand in hand with the theme of God's exalting the poor and lowly is the theme of relying on God. The proud and self-reliant do not look to God for help; they trust in their own ability. Highlighting this theme, Hannah prays,

> *Do not keep talking so proudly*
> *or let your mouth speak such arrogance,*

---

[12] 1 Sam. 24:14; cf. 26:20.

[13] 2 Sam. 6:20.

[14] 2 Sam. 6:21–22.

> *for the LORD is a God who knows,*
> *and by him deeds are weighed.*
>
> . . .
>
> *He will guard the feet of his faithful servants,*
> *but the wicked will be silenced in the place of darkness.*
> *It is not by strength that one prevails;*
> *those who oppose the LORD will be broken.*
> *The Most High will thunder from heaven;*
> *the LORD will judge the ends of the earth.*
> *He will give strength to his king*
> *and exalt the horn of his anointed.*
> (3, 9–10)

Hannah's remarks underline that God is not oblivious to the thoughts and actions of people. In his oversight of all that happens, God judges the proud and arrogant. Despite their boasting, they will not prevail. On the other hand, God sides with the weak and humble, giving them the strength to prevail in a hostile world. Beyond this, however, 'Hannah's Song provides a subtle indication that the narrative is moving towards kingship.'[15] As Stephen Dempster observes, Hannah 'has discerned in the resolution of her personal pain, suffering and frustration, a future resolution to the pain, suffering and frustration of the world. In short she sees the coming of a new world order.'[16] Building on her own experience, and drawing on traditions that go back to Abraham, Hannah anticipates the divine establishment of a monarchy. As God has raised high Hannah's horn (1), so he will *exalt the horn of his anointed*. Importantly, 'Yahweh's king must understand the paradox that real authority comes from yielding power to Yahweh.'[17] How this becomes a reality is described in the narrative that follows.[18]

a. Example 1: Saul

In the early years of his reign, Saul displays a strong trust in God for help. After being anointed as king, Saul rescues the people of Jabesh Gilead from

---

[15] D. G. Firth, *1 & 2 Samuel* (Nottingham: Apollos, 2009), p. 61.

[16] Dempster, 'Hannah's Song', p. 4.

[17] Firth, *1 & 2 Samuel*, p. 62.

[18] R. P. Gordon, *I & II Samuel: A Commentary* (Grand Rapids: Zondervan, 1986), pp. 78–79, observes, 'Throughout its several movements the psalm focuses on the illimitable power of God as it is deployed in the reversal of human fortunes. The climax is reached with an assertion of universal sovereignty and a declaration that the same divine power is at work for the good of God's earthly vicegerent the king.'

the Ammonites.[19] In doing so, he acknowledges publicly that 'this day the LORD has rescued Israel'.[20] However, soon after this, a Philistine invasion tests Saul's reliance on God. Disregarding Samuel's instructions, Saul offers up a burnt offering (1 Sam. 13:7–14). While this action has the appearance of looking to God for help, true dependence is marked by wholehearted obedience. For ignoring God's command, Samuel condemns Saul:

> 'You have done a foolish thing,' Samuel said. 'You have not kept the command the LORD your God gave you; if you had, he would have established your kingdom over Israel for all time. But now your kingdom will not endure; the LORD has sought out a man after his own heart and appointed him ruler of his people, because you have not kept the LORD's command.'[21]

Tragically for Saul, he commits further acts of disobedience. When the Lord, through Samuel, instructs Saul to attack the Amalekites and destroy totally all that belongs to them, Saul disobeys by sparing 'Agag and the best of the sheep and cattle, the fat calves and lambs – everything that was good'. Subsequently, the Lord says to Samuel: 'I regret that I have made Saul king, because he has turned away from me and has not carried out my instructions.'[22]

Despite Samuel's prophetic warnings, Saul expresses no genuine remorse for having disobeyed God. His actions lead him further and further from God. This becomes especially evident when later in life Saul turns to a woman in Endor, a medium, in order to discern God's will (1 Sam. 28:4–25). The consequences are chilling. Through the medium, the deceased Samuel addresses Saul:

> Why do you consult me, now that the LORD has departed from you and become your enemy? The LORD has done what he predicted through me. The LORD has torn the kingdom out of your hands and given it to one of your neighbours – to David. Because you did not obey the LORD or carry

---

[19] By rescuing the population of Jabesh Gilead from the Ammonites Saul possibly seeks to atone for past wrongs done to the city (see Judg. 21:1–25).

[20] 1 Sam. 11:13.

[21] 1 Sam. 13:13–14.

[22] 1 Sam. 15:9–11.

out his fierce wrath against the Amalekites, the LORD has done this to you today. The LORD will deliver both Israel and you into the hands of the Philistines, and tomorrow you and your sons will be with me. The LORD will also give the army of Israel into the hands of the Philistines.[23]

Despite having been exalted by God and placed on a throne of honour, Saul's pride and self-reliance cause him to be brought down to the grave. Hannah's words prove to be all too true.

b. Example 2: David

In contrast to Saul, who turns away from God, David is portrayed as trusting and obeying the Lord. As a boy, he courageously goes out against Goliath, a 9-ft tall Philistine warrior. Despite his lack of physique and training as a soldier, David is confident that God will protect him: 'The LORD who rescued me from the paw of the lion and the paw of the bear will rescue me from the hand of this Philistine.'[24] David's victory over the boastful Philistine confirms Hannah's insight:

> He will guard the feet of his faithful servants,
>> but the wicked will be silenced in the place of darkness.
> It is not by strength that one prevails;
>> those who oppose the LORD will be broken.
> (9–10)

When in manhood David engages in military activity, he looks to God for guidance before taking up arms (1 Sam. 23:2, 4; 30:8; 2 Sam. 2:1; 5:19, 23). Not only does this underline his dependence upon God, but it also highlights God's role in overcoming aggressive enemies.

David's reliance on God is apparent in his reluctance to kill Saul. Despite knowing that Samuel has anointed David to be the next king, Saul seeks on various occasions to murder David. Tragically, Saul's opposition to David even results in the deaths of some of those who give assistance to David (1 Sam. 22:6–23). Despite Saul's murderous actions, David does not respond in kind. When his men encourage him on several occasions to assassinate Saul, David refuses to kill 'the LORD's anointed'.[25] David is

---

[23] 1 Sam. 28:16–19.

[24] 1 Sam. 17:37.

[25] 1 Sam. 24:6, 10; 26:9–11, 23; cf. 2 Sam. 1:1–16.

unwilling to seize the throne by taking Saul's life, even though he has been anointed by Samuel to be king (16:13), a fact acknowledged by Achish (21:11), Jonathan (23:17) and Saul himself (24:20). David waits patiently for God to establish him as king. Even when he learns of the deaths of Saul and Jonathan, David does not rejoice. He laments their passing, rather than focusing on the opportunity that it presents for him (2 Sam. 1:19–27).

David's attitude recalls the central message of Hannah's prayer that God raises up and brings down. This same message is highlighted by another woman, Abigail, who encourages David to remain faithful to God in the face of provocation from her husband:

> Please forgive your servant's presumption. The LORD your God will certainly make a lasting dynasty for my lord, because you fight the LORD's battles, and no wrongdoing will be found in you as long as you live. Even though someone is pursuing you to take your life, the life of my lord will be bound securely in the bundle of the living by the LORD your God, but the lives of your enemies he will hurl away as from the pocket of a sling. When the LORD has fulfilled for my lord every good thing he promised concerning him and has appointed him ruler over Israel, my lord will not have on his conscience the staggering burden of needless bloodshed or of having avenged himself.[26]

In the face of Saul's malevolent efforts to prevent him becoming king, David's patience in trusting God illustrates well the sentiments expressed by Hannah in her prayer. It is God who exalts the humble and brings down the proud.

David, however, is not always portrayed as obeying God consistently. His shortcomings are not overlooked by the author of Samuel, who records David's sordid affair with Bathsheba, the wife of Uriah the Hittite (2 Sam. 11:1–27). Attracted by her beauty, David has an adulterous relationship with her, causing her to become pregnant when her husband is undertaking military duties. Uriah's single-minded commitment to duty contrasts sharply with David's nefarious behaviour, especially when David deliberately plots to have Uriah killed in battle. Not surprisingly, David's actions are sternly rebuked by the prophet Nathan (12:1–14).

---

[26] 1 Sam. 25:28–31.

Soon afterwards David is deposed as king by his son Absalom, an event that recalls Saul's fate. However, unlike Saul, David is filled with remorse (cf. Ps. 51) and accepts the humiliation of being ousted by his son. David's acceptance of what occurs is reflected in his attitude towards Shimei, who curses David when he is forced to abandon his palace in Jerusalem (2 Sam. 16:5–14). While God punishes David by removing him from the throne, he later reinstates him, following the death of Absalom (18:1–33). Through all that happens, Hannah's insights remain true: God exalts the lowly and brings down the proud.

5. In tune with Hannah

Hannah's prayer at the start of 1 Samuel is balanced at the end of 2 Samuel by a song composed by David (see 2 Sam. 22). In a significant way, these poetic passages frame the books of Samuel. The song is located at the end of 2 Samuel for thematic and not chronological reasons. According to its introduction, David's song was composed shortly after the death of Saul, when David was first appointed king over Israel. At that time, the Lord delivered David 'from the hand of all his enemies and from the hand of Saul'.[27] Remarkably, this lengthy song, which is replicated in Psalm 18:1–50, echoes the themes of Hannah's prayer.[28] In David's own words, addressing God, 'You save the humble, but your eyes are on the haughty to bring them low.'[29] Acknowledging the Lord's role in making him king, David concludes his psalm with these words:

> The LORD lives! Praise be to my Rock!
> Exalted be my God, the Rock, my Saviour!
> He is the God who avenges me,
> who puts the nations under me,
> who sets me free from my enemies.
> You exalted me above my foes;
> from a violent man you rescued me.
> Therefore I will praise you, LORD, among the nations;
> I will sing the praises of your name.

---

[27] 2 Sam. 22:1.

[28] Apart from sharing common themes, both Hannah and David use the image of God being a rock (1 Sam. 2:2; 2 Sam. 22:2–3, 32, 47) and thundering from heaven (1 Sam. 2:10; 2 Sam. 2:14).

[29] 2 Sam. 22:28.

He gives his king great victories;
> he shows unfailing kindness to his anointed,
> to David and his descendants for ever.[30]

With its concluding references to 'his king' and 'his anointed', David's composition recalls the ending to Hannah's prayer. David's exaltation as king marks an important development in the fulfilment of God's plan to establish his kingdom on earth. As we shall see in subsequent chapters, through a future 'son of David' God will establish his kingdom of righteousness and peace, bringing blessing to all the nations of the earth. In the light of this anticipated development, two final observations regarding Hannah's prayer are noteworthy.

6. Mary's song

Hannah's prayer is echoed in a most remarkable way in Mary's song, the Magnificat (Luke 1:46–55). As Joyce Baldwin observes, 'A careful comparison of the two poems shows the same wonder at God's mercy to a humble woman in Israel, in keeping with his character through the ages as the just God who accomplishes his good purposes.'[31] True to his nature, God acts through those whom others regard as insignificant. Confounding the normal expectations of society, God chooses an ordinary young woman to give birth to the Saviour of the world. Like Hannah, Mary rejoices at how God favours those who are insignificant in the world's eyes.

My soul glorifies the Lord
> and my spirit rejoices in God my Saviour,
for he has been mindful
> of the humble state of his servant.
From now on all generations will call me blessed,
> for the Mighty One has done great things for me –
> holy is his name.
His mercy extends to those who fear him,
> from generation to generation.
He has performed mighty deeds with his arm;
> he has scattered those who are proud in their inmost thoughts.

---

[30] 2 Sam. 22:47–51.
[31] Baldwin, *1 and 2 Samuel*, p. 63.

> He has brought down rulers from their thrones
>> but has lifted up the humble.
> He has filled the hungry with good things
>> but has sent the rich away empty.
> He has helped his servant Israel,
>> remembering to be merciful
> to Abraham and his descendants for ever,
>> just as he promised our ancestors.

With words that echo Hannah's prayer, Mary rejoices in a holy and merciful God who exalts the humble and brings down the proud. Capturing the essence of Mary's expectations, Stephen Dempster remarks,

> When she finds out that she is to be the mother of the Messiah, she, like Hannah, her ancient forebearer, also celebrates nothing less than a new world order in which the rich, the powerful and the prideful are swept away before the humble and the hungry in the coming of a new world order.[32]

With this 'new world order' we witness the arrival of God's kingdom.

7. Christ the perfect example

Learning from both Hannah and Mary, the challenge for all of us is how to have an attitude of genuine humility, devoid of selfish ambition and pride. Addressing this issue, the apostle Paul exhorted the followers of Jesus Christ in Philippi to have the mindset of their Lord and Saviour. He writes,

> In your relationships with one another, have the same mindset as Christ Jesus:

> who, being in very nature God,
>> did not consider equality with God something to be used to his
>>> own advantage;
> rather, he made himself nothing
>> by taking the very nature of a servant,
>> being made in human likeness.

---

[32] Dempster, 'Hannah's Song', p. 25.

And being found in appearance as a man,
    he humbled himself
    by becoming obedient to death –
        even death on a cross!
Therefore God exalted him to the highest place
    and gave him the name that is above every name,
that at the name of Jesus every knee should bow,
    in heaven and on earth and under the earth,
and every tongue acknowledge that Jesus Christ is Lord,
    to the glory of God the Father.[33]

In Christ's humiliation and exaltation, we witness the ultimate fulfilment of Hannah's prayer.

8. Conclusion

The books of Samuel provide a profound insight into God's attitude regarding human kingship. Importantly, his approach is counter-cultural. His choice of king is not determined by those qualities that people usually associate with kingship. As his choice of David reveals, God does not look on the outward appearance but on the heart. To this end, it is in God's nature to appoint those who are humble and lowly rather than the proud and arrogant. As Hannah perceptively states,

The LORD sends poverty and wealth;
    he humbles and he exalts.
He raises the poor from the dust
    and lifts the needy from the ash heap;
he seats them with princes
    and makes them inherit a throne of honour.
(7–8)

As the biblical story moves towards the coming of a divinely promised vicegerent who will mediate God's blessing to the nations of the earth, the expectation is created that he will be exalted by God from humble origins that are associated with the poor and needy. The Gospels confirm that this is true of Jesus Christ.

---

[33] Phil. 2:5–11.

1 Kings 3:1–28

10. Royal wisdom

As parents we are always keen to impart wise advice to our children. When my teenage daughter mentioned to my wife that one of the boys in her class often missed lessons because he was playing golf, my wife was quick to question the wisdom of this. How would he possibly pass his exams? Why were his parents letting him neglect his studies? He would live to regret missing school. At the time it sounded like wise advice. With hindsight this reaction seems less wise. The boy in question was Rory McIlroy, who went on to become the number one golfer in the world. True wisdom is not always immediately obvious.

The inauguration of the Davidic dynasty is an important landmark in the journey towards the perfect vicegerent who will establish God's kingdom on the earth. The next stage of the story is recorded in the books of 1 and 2 Kings, which provide a theologically shaped history of the Davidic dynasty from David's death through to the release of Jehoiachin from a Babylonian prison in the year 562 BC.[1] The overall picture of the Davidic dynasty is coloured by failure, resulting in its removal from the throne in Jerusalem after the capture of the city by the Babylonians in 586 BC. Despite this setback the author of Kings offers hope that a future Davidic king will mediate God's blessing to the nations in fulfilment of God's commitment to Abraham.

---

[1] On the significance of Jehoiachin's release, see S. G. Dempster, 'The End of History and the Last Man', in P. R. Williamson and R. F. Cefalu (eds.), *The Seed of Promise: The Sufferings and Glory of the Messiah; Essays in Honor of T. Desmond Alexander*, GlossaHouse Festschrift Series 3 (Wilmore: GlossaHouse, 2020), pp. 113–141.

This optimism comes in part through the special attention that is given to three kings, Solomon, Hezekiah and Josiah. Gary Millar helpfully summarizes the significance of these monarchs in the books of Kings:

> At a macro level, the text of Kings is bookended by the extended discussion of the rule of Solomon the Wise in 1 Kgs 1–11 at the beginning, and the rule of Hezekiah and his great grandson Josiah in 2 Kgs 18–23 at the end. There are significant similarities between these great kings. On the positive side, each of them is described in ways which set them apart as uniquely godly. Solomon loved Yahweh like none before or since. Hezekiah trusted Yahweh like no other, and Josiah turned to Yahweh as the embodiment of Deuteronomic piety.[2]

While all three kings display positive qualities, they exhibit weaknesses that exclude them from being God's perfect vicegerent. Nevertheless, their lives provide an insight into those qualities that will be the hallmark of the promised king. To appreciate how they prefigure the promised vicegerent, we shall focus on Solomon.

Solomon is associated especially with wisdom. His wisdom is proverbial.[3] While it is true that Solomon and wisdom go together, the biblical story of Solomon's wisdom is more complex than is often recognized. Central to understanding the significance of his wisdom are the events recorded in 1 Kings 3. These come on the heels of the narrator's statement 'The kingdom was now established in Solomon's hands.'[4]

1. Solomon's love for God (3:1–4)

As Solomon consolidates his position as king, his actions convey a sense of ambiguity regarding his commitment to God. On the one hand, we learn that *Solomon showed his love for the* LORD *by walking according to the*

---

[2] J. G. Millar, '"We Three Kings . . ." – An Examination of the Messianic Trajectory of the Book of Kings with Special Reference to Solomon, Hezekiah, and Josiah', in P. R. Williamson and R. F. Cefalu (eds.), *The Seed of Promise: The Sufferings and Glory of the Messiah; Essays in Honor of T. Desmond Alexander*, GlossaHouse Festschrift Series 3 (Wilmore: GlossaHouse, 2020), p. 111. Importantly, despite these positive attributes, Millar observes that each of these kings has shortcomings: 'Solomon's wisdom did not save him from decadence. Hezekiah's faith did not protect him from self-pity and self-preoccupation. Josiah's piety did not prevent him from getting involved in a conflict he could not possibly win' (p. 111).

[3] A major reason for this is his identification as the author of most of the sayings recorded in the biblical book of Proverbs. See 1 Kgs 4:32.

[4] 1 Kgs 2:46.

instructions given him by his father David (3). Solomon's love for Yahweh prompts him to obey David's instructions. However, the second half of verse 3 states that Solomon does not follow David's directions when he offers sacrifices at *the high places.* Within the books of Kings 'high places' are usually viewed negatively and associated with idolatry (1 Kgs 22:43; 2 Kgs 12:3; 14:4; 15:4, 35; cf. 1 Kgs 11:7–8; 2 Kgs 18:4; 21:3–9). In 1 Kings 3:4, Solomon's actions at Gibeon do not involve the worship of idols. He goes there to worship Yahweh. According to Donald Wiseman, '*Gibeon* (El-Jīb, ten kilometres north-west of Jerusalem) as *the most important high place* or "chief shrine" (REB) was the site of the tabernacle and altar after the sack of Shiloh (1 Chr. 21:29; 2 Chr. 1:2–6).'[5] While the narrator does not explicitly condemn Solomon for going to Gibeon to offer *a thousand burnt offerings,* his journey there possibly detracts from the importance of Jerusalem as the location that God has chosen for his dwelling-place. In due course, Solomon's attitude towards Jerusalem will change when he builds there *the temple of the* LORD.

A further indicator that Solomon's love for Yahweh is not quite perfect is his marriage to the daughter of *Pharaoh king of Egypt.* While little is said about this marriage motivated by political considerations, it later becomes evident that Solomon's marriages to various wives introduce into Israel the worship of other deities (see 11:1–13). As Iain Provan observes,

> First Kings 3:1–3 presents us, then, with a Solomon who loves God – who does share his father David's basic commitment to God (3:3) – but who right at the beginning of his reign also carries with him the seeds of his own destruction.[6]

While the observation in verse 3 that Solomon loves God is significant, it is noteworthy that in chapter 11 the narrator links Solomon's love for foreign wives to his turning away from Yahweh (see 11:1–6). With disastrous consequences, our love for God can too easily be replaced by our love for other people.

---

[5] D. J. Wiseman, *1 and 2 Kings: An Introduction and Commentary*, Tyndale Old Testament Commentaries 9 (Leicester: Inter-Varsity Press, 1993), p. 91.

[6] I. W. Provan, *1 and 2 Kings*, New International Biblical Commentary Old Testament Series (Peabody: Hendrickson; Carlisle: Paternoster, 1995), p. 46.

2. Solomon as David's successor (3:5–7a)

Responding to Solomon's many sacrifices, God makes a request of him in a dream. God encourages Solomon to ask for anything that he might wish. This request gives a telling insight into the heart of Solomon. What are his priorities? What does he desire more than all else? It is a request that should cause all of us to reflect on our own priorities. What is my heart's desire that dominates my thoughts and actions?

Replying to God's request, Solomon focuses initially on what God has already done for him. In particular, he highlights God's *great kindness* in establishing the Davidic dynasty, making Solomon king after his father David. Solomon uses the expression *great kindness* twice in verse 6. He repeats the Hebrew word *ḥesed* 'kindness', a difficult term to translate into English because no single word conveys sufficiently the nuances of the original Hebrew. William Barnes suggests that 'faithful love' comes close to capturing how *ḥesed* means 'love and mercy on the one hand, and faithfulness and loyalty (to a covenantal relationship) on the other'.[7] Ultimately, God's enthronement of David as king and God's commitment to establish David's dynasty for ever rest on God's *ḥesed*, his merciful love and faithfulness. This important truth was previously affirmed by God when he first promised David that his dynasty would be established for ever. God says,

> When your days are over and you rest with your ancestors, I will raise up your offspring to succeed you, your own flesh and blood, and I will establish his kingdom. He is the one who will build a house for my Name, and I will establish the throne of his kingdom for ever. I will be his father, and he shall be my son. When he does wrong, I will punish him with a rod wielded by men, with floggings inflicted by human hands. But my love will never be taken away from him, as I took it away from Saul, whom I removed from before you. Your house and your kingdom shall endure for ever before me; your throne shall be established for ever.[8]

The term translated 'love' in verse 15 ('But my love will . . .') is *ḥesed*. God promises David that his 'faithful love' will sustain the heirs to David's

---

[7] W. H. Barnes, *1 – 2 Kings*, Cornerstone Biblical Commentary 4b (Carol Stream: Tyndale House, 2012), p. 53.

[8] 2 Sam. 7:12–16.

throne. God's commitment to David will continue to have an important bearing on future events, a fact reflected in the positive messages associated with the refrain 'for the sake of David my/his servant'.[9]

Recognizing the importance of God's devotion to David, Solomon also appreciates that his appointment as king depends on God's *hesed*, his *great kindness*. As the opening chapter of 1 Kings reveals, Solomon did not promote himself as heir to the Davidic throne. In contrast to his older brother Adonijah, Solomon makes no effort to present himself as David's successor. However, when we recall Hannah's prayer that God exalts the humble but brings down the proud, it is perhaps no surprise that Solomon is made king rather than Adonijah, who puts himself forward as Israel's king in waiting (1 Kgs 1:5).

Solomon speaks positively of his father David. While David is not without his faults, he nevertheless displays a faith in God that is exemplary. His willingness as a youth to confront Goliath, the champion of the Philistines, highlights David's deep trust in God (see 1 Sam. 17:1–58). As regards David's being *righteous and upright in heart*, the many psalms associated with his name convey something of his abhorrence of evil and his desire to ensure justice and righteousness (e.g. Pss 3; 4; 5). Even his own lapse into sin by committing adultery with Bathsheba evokes in David a response of repentance and a desire to be forgiven (see Ps. 51).

3. Solomon's request for help (3:7b–9)

After focusing on God's *great kindness* in establishing him as king after David, Solomon confesses his inadequacy *to govern* [God's] *people* (9). The Hebrew word translated 'to govern' in the NIV is *lišpōṭ*, which carries the sense 'to judge' (KJV; CSB) or 'to make judicial decisions' (NET). This term draws attention to Solomon's role in governing judicially, dispensing justice in an equitable and impartial manner, and pronouncing judgments that are appropriate. Solomon senses his own inadequacy to undertake this task effectively. The reason for his confession of failure may be best appreciated by reflecting on the judgments that he has already made involving Adonijah, Joab and Shimei. These judgments are recorded in 1 Kings 2 and in each case there are strong grounds for believing that Solomon has not delivered the best possible judgment. In each instance

---

[9] 1 Kgs 11:13, 32, 34; 2 Kgs 8:19; 19:34; 20:6; cf. 1 Kgs 11:12.

Solomon fails to judge with equity and impartiality, delivering justice to those involved.

When Adonijah asks to marry Abishag, Solomon reacts hastily, executing his older brother out of fear that Adonijah will seize the kingdom from him (2:13–25). Various observations suggest that Solomon does not judge Adonijah with true wisdom. First, Adonijah, conscious of how his request to marry Abishag may be misunderstood, approaches Bathsheba, the queen mother, asking her to intercede with Solomon on his behalf. Adonijah is exceptionally cautious about going directly to Solomon in the light of Solomon's warning in 1 Kings 1:52: 'If he shows himself to be worthy, not a hair of his head will fall to the ground; but if evil is found in him, he will die.' To dispel any concern that Bathsheba might have, Adonijah acknowledges to her that Yahweh has made Solomon king (2:15). If Adonijah is intent on replacing his half-brother as king, it is surprising that he should ask Bathsheba, Solomon's mother, to intercede on his behalf. Second, when Bathsheba approaches Solomon, he promises to grant his mother any request that she might make. When she presents her request, Solomon proceeds to break the oath that he just made to her. Finally, Solomon's actions sit uncomfortably with his claim that Yahweh has established him as king in the place of his father David (2:24; cf. 2:15). If God has made Solomon king, there should be no need for him to consolidate his position by executing a possible rival. In his dealings with Adonijah, Solomon displays both a lack of trust in God's sovereign protection and no magnanimity towards his brother, who has not been made king despite being the eldest of David's surviving sons.[10] There is no legitimate justification for Solomon's execution of Adonijah. His brother is not the threat that Solomon perceives him to be.[11]

The account of Adonijah's execution is followed by two more executions, involving Joab and Shimei. Both men have been mentioned by David, who says to Solomon regarding Joab, 'Deal with him according to your wisdom, but do not let his grey head go down to the grave in peace', and regarding Shimei, 'But now, do not consider him innocent. You are a man of wisdom;

---

[10] His older brothers are Amnon, Kileab and Absalom (2 Sam. 3:2–4). Amnon and Absalom are both killed (13:28; 18:15); since no mention is made of Kileab we must presume that he is also dead. When Solomon is anointed king, Adonijah fears that he will be put to death and takes hold of the horns of the altar to secure protection for himself (see 1 Kgs 1:50–53).

[11] J. T. Walsh, *1 Kings*, Berit Olam (Collegeville: Liturgical Press, 1996), p. 67, writes, 'The inference is that Solomon does not have Adonijah executed simply because of the request for Abishag; rather the request supplies Solomon with a convenient excuse to eliminate a rival he still perceives as a danger.'

you will know what to do to him. Bring his grey head down to the grave in blood.'[12] In addressing Solomon, it is noteworthy that David instructs him to deal with Joab and Shimei on the basis of his wisdom. However, this is not wisdom given by God, but Solomon's own human wisdom. As becomes evident, Solomon misuses his wisdom to bring about the deaths of Joab and Shimei.

Regarding the death of Joab, he is executed by Benaiah, despite seeking sanctuary by clinging to the horns of the altar. According to Iain Provan,

> There is, in truth, poetic justice in all of this. Joab had lived by the sword, killing (among others) two army commanders who happen to be his professional rivals. Now he dies by the sword and is immediately replaced by his killer as commander of the army (v. 35).[13]

Yet, despite Solomon's claim that Joab's execution is justified in order to clear him and his 'whole family of the guilt of the innocent blood that Joab shed',[14] Solomon appears to be motivated not by a genuine desire for justice but by fear that Joab poses a threat to his kingship.

Adding to this, we should note that Solomon's instruction to Benaiah to slay Joab at the altar runs counter to Exodus 21:14, which requires a murderer to be removed from the altar before being executed. Joab's death at the altar, a place of sanctuary, offers him no opportunity to argue his case in a properly convened judicial setting.[15] Solomon deliberately subverts the normal course of justice.

As for Solomon's treatment of Shimei, his execution for leaving Jerusalem appears extremely harsh and unwarranted. His journey does not merit the death penalty. Moreover, strictly speaking Shimei does not break the oath that he swore when he stated that he would not leave Jerusalem by crossing the Kidron Valley (2:36–37). His oath prohibits a journey eastward out of Jerusalem, but Shimei goes westward to Gath and does not cross the Kidron Valley.[16]

While the Kings narrative offers pretexts for Solomon's decisions to kill Adonijah, Joab and Shimei, his judgments are far from equitable and

---

[12] 1 Kgs 2:6, 9.

[13] Provan, *1 and 2 Kings*, p. 39.

[14] 1 Kgs 2:31.

[15] See Walsh, *1 Kings*, p. 67.

[16] See ibid., p. 68.

impartial. 'What we have here, in fact, is a fairly sordid story of power-politics thinly disguised as a morality tale.'[17] As the events recorded in 1 Kings 2 reveal, Solomon's judgments are troubling. They do not inspire confidence in the one who is meant to oversee the judicial processes in Israel. Solomon may have sensed the unease of others or perhaps his own conscience troubled him when he reflected on what he had done. Such thoughts may explain his sense of inadequacy in dispensing justice in Israel. This prompts his request to God for *discernment in administering justice* (3:11).

4. God's gift of wisdom (3:10–28)

Solomon's honest request for wisdom pleases God. Having already executed some of his enemies, it would have been easy for Solomon to ask for the death of other enemies. As God mentions, he might also have asked for long life or wealth, but Solomon requests discernment for administering justice. In response God promises him, *I will give you a wise and discerning heart, so that there will never have been anyone like you, nor will there ever be* (12).

God's answer to Solomon's prayer is illustrated immediately when two women come to the king, each claiming to be the mother of a young baby. With wisdom Solomon identifies the child's true mother by threatening to cut the baby in half, giving a portion to each woman. When the birth mother objects, looking to save the child's life, Solomon gives her custody of the baby. Underscoring the wisdom of Solomon's judgment, the narrator comments, *When all Israel heard the verdict the king had given, they held the king in awe, because they saw that he had wisdom from God to administer justice* (28).

Building on this episode, the Kings narrative proceeds to highlight how Solomon's administration of the nation brings prosperity to the people. Capturing the impact of this, 1 Kings 4:20 states, 'The people of Judah and Israel were as numerous as the sand on the seashore; they ate, they drank and they were happy.' Prosperity is accompanied by peace. Solomon's reign is characterized by a period of national security for the whole nation, as noted in 4:25: 'During Solomon's lifetime Judah and Israel, from Dan to Beersheba, lived in safety, everyone under their own vine and under their

---

17 Provan, *1 and 2 Kings*, pp. 40–41.

own fig tree.' Confirmation that all these benefits for the nation of Israel are due to Solomon's God-given wisdom comes in 4:29–34. This passage records how Solomon becomes internationally famous for his knowledge and understanding:

> God gave Solomon wisdom and very great insight, and a breadth of understanding as measureless as the sand on the seashore. Solomon's wisdom was greater than the wisdom of all the people of the East, and greater than all the wisdom of Egypt. He was wiser than anyone else, including Ethan the Ezrahite – wiser than Heman, Kalkol and Darda, the sons of Mahol. And his fame spread to all the surrounding nations. He spoke three thousand proverbs and his songs numbered a thousand and five. He spoke about plant life, from the cedar of Lebanon to the hyssop that grows out of walls. He also spoke about animals and birds, reptiles and fish. From all nations people came to listen to Solomon's wisdom, sent by all the kings of the world, who had heard of his wisdom.

Solomon's influence on the establishment of God's kingdom on the earth extends well beyond his own lifetime through the numerous proverbs that he composed. Many of these are now preserved in the book of Proverbs. These sayings, reflecting God's nature, seek to inculcate positive values that shape the attitudes and behaviour of those who are kingdom people. By contrasting the ways of wisdom and folly, Solomon offers practical instructions covering a wide range of human experiences. Composed around three thousand years ago, Solomon's proverbs remain a source of divine wisdom for followers of Jesus today.

Unfortunately, despite his great wisdom, Solomon's reign does not end well. The Kings narrative introduces this possibility by describing a second occasion when God speaks to Solomon (9:1–9). God's speech underlines the importance of obedience and warns Solomon against worshipping other gods. Despite this intervention, Solomon fails to obey God in ways that recall three prohibitions linked to kingship in Deuteronomy 17:16–17:

> The king, moreover, must not acquire great numbers of horses for himself or make the people return to Egypt to get more of them, for the Lord has told you, 'You are not to go back that way again.' He must not

take many wives, or his heart will be led astray. He must not accumulate large amounts of silver and gold.

According to the Kings narrative, Solomon ignores all three proscriptions. He amasses great wealth (9:10 – 10:25), imports horses from Egypt (10:26–29) and marries numerous foreign wives, who encourage him to worship other gods (11:1–8). Not surprisingly, despite his great wisdom and his construction of the temple in Jerusalem (5:1 – 8:66), Solomon is strongly condemned by God, who says to him in 11:11–13:

> Since this is your attitude and you have not kept my covenant and my decrees, which I commanded you, I will most certainly tear the kingdom away from you and give it to one of your subordinates. Nevertheless, for the sake of David your father, I will not do it during your lifetime. I will tear it out of the hand of your son. Yet I will not tear the whole kingdom from him, but will give him one tribe for the sake of David my servant and for the sake of Jerusalem, which I have chosen.

Remarkably, God's punishment of Solomon is tempered by his commitment to David. Twice God indicates that Solomon's sentence is less severe 'for the sake of David'.[18] While God could have justifiably removed the kingdom from Solomon, he refrains from doing this because of his promise to maintain the Davidic dynasty in Jerusalem (2 Sam. 7:11–16). This commitment provides the basis for hope that there will eventually be a perfect vicegerent, a son of David, one wiser than Solomon.[19] As we shall see, this expectation finds its fulfilment in Jesus Christ, who comes to establish God's kingdom on earth.

5. Conclusion

As the story of God's rescue plan for humanity continues, the books of Kings confirm God's pledge to establish the Davidic dynasty as the lineage

---

[18] 1 Kgs 11:12–13.

[19] Millar, '"We Three Kings . . ."', pp. 111–112, writes, 'By framing the history of Israel and Judah with these towering figures (Solomon; Hezekiah; Josiah) who all ultimately fall short of fulfilling their potential, and more importantly, seeing the fulfilment of the kingdom promises of God, the focus of the reader is inexorably thrown forward to look for a king who does display Solomon's wisdom, Hezekiah's faith and Josiah's relentless, word-driven piety, to the extent that when Jesus Christ announces that "one greater than Solomon is here" (Matt 12:42), it comes as no surprise. The quest for the one who will crush the serpent's head, which begins in Gen 3:15, is significantly advanced by the extended treatment of the best of Israel and Judah's rulers.'

that will lead to the perfect vicegerent. This commitment on God's part explains why Matthew begins his Gospel by describing Jesus as the 'son of David'. Solomon's reign exemplifies both the potential benefits associated with the establishment of God's kingdom under a supremely wise ruler, and the inherent tendency of Davidic kings to turn away from serving God wholeheartedly. While the dynasty's shortcomings will eventually result in the destruction of Jerusalem and the end of the Davidic monarchy's rule over the nation, nevertheless there remains the hope that 'for the sake of David' God will not abandon his commitment to establish his kingdom on earth by giving universal authority to one of David's descendants. This comes to fulfilment in Jesus Christ. This hope of a future Davidic king permeates the teaching of the Old Testament prophets and is reflected in other Old Testament books composed after the fall of Jerusalem in 586 BC. With this in view, we turn to consider how the books of Isaiah and Psalms foresee the coming of a unique king who will subdue God's enemies and establish God's authority over all the nations of the earth.

Isaiah 52:13 – 53:12

11. The servant king

Life is full of twists and turns. Occasionally it may seem that we are motoring along on a flat, straight motorway, but more often life resembles a road that snakes up the side of a mountain. The same is true for the establishment of God's kingdom on the earth. Our journey has taken us from the garden of Eden, via Mount Sinai, to Jerusalem. With the inauguration of the Davidic dynasty and the construction of the temple, God's plan of redemption takes an important step forward. Hope for a future, perfect vicegerent is linked to King David's descendants. As the location of Yahweh's earthly temple, Jerusalem takes on special significance as the city that lies at the heart of God's plans for the establishment of his kingdom on the earth. Although we have not yet reached our destination, we have made progress and the direction of travel is mapped out in more detail. Yet the onward journey is far from smooth. We have already witnessed something of this in the life of Solomon. Despite receiving the gift of divine wisdom, he is led astray by his foreign wives. Unfortunately, subsequent generations of Davidic kings are also prone to failure.

In this chapter, we turn to see how these shortcomings are addressed in the book of Isaiah, a remarkable collection of divine oracles that are associated with the reigns of Uzziah, Jotham, Ahaz and Hezekiah, kings of Judah who ruled in the second half of the eighth century BC through to the first half of the seventh century BC. Importantly, Isaiah foresees that the establishment of God's kingdom will ultimately be realized through the creation of a new Jerusalem.

1. From judgment to salvation

The book of Isaiah consists of prophetic sayings that have been brought together to convey a movement from judgment to salvation. This centres on the transformation of a corrupt Jerusalem into a resplendent, holy city.[1] The book begins by highlighting how the inhabitants of eighth-century Jerusalem have deserted God. As Isaiah remarks in 1:4:

> They have forsaken the LORD;
>> they have spurned the Holy One of Israel
>> and turned their backs on him.

Remarkably, their abandonment of God is not an outward rejection of him. The citizens of Jerusalem have not chosen to worship another deity. They continue to offer sacrifices to Yahweh, celebrate his religious festivals and pray to him. Yet their outward show of devotion is not matched by a true adherence to God's values. From Yahweh's perspective, their activities merely add to his outrage concerning the immoral behaviour of the civil and religious leaders of Jerusalem. With passion, in 1:16–17 the prophet Isaiah calls on the people to repent:

> Wash and make yourselves clean.
>> Take your evil deeds out of my sight;
>> stop doing wrong.
> Learn to do right; seek justice.
> Defend the oppressed.
> Take up the cause of the fatherless;
>> plead the case of the widow.

With considerable detail the opening chapters of Isaiah highlight the moral corruption of Jerusalemite society. Isaiah denounces the pride and arrogance of the people; their unrestrained selfish indulgence; their religious hypocrisy; their complacency towards social injustice; their exploitation of the poor and disadvantaged.[2] Isaiah's message is one of condemnation. The

---

[1] For a fuller discussion, see B. G. Webb, 'Zion in Transformation: A Literary Approach to Isaiah', in D. J. A. Clines, S. E. Fowl and S. E. Porter (eds.), *The Bible in Three Dimensions*, JSOTSup 87 (Sheffield: JSOT Press, 1990), pp. 65–84.

[2] Commenting on the historical situation that developed in Jerusalem towards the end of the eighth century BC, B. G. Webb, *The Message of Isaiah: On Eagles' Wings*, The Bible Speaks Today (Leicester:

people's lack of contrition means that punishment will surely come. The outlook is bleak.

God's sense of disappointment is vividly illustrated in a short parable that Isaiah addresses to the inhabitants of Jerusalem and the people of Judah. After describing the effort that its owner has put into creating a walled vineyard, Isaiah conveys his sense of disappointment when the vines produce 'only bad fruit'.[3] The owner of the vineyard has done all that is possible to produce a crop of good grapes. When the vineyard yields only bad fruit, he decides to destroy his unproductive vines. In 5:5–6 he states,

> I will take away its hedge,
>   and it will be destroyed;
> I will break down its wall,
>   and it will be trampled.
> I will make it a wasteland,
>   neither pruned nor cultivated,
>   and briers and thorns will grow there.
> I will command the clouds
>   not to rain on it.

As an illustration that Isaiah's hearers would easily understand, the parable sends a solemn warning to the people of Jerusalem. Despite everything that God has done for the city, the people have not produced 'good fruit'. Centuries later, possibly recalling this passage, Jesus Christ reminds his listeners that God assesses people not by their words of devotion, but by the fruit of their actions (see Matt. 7:15–20).

The parable of the vineyard warns of Jerusalem's destruction. Adding to the severity of the penalty, the vineyard is not simply abandoned by its owner. The walls, patiently built to protect it, are intentionally pulled down. God will not simply leave the people of Jerusalem to continue living as they please. He himself will actively participate in their punishment.

The theme of Jerusalem's corruption, which dominates the early chapters of the book, stands in marked contrast to how Jerusalem is

---

Inter-Varsity Press, 1996), p. 56, observes, 'A new, wealthy élite emerged, who grew more and more corrupt and oppressive as they became intoxicated (in more ways than one!) with materialism and the pursuit of pleasure.'

[3] Isa. 5:2.

portrayed in the final chapters of Isaiah. Here we encounter a future Jerusalem that will be characterized by peace and well-being (60:17). It will be a place of safety, where people will feel secure (60:18). No enemy will besiege the city or threaten those who dwell there. With good reason its inhabitants will call the city walls 'Salvation' and its gates 'Praise'. Jerusalem will stand as a testimony to the salvation that God brings. Building on this, in 60:19–20 Isaiah says,

> The sun will no more be your light by day,
> > nor will the brightness of the moon shine on you,
> for the LORD will be your everlasting light,
> > and your God will be your glory.
> Your sun will never set again,
> > and your moon will wane no more;
> the LORD will be your everlasting light,
> > and your days of sorrow will end.

Darkness gives way to light, but this is no ordinary light. This light radiates from God himself, highlighting his presence within the city.

As God's presence radiates light throughout the entire city, this transformed Jerusalem will be characterized by peace and righteousness. The hope expressed here recurs throughout chapters 40–66, as John Bright observes,

> There is vaulting hope in these chapters [of Isaiah]. From first (40:1–11) to last (65:17–25; 66:10–14) there runs through them an overtone of joy like the strains of triumphant music. The pages are suffused with light – light rising from the sun (60:1–3). It is as if the hell and horror had been left behind, and one is moving up a high, sun-drenched summit to the very doors of the Kingdom of God. There is good news to tell (40:9–11; 52:1–12): the night of humiliation has ended, a glorious future lies ahead.[4]

Bright's remarks remind me of an experience that I had many years ago in North Wales when I joined a group to hike to the top of Snowdon. It was the middle of summer, but thick cloud covered the mountain. The conditions

---

[4] J. Bright, *The Kingdom of God: The Biblical Concept and Its Meaning for the Church* (Nashville: Abingdon Press, 1953), pp. 137–138.

were anything but pleasant. Visibility was minimal due to the mist and light rain. It was impossible to appreciate the beauty of the mountain. However, something very unexpected happened as we neared the summit. We suddenly emerged out of the thick mist into bright sunlight. We found ourselves above the clouds, looking out over the top of them. It was a remarkable view. The summit of the mountain was visible and we enjoyed the warmth of the sun. None of us had anticipated this when we stood at the foot of Snowdon. In certain regards, reading through the book of Isaiah is like this. The gloom and doom of the first half of the book gives way to a 'sun-drenched summit', to quote John Bright.

In marked contrast to God's rejection of Jerusalem at the start of Isaiah, a different outlook emerges in the second part of the book. Picturing the future Jerusalem as a crown or royal diadem, Isaiah speaks of how the city will be treasured by God (62:3). In 62:4 he proclaims,

> No longer will they call you Deserted,
> or name your land Desolate.
> But you will be called Hephzibah,
> and your land Beulah;
> for the Lord will take delight in you,
> and your land will be married.

God proudly claims ownership of Jerusalem. No longer do we see an abandoned vineyard overgrown with weeds. The nickname previously given to Jerusalem, 'Deserted', will be replaced by 'Hephzibah', meaning 'My delight is in her'. The land that had been named 'Desolate' will be called 'Beulah', meaning 'Married'. These name changes poignantly capture how God's attitude towards Jerusalem will shift dramatically. The city that God abandoned to the Babylonians will be precious to him. As Isaiah comments, it 'will be a crown of splendour in the Lord's hand'.[5] Having previously been rejected by God, Jerusalem will be married to him.

As the book of Isaiah moves from judgment to salvation, it becomes apparent that chapters 40–66 look beyond the reigns of Ahaz and Hezekiah to a future time when Jerusalem will be restored after judgment. In broad terms, chapters 40–48 highlight the rebuilding of Jerusalem after its destruction by the Babylonians in 586 BC. This restoration of the city

---

[5] Isa. 62:3.

is attributed to a foreign king called Cyrus, who is mentioned by name in 44:28 – 45:1, 13. Remarkably, Cyrus is portrayed as a Davidic king and referred to as the Lord's anointed (45:1). Other passages in the Old Testament record how the Persian Cyrus issues a decree that initiates the rebuilding of the temple in Jerusalem (2 Chr. 36:22–23; Ezra 1:1–8). This process of restoration begins around 538 BC.

The image of a foreign king restoring Jerusalem is noteworthy. However, in Isaiah 49 – 66 we encounter another individual who, like Cyrus, is linked to the restoration of Jerusalem. This restoration stands apart from that undertaken by Cyrus. Importantly, the book of Isaiah links this restored Jerusalem to the divine creation of new heavens and a new earth (see 65:17–19).

The resplendent, holy Jerusalem described in the final chapters of Isaiah has an eschatological feel to it.[6] It is the climactic result of God's redemptive activity. As Gary Smith observes, the description of this radically transformed Jerusalem, this new Jerusalem, draws together ideas that are sprinkled throughout Isaiah's oracles:

> When chapters 65–66 refer to the new heavens and new earth, they recall earlier texts, in which Jerusalem will be called 'the city of righteousness, a faithful city' (1:26), where God will teach the Torah to people from many nations (2:3), where the Prince of Peace will reign forever on the throne of David (9:6–7), and where the remnant of God's people will gather (11:10–11).[7]

This new Jerusalem is undoubtedly the goal towards which God is working as he establishes his kingdom on earth, but it would be a mistake to assume that it will exist only for the benefit of those who are yet to be born in the future. Isaiah's oracles contain hints that associate this unique city with the life to come. To this end, various passages contain imagery that suggests the citizens of New Jerusalem will experience a quality of life that far

---

[6] This picture of an eschatological Jerusalem is widespread in the prophetic books. See D. E. Gowan, *Eschatology in the Old Testament* (Philadelphia: Fortress, 1986); W. J. Dumbrell, *The End of the Beginning: Revelation 21 – 22 and the Old Testament* (Grand Rapids: Baker, 1985), pp. 5–27.

[7] G. V. Smith, 'Isaiah 65 – 66: The Destiny of God's Servants in a New Creation', *Bibliotheca Sacra* 171 (2014), p. 50. He goes on to say, 'Believers from Egypt and Assyria and many other nations will be there with all the faithful and humble Israelites (19:19–25; 66:18–22), enjoying God's lavish banquet (25:6). Death will have vanished from the new earth (25:8; 30:19). In the heavens the light from the sun will change (30:26; 60:19), God's Spirit will be poured out on His people (32:15), and Zion will be filled with gladness and joyful shouting (35:10).'

exceeds anything that earthly Jerusalem can ever offer. It will be a place of everlasting joy, where life will be enjoyed to the full. Something of this transformation is communicated in 35:5–6, 10:

> Then will the eyes of the blind be opened
>   and the ears of the deaf unstopped.
> Then will the lame leap like a deer,
>   and the mute tongue shout for joy.
> Water will gush forth in the wilderness
>   and streams in the desert.
>
> . . .
>
> They will enter Zion with singing;
>   everlasting joy will crown their heads.
> Gladness and joy will overtake them,
>   and sorrow and sighing will flee away.

Isaiah's expectations in this passage go far beyond what Judean exiles would have experienced in returning from Babylon to rebuild Jerusalem at the end of the sixth century BC. As we shall see later, Christ's healing miracles, which resemble those mentioned here, signal the coming of the kingdom and anticipate the wholeness of life that will be experienced in the eternal city of God.

Looking to the new Jerusalem, Isaiah's oracles point to the acquisition of eternal life. He speaks of how those returning to Zion will experience 'everlasting joy'.[8] In a noteworthy passage, Isaiah associates a divinely prepared banquet of exquisite food and drink with the annihilation of death (25:6–8).[9] Highlighting the importance of this 'new creation' event, Sigurd Grindheim remarks,

> On that day, there will be no more sorrow because all reasons for sorrow will no longer exist. No one will ever lose their loved ones. No one will have their life ruined by poor health. No one will experience heart-

---

[8] Isa. 35:10; cf. 51:11; 61:7.

[9] Jesus Christ picks up on the imagery of this passage when he says of a Gentile centurion: 'Truly I tell you, I have not found anyone in Israel with such great faith. I say to you that many will come from the east and the west, and will take their places at the feast with Abraham, Isaac and Jacob in the kingdom of heaven. But the subjects of the kingdom will be thrown outside, into the darkness, where there will be weeping and gnashing of teeth' (Matt. 8:10–12). The references to 'peoples' and 'nations' in Isa. 25:6–7 draw attention to the cosmopolitan nature of the new Jerusalem.

wrenching relationship breakups. The prophet looks forward to a day of unbridled happiness, a happiness that will not give way to disappointment, as happens with all our happiness in this world. This is an eternal joy, the joy that our Lord will bring to those who trust in him.[10]

Remarkably, these comments about death being swallowed up for ever are not restricted to the people of Judah. They apply to 'all peoples' and 'all nations'.[11]

As we have observed, the book of Isaiah moves from judgment to salvation. Beyond the destruction of Jerusalem by the Babylonians in 586 BC, it anticipates a restoration of the city. This, however, is not the only restoration envisaged. Isaiah foresees the coming of a new Jerusalem that will entail the creation of new heavens and a new earth. Importantly, as the restoration of Jerusalem after its destruction by the Babylonians centres on the actions of a divinely anointed foreign king, another individual plays a significant role in the establishment of the new Jerusalem. This individual comes to the fore in Isaiah 49 – 53, where he is mentioned in three different passages.[12] The longest of these is 52:13 – 53:12, which highlights how this unique individual suffers vicariously, bearing the punishment due to others.

2. The arm of the Lord (52:13 – 53:1)

God introduces the central character of 52:13 – 53:12 by referring to him as *my servant*. This designation is not intended to demean this individual but to underscore his obedience to God. As we observed in the book of Joshua, Moses is honoured by being regularly described as Yahweh's servant.[13] The servant hears and obeys what God has to say. In Isaiah 50:4–5, he is portrayed as being attentive and obedient to God:

> The Sovereign LORD has given me a well-instructed tongue,
> to know the word that sustains the weary.

---

[10] S. Grindheim, *Living in the Kingdom of God: A Biblical Theology for the Life of the Church* (Grand Rapids: Baker Academic, 2018), p. 14.

[11] Isa. 25:7.

[12] Isa. 49:1–7; 50:4–9; 52:13 – 53:12.

[13] Josh. 1:1, 13, 15; 8:31, 33; 11:12; 12:6 (x2); 13:8; 14:7; 18:7; 22:2, 4–5; 24:29.

He wakens me morning by morning,
> wakens my ear to listen like one being instructed.

The Sovereign LORD has opened my ears;
> I have not been rebellious,
> I have not turned away.

The servant's willing obedience sets him apart from others in the book of Isaiah who are condemned for failing to follow God faithfully.

Speaking of his servant in 52:13 – 53:1, God indicates that he will evoke very different responses. On the one hand, many will be *appalled at him*, for they will see nothing attractive in him. He will be an object of contempt. On the other hand, many will perceive him for who he truly is, recognizing him as *the arm of the LORD* (53:1).[14]

This is not the first reference to *the arm of the LORD*. It has already been mentioned in 51:9, where it is associated with God's deliverance of the Israelites from slavery in Egypt. By recalling with poetic imagery God's defeat of the Egyptian army, this passage implies that the arm of the Lord will bring about an even greater exodus. This will result in those who are rescued entering Zion with singing. Crowned with everlasting joy, 'gladness and joy will overtake them, and sorrow and sighing will flee away'.[15] Picking up on the significance of this, Mark Boda observes that 'the arm of the LORD' is associated with the 'inbreaking of the reign of God'.[16] Remarkably, however, as 53:1 reveals, the arm of the Lord, which we might naturally associate with God's power, is his suffering servant. Bizarre as it may seem, God's salvation comes through an individual who, as we shall see in more detail shortly, will silently suffer and die for others.

3. The servant suffers for others (53:2–9)

Having identified the *servant* as *the arm of the LORD*, Isaiah proceeds to focus on what he will accomplish. Before doing so, however, he highlights how the servant will be despised by many people. In their eyes he is like a spindly plant that has not grown fully due to a lack of moisture (53:2).

---

[14] They will see and understand, a motif that recalls God's words to Isaiah in 6:9–10.

[15] Isa. 51:11.

[16] M. J. Boda, '"Declare His Glory among the Nations": The Psalter as Missional Collection', in S. E. Porter and C. L. Westfall (eds.), *Christian Mission: Old Testament Foundations and New Testament Developments*, McMaster New Testament Studies (Eugene: Pickwick, 2010), p. 39.

Unfortunately, those who despise him fail to recognize that despite his appearance he is the one who can bring them healing.

Through the repetition of the nouns *suffering* and *pain* in verses 3 and 4, a chiasm is created that binds the two verses together.[17] Importantly, the very factors that are a cause for despising the servant in verse 3 – *suffering* and *pain* – are present due to the fact that he has taken *our pain* and *our suffering*.

Picture a woman whose hands and face have been scarred by serious burns. Her scars are so repulsive that people look away from her. Yet to her daughter they are an ever-present reminder of exceptional love and courage. She would have been burnt to death but for her mother's sacrificial intervention. While others are repelled by the woman's scars, for her daughter they are wounds of love. It is so with the servant. He is despised for bearing pain and suffering. Yet to those who understand, he is bearing their pain and suffering. As Shalom Paul comments, 'We were totally taken by surprise when we realized that his maladies were actually in atonement for our own wrongdoings, for he . . . was, in effect, bearing the sickness that we should have suffered.'[18]

Isaiah drives home the vicarious nature of the servant's suffering. In rapid succession he emphasizes how the servant has taken on himself *our pain, our suffering, our transgressions* and *our iniquities*. Consequently, he has been *punished, stricken, afflicted, pierced, crushed* and *oppressed* (4–7). Succinctly, in verse 6 Isaiah states,

> *We all, like sheep, have gone astray,*
>   *each of us has turned to our own way;*
> *and the* Lord *has laid on him*
>   *the iniquity of us all.*

As Isaiah's description of the servant unfolds, various interrelated ideas are developed. First, the servant bears the pain and suffering of punishment without complaint. He willingly gives his life, offering no resistance. Second, although he is punished for the wrongs of others, he himself is entirely

---

[17] J. A. Motyer, *Isaiah: An Introduction and Commentary*, Tyndale Old Testament Commentaries 20 (Leicester: Inter-Varsity Press, 1999), p. 377, comments, '*Sorrows* ['suffering' in NIV] makes a "domino" link between verses 3 and 4, and it is only in 4 that we discover that his sorrow and suffering arose not from a sickly constitution but because he took our sorrows [suffering] as his own.'

[18] S. M. Paul, *Isaiah 40 – 66: Translation and Commentary* (Grand Rapids/Cambridge: William B. Eerdmans, 2012), p. 404.

innocent. He has not acted violently, *nor was any deceit in his mouth* (9). God declares him righteous (11). Third, in the light of his innocence the process by which he is declared guilty and punished is unjust. Despite this, no-one protests in support of him. Remarkably, all that happens is divinely intended so that his death will be *an offering for sin* (10). In the light of humanity's disobedience of God and their subsequent alienation from him, this act of atonement offers hope to those who are estranged from God. By offering himself in the place of others, the servant fulfils a vital and necessary role, a role essential for the restoration of harmony between God and rebellious humanity.

4. The servant is vindicated (53:10–12)

Isaiah's portrayal of the servant is permeated with remarks that underline the vicarious nature of his suffering. Bearing the *iniquities* of others (11), he is *numbered with the transgressors* (12). He is even willing to pour out *his life unto death* (12). Despite everything that happens to him, remarkably, death is not the end for him. God speaks of a positive outcome, stating, *After he has suffered, he will see the light of life and be satisfied* (11). Although the servant will suffer on behalf of others, he will ultimately be vindicated by God. God will not abandon him. This expectation recalls an earlier passage in which the servant expresses his confidence in God's assistance:

> I offered my back to those who beat me,
>> my cheeks to those who pulled out my beard;
> I did not hide my face
>> from mocking and spitting.
> Because the Sovereign Lord helps me,
>> I will not be disgraced.
> Therefore have I set my face like flint,
>> and I know I will not be put to shame.[19]

In the light of the servant's willingness to bear the sin of others, God promises to give him *a portion among the great, and he will divide the spoils with the strong* (12). Ultimately, the servant, who has been despised by others,

---

[19] Isa. 50:6–7.

will be exalted to a position of honour. This outcome has already been mentioned in Isaiah 49. Addressing the servant, 'the Redeemer and Holy One of Israel' says in 49:7:

> Kings will see you and stand up,
>> princes will see and bow down,
> because of the LORD, who is faithful,
>> the Holy One of Israel, who has chosen you.

While the servant is not specifically designated a king, he will receive the homage of kings and princes. Such an outcome suggests that he may well be the promised vicegerent who will mediate God's blessing to the nations of the earth.[20]

5. Conclusion

With its focus on the transformation of Jerusalem, the book of Isaiah contributes in a special way to Old Testament expectations regarding the establishment of God's kingdom on the earth. As the prophet Isaiah looks to the future, he proclaims that beyond judgment there is salvation. Importantly, he anticipates the creation of a new Jerusalem, which will offer an experience of life that transcends anything known by the inhabitants of earthly Jerusalem. Isaiah's hope rests on the expectation that God will create new heavens and a new earth (65:17), resulting in a city where God will dwell surrounded by the nations of the earth. However, this goal cannot be attained without a process of atonement that addresses human sinfulness. As Isaiah discovers for himself when he sees the Holy One of Israel on his throne, he is 'a man of unclean lips' living 'among a people of unclean lips'.[21] Taking the reality of human sinfulness into account, Isaiah 52:13 – 53:12 reveals that God's salvation comes through an exceptional individual who bears the punishment due to others. Isaiah's predictions regarding this suffering servant find their fulfilment in Jesus Christ.

---

[20] For a fuller discussion, see M. Zehnder, 'The Enigmatic Figure of the "Servant of the Lord": Observations on the Relationship between the "Servant of the Lord" in Isaiah 40 – 55 and Other Salvific Figures in the Hebrew Bible', in M. Zehnder (ed.), New Studies in the Book of Isaiah, Perspectives on Hebrew Scriptures and Its Contexts 21 (Piscataway: Gorgias Press, 2014), pp. 231–282; M. S. Harmon, The Servant of the Lord and His Servant People: Tracing a Biblical Theme through the Canon, New Studies in Biblical Theology 54 (London: Apollos, 2020), pp. 109–142.

[21] Isa. 6:5.

Psalm 2:1–12

12. The divine king and his anointed

On 28 August 1963, Martin Luther King Jr delivered one of the greatest speeches of modern times. Addressing some 250,000 people at the Lincoln Memorial in Washington DC, King departed from his prepared notes and shared his dream of a transformed nation. Contemplating a better future, King set out his vision of the future with a series of images. Among these, he spoke of his children being judged by their character and not their appearance. To highlight the transformation that he dreamed about, King drew on the words of the prophet Isaiah:

> Every valley shall be raised up,
> every mountain and hill made low;
> the rough ground shall become level,
> the rugged places a plain.
> And the glory of the Lord will be revealed,
> and all people will see it together.'[1]

King's powerful oratory offered hope to oppressed people in a time of political turmoil and social unrest. In a similar way, the book of Psalms also provides hope to those suffering oppression.

There is no record of when and how it happened, but we can be reasonably sure that at some point in the final decades of the sixth century or early decades of the fifth century BC, an individual or small group brought together various collections of songs to compile the biblical book of Psalms. This anthology of 150 songs was compiled for use in the early

---

[1] Isa. 40:4–5.

post-exilic period, possibly accompanying the rebuilding of the temple in Jerusalem and the restoration of public worship at this sacred location. Whoever was responsible for its compilation appears to have ordered the entire Psalter with some care, drawing on earlier collections, some of which may have existed for several centuries. Its structure mirrors something of the history of Jerusalem from its capture c.1000 BC by King David down to the time of the compiler(s).

In the light of the historical circumstances when the Psalter was created, one of its most noteworthy features is the prominence that it gives to the royal house of David. On one level, this is evident from the number of psalms that mention David in their titles. A strong tradition within the Old Testament associates him with the composition of songs (e.g. 2 Sam. 22 – 23). For this reason, David has been considered by many to be the author of those psalms that name him in their titles. On another level, the content of many psalms draws attention to the importance of the monarchy, addressing different aspects of royal life, especially David's own experiences as king. Some of these 'royal' psalms are strategically located within the Psalter, giving further emphasis to the importance of the Davidic dynasty.

The Psalter's interest in royalty is especially noteworthy. Following the destruction of Jerusalem in 586 BC, no Judean king exercises authority over the inhabitants of the city. With the overthrow of the Babylonians by the Persian king Cyrus in 539 BC, the task of governing Jerusalem is delegated to officials appointed by the Persians. In this post-exilic world there is no role for a king descended from the line of David.

Against a background of foreign domination and the absence of a Davidic king, the compiler(s) of the Psalter deliberately places two songs at the start of the collection to introduce concepts that were especially important for those living in Jerusalem.[2] Taken together Psalms 1 and 2 offer a worldview that stresses the concepts of good and evil, with God's blessing being assured to those who live by his righteous instructions. With imagery drawn from agricultural practices, Psalm 1 contrasts the fate of the righteous and the wicked:

> Blessed is the one
> who does not walk in step with the wicked

---

[2] Psalms 1 and 2 stand apart from those that follow because they both lack titles.

    or stand in the way that sinners take
        or sit in the company of mockers,
    but whose delight is in the law of the Lord,
        and who meditates on his law day and night.
    That person is like a tree planted by streams of water,
        which yields its fruit in season
    and whose leaf does not wither –
        whatever they do prospers.
    Not so the wicked!
        They are like chaff
        that the wind blows away.[3]

Building on this striking contrast between the righteous and the wicked, Psalm 2 introduces a further perspective that focuses, perhaps surprisingly, on the significance of the Davidic monarchy in God's dealings with the nations of the world.

1. The Lord and his anointed (2:1–5)

The opening verses of Psalm 2 portray humanity's rebellion against Yahweh and his anointed:

Why do the nations conspire
    and the peoples plot in vain?
The kings of the earth rise up
    and the rulers band together
    against the Lord and against his anointed, saying,
'Let us break their chains
    and throw off their shackles.'
(1–3)

With references to *nations, peoples, kings* and *rulers*, Psalm 2 conveys a sense of widespread and weighty opposition to God. In the light of this challenge to his authority, which is understandably derisible given the contrast that exists between God's omnipotence and humanity's impotence (see verse 4), God speaks of how he has installed his king *on Zion, my holy*

---

[3] Ps. 1:1–4.

mountain (6). As God's special representative this king will subdue defiant kings and rulers. In the light of this expectation, the psalm writer challenges those opposed to God to reconsider their rebellious stance. If they submit to God and his chosen king, fearfully acknowledging *his rule with trembling* (11), they will placate God's anger and escape destruction. By submitting to God's anointed, they will find refuge and blessing.

The prominence given to the divinely appointed king in Psalm 2 is surprising, especially given the circumstances surrounding the Psalter's compilation. It is noteworthy that the compiler of the Psalter should attribute such an important role to a divinely appointed king when there is no Davidic king ruling in Jerusalem. Yet his expectations reflect long-standing traditions, the roots of which may be traced back to (1) the opening chapters of Genesis and (2) the account of the establishment of the Davidic dynasty in Jerusalem in 2 Samuel 5 – 7.

Humanity's desire for independence from God, for autonomy to go their own way, originates with Adam and Eve's actions in the garden of Eden (Gen. 3:1–24). Although appointed by God to be his vicegerents, they are tempted by a mysterious 'serpent' to betray God. Out of a misguided desire to become like God, 'knowing good and evil', they disregard their Creator's instructions. Their rebellious attitude has devastating consequences, resulting in a world marked by human aggression and violence. However, in response to Adam and Eve's actions, God promises to send a vicegerent, descended from Eve, who will overcome the 'serpent' (3:15). God's plan of restoration requires the coming of a divinely appointed ruler who will establish God's kingdom on the earth.

2. Zion the City of David (2:6)

Psalm 2 picks up the theme of God's intention to send a vicegerent and links it to the Davidic dynasty in Jerusalem. In verse 6 of the psalm, God states,

> *I have installed my king*
> *on Zion, my holy mountain.*

The first reference to Zion in the Old Testament comes in 2 Samuel 5:7 in the account of David's conquest of Jerusalem: 'David captured the fortress of Zion – which is the City of David.' Zion is the name given to David's city.

Strikingly, the same connection is made when Zion is next mentioned. In the context of Solomon's dedication of the temple in Jerusalem, 1 Kings 8:1 states,

> Then King Solomon summoned into his presence at Jerusalem the elders of Israel, all the heads of the tribes and the chiefs of the Israelite families, to bring up the ark of the LORD's covenant from Zion, the City of David.[4]

In 2 Samuel 4 – 6 a strong association is created between David's confirmation as king over Israel, the establishment of Jerusalem/Zion as the capital of David's kingdom and the presence of the ark of the covenant in the city.[5] As the footstool of the divine throne, the ark's arrival in Jerusalem confirms Yahweh's approval of David as king over Israel. Immediately after describing this significant event, the author of 2 Samuel observes that Yahweh gave David 'rest from all his enemies around him'.[6]

With the consolidation of his position as king over Israel, David expresses a desire to construct a palace/temple for Yahweh. Out of a desire to acknowledge appropriately God's divine kingship, David wants to construct a temple for God in Jerusalem (2 Sam. 7:2). David is troubled by the fact that he dwells in a 'house of cedar' whereas the ark of Yahweh is situated inside a tent. For David it is incongruous that the earthly residence of the king of heaven and earth should be inferior to his palace.

Although Yahweh forbids David from constructing a temple in Jerusalem, he responds by promising to make David the head of a dynasty that will rule from Jerusalem. God's proposal mirrors David's offer. David's desire to build a 'house' for God is met by God's promise to build a 'house' for David. The same Hebrew word *bayit* denotes both types of 'house'. Importantly, this is the first time that God commits to establishing a dynasty within the nation of Israel. With this development God's plan to establish his kingdom on earth through a perfect vicegerent takes an important step forward.

---

[4] The expression 'Mount Zion' comes in 2 Kgs 19:31; Pss 48:2, 11; 74:2; 78:68; 125:1; 133:3; Isa. 4:5; 8:18; 10:12; 18:7; 24:23; 29:8; 31:4; 37:32; Lam. 5:18; Joel 2:32; Obad. 1:17, 21; Mic. 4:7; Heb. 12:22; Rev. 14:1. The idea of Zion being a 'holy mountain' is a theme developed in Ps. 48. See T. D. Alexander, *The City of God and the Goal of Creation*, Short Studies in Biblical Theology (Wheaton: Crossway, 2018), pp. 43–63.

[5] David's capture of Jerusalem marks the end of the Israelites' conquest of Canaan. As J. A. Groves, 'Zion Traditions', in Bill T. Arnold, and H. G. M. Williamson, *Dictionary of the Old Testament: Historical Books* (Downers Grove: InterVarsity Press, 2005), p. 1023, observes, 'In the biblical narrative Zion was the final Canaanite holdout in the promised land. With its fall, the conquest of Canaan begun by Joshua was completed. Having chosen David to act on his behalf, Yahweh took Zion and completed the conquest. In the same stroke, David and Zion were bound inextricably together.'

[6] 2 Sam. 7:1.

While God bars David from building a temple in Jerusalem, he extends this privilege to David's son. Solomon will construct a temple for Yahweh in Jerusalem (1 Kgs 6 – 7), confirming the importance of both the Davidic dynasty and the city of Jerusalem. This connection between the monarchy, the temple and the city will play an important role in the out-working of God's purposes.

3. A father–son relationship (2:7)

To emphasize the special relationship that God will create between himself and future Davidic kings, in 2 Samuel 7:14 God promises David: 'I will be his father, and he shall be my son.' This is the decree alluded to in Psalm 2:7 when Yahweh's anointed speaks:

> I will proclaim the LORD's decree:
>
> He said to me, 'You are my son;
>   today I have become your father.'

This father–son relationship highlights the close bond that will exist between Yahweh and the anointed king. However, God's words in 2 Samuel 7:14 do not imply that the king will be divine like God. God will be the king's father in a metaphorical sense.[7] This is confirmed by God's subsequent remark in the same verse that the king can potentially do wrong: 'When he does wrong, I will punish him with a rod wielded by men, with floggings inflicted by human hands.' In speaking of a father–son relationship, God signals that the king will be his vicegerent, enjoying the status that Adam and Eve had prior to their expulsion from the garden of Eden. In Luke's genealogy of Jesus, it is noteworthy that Adam is designated 'son of God'.[8] Jesus Christ is often viewed as the 'son of God' due to his divine nature, but he is also the 'son of God' as God's appointed human king.[9]

While God assures David that his son will reign after him and construct God's house in Jerusalem, his remarks contain the warning we noted

---

[7] See P. R. Williamson, *Abraham, Israel and the Nations: The Patriarchal Promise and Its Covenantal Development in Genesis*, JSOTSup 315 (Sheffield: Sheffield Academic, 2000), p. 159.

[8] Luke 3:38.

[9] Whereas the Gospel of Mark focuses particularly on Jesus Christ as the divine 'son of God', the Gospel of Matthew emphasizes how Jesus is the 'son of David' and as such is also the royal 'son of God'. See T. D. Alexander, *Discovering Jesus: Four Gospels, One Person* (Nottingham: Inter-Varsity Press, 2010). The Gospel writers view these two sides of Jesus' sonship as complementary, reflecting his twofold nature; he is at the same time fully human and fully divine.

above: 'When he does wrong, I will punish him with a rod wielded by men, with floggings inflicted by human hands.' David's son will not be faultless; his actions will require him to be disciplined. This observation is in keeping with earlier warnings in 1 Samuel regarding the dangers associated with having a monarch. Despite recording in detail how God establishes the Davidic monarchy in Jerusalem, the books of Samuel contain some of the severest warnings against monarchy in the Old Testament. God recognizes that those appointed as kings will be prone to abuse their royal power (e.g. 1 Sam. 8:11–18).

God's warnings against the abuse of power are not meaningless. A recurring theme in the pre-exilic prophetic writings is the failure of successive kings to ensure social harmony and prosperity for all. All too often those in power are guilty of exploiting the vulnerable members of society. Even David himself succumbs to this temptation when he has an adulterous relationship with Bathsheba, which results in his manipulating circumstances to cause the death of Bathsheba's husband, Uriah. When the prophet Nathan confronts David regarding his immoral actions, he astutely uses the story of a wealthy man taking and killing a poor man's one and only ewe lamb (2 Sam. 12:1–10).

Despite God's warning that David's son will do wrong and be punished, God tells David that his throne will be established for ever (2 Sam. 7:13, 16). This promise, which is repeated for emphasis, is highly significant. The author of Psalm 89, Ethan the Ezrahite, expresses God's commitment to David with these words:

> I will maintain my love to him for ever,
>> and my covenant with him will never fail.
> I will establish his line for ever,
>> his throne as long as the heavens endure.
>
> . . .
>
> Once for all, I have sworn by my holiness –
>> and I will not lie to David –
> that his line will continue for ever
>> and his throne endure before me like the sun;
> it will be established for ever like the moon,
>> the faithful witness in the sky.[10]

---

10 Ps. 89:28–29, 35–37.

Viewed as a divine oath, God's promise to David is understood to be a 'covenant'. While 2 Samuel 7 does not use the term 'covenant', David himself refers to God's promise as a covenant in 2 Samuel 23:1–7. In this poetic passage, which is described as David's 'last words' (1), David offers a critical assessment of his reign:

> The Spirit of the LORD spake by me, and his word was in my tongue.
>
> The God of Israel said, the Rock of Israel spake to me, He that ruleth over men must be just, ruling in the fear of God.
>
> And he shall be as the light of the morning, when the sun riseth, even a morning without clouds; as the tender grass springing out of the earth by clear shining after rain.
>
> Although my house be not so with God; yet he hath made with me an everlasting covenant, ordered in all things, and sure: for this is all my salvation, and all my desire, although he make it not to grow.
>
> But the sons of Belial shall be all of them as thorns thrust away, because they cannot be taken with hands:
>
> But the man that shall touch them must be fenced with iron and the staff of a spear; and they shall be utterly burned with fire in the same place.[11]

The KJV translation is adopted here because most English versions mistakenly interpret verse 5 as a question.[12] In verses 3–4 David notes the impact that comes when a king rules justly and 'in the fear of God'. Such a king shines brightly like the sun in a cloudless sky. David, however, acknowledges that this has not been the case as regards his own reign. Nevertheless, he looks with hope to the future because of God's commitment to establish his dynasty for ever. On the basis of God's covenant, David anticipates that there will be a future king who will be God's perfect vicegerent.

4. A universal rule (2:8–12)

The author of Psalm 2 shares David's expectation, recording Yahweh's words to his anointed one. These words are not preserved elsewhere in

---

[11] 2 Sam. 23:2–7, KJV.

[12] Almost all modern English versions take David's words in verse 5 to be a question, presenting a positive reading of what David says. However, the Hebrew text of verse 5 is better interpreted as expressing a negative assessment of David's reign when measured against the words of verse 4.

the Old Testament, although they echo part of God's speech to David in 2 Samuel 7:14. God says to his anointed:

> ... *You are my son;*
> *today I have become your father.*
> *Ask me,*
> *and I will make the nations your inheritance,*
> *the ends of the earth your possession.*
> *You will break them with a rod of iron;*
> *you will dash them to pieces like pottery.*
> (7–9)

As God's son, the king is invited to petition God to give him authority over the whole earth. By looking to God, the Davidic king recognizes that he serves as God's vicegerent. With God on his side, the king will be invincible. The nations will be subject to him and his rule will extend to the *ends of the earth* (8). Importantly, as the final stanza of Psalm 2 indicates, those who have rebelled against God are offered the opportunity to submit to the son's authority. Through doing this, they will not only avoid destruction, but will experience God's blessing.

By placing Psalms 1 and 2 at the start of the Psalter, the compiler(s) creates an expectation that a godly and righteous Davidic king will play a vital role in establishing God's rule throughout the earth. In the light of this prospect, other 'royal' psalms contribute in a significant way to the structuring of the Psalter.[13]

As has long been recognized, the Psalter consists of five sections or books each marked by a concluding doxology (Pss 41:13; 72:18–19; 89:52; 106:48; 150:1–6). The first two books are dominated by psalms associated with King David. Psalm 72 brings this material to a conclusion. Of all the 'royal' psalms it is by far the most significant in speaking of a future king exercising authority to *the ends of the earth* (2:8). As a prayer for the coming of such a king, Psalm 72 anticipates a time of universal peace and prosperity with justice for the oppressed. To add to its positive picture of a transformed world, Psalm 72 portrays the king as ruling for ever:

---

13 See G. H. Wilson, 'The Structure of the Psalter', in P. Johnston and D. G. Firth (eds.), *Interpreting the Psalms: Issues and Approaches* (Leicester: Apollos, 2005), pp. 229–246; D. C. Mitchell, *The Message of the Psalter: An Eschatological Programme in the Book of Psalms*, JSOTSup 252 (Sheffield: Sheffield Academic, 1997); D. C. Mitchell, 'Lord, Remember David: G H Wilson and the Message of the Psalter', *Vetus Testamentum* 56 (2006), pp. 526–548.

> May he defend the afflicted among the people
> and save the children of the needy;
> may he crush the oppressor.
> May he endure as long as the sun,
> as long as the moon, through all generations.
> May he be like rain falling on a mown field,
> like showers watering the earth.
> In his days may the righteous flourish
> and prosperity abound till the moon is no more.[14]

The hopes expressed in Psalm 72 are not limited to the people of Israel. As verse 17 states,

> Then all nations will be blessed through him,
> and they will call him blessed.

In the light of this vision of the future, Psalm 72 concludes with a wonderful doxology:

> Praise be to the LORD God, the God of Israel,
> who alone does marvellous deeds.
> Praise be to his glorious name for ever;
> may the whole earth be filled with his glory.
> Amen and Amen.[15]

5. The absence of the king

In marked contrast to the hope that flows through Psalm 72, the next section of the Psalter ends on a very different note. Psalm 89 addresses the situation that develops after the Babylonian capture of Jerusalem in 586 BC. The author of the psalm, Ethan the Ezrahite, is deeply troubled by the absence of a Davidic king on the throne in Jerusalem. His anxiety is fuelled by the dissonance that he observes between God's faithfulness to his promises and the expectations associated with God's covenant with David. Ethan's words convey well the inner struggle that he faces as he

---

[14] Ps. 72:4–7; cf. v. 17.

[15] Ps. 72:18–19. This doxology brings Book 2 to a conclusion. It is followed by the observation: 'This concludes the prayers of David son of Jesse' (72:20).

tries to reconcile his understanding of God's commitment to the Davidic dynasty and the realities of circumstances after the fall of Jerusalem. God's promises to David, especially in the light of the universal victory promised in Psalm 2, appear to have been reversed:

> You have exalted the right hand of his foes;
>> you have made all his enemies rejoice.
> Indeed, you have turned back the edge of his sword
>> and have not supported him in battle.
> You have put an end to his splendour
>> and cast his throne to the ground.[16]

The situation reflected in Psalm 89 suggests that the nations and kings hostile to God have won the day. With the demise of the Davidic dynasty, God's enemies appear to have triumphed. With such a reversal in view, Ethan concludes his psalm with a series of questions and pleas:

> How long, LORD? Will you hide yourself for ever?
>> How long will your wrath burn like fire?
> Remember how fleeting is my life.
>> For what futility you have created all humanity!
> Who can live and not see death,
>> or who can escape the power of the grave?
> Lord, where is your former great love,
>> which in your faithfulness you swore to David?
> Remember, Lord, how your servant has been mocked,
>> how I bear in my heart the taunts of all the nations,
> the taunts with which your enemies, LORD, have mocked,
>> with which they have mocked every step of your anointed one.[17]

If the Psalter had finished with Psalm 89, we might well conclude that God has revoked his plans for the Davidic dynasty. Yet this is not the end of the story; all is not lost. With frequent bursts of hallelujahs ringing loud and clear, the compiler(s) of the Psalter offers hope to his post-exilic community as Books 4 and 5 move towards a positive conclusion (Pss 104 – 106; 111 – 113; 115 – 117; 135; 146 – 150).

---

[16] Ps. 89:42–44.
[17] Ps. 89:46–51.

6. Future expectations

Hope comes through focusing on the divine king. Many of the psalms in Book 4 affirm confidently that the Lord reigns (e.g. Pss 93 – 99). Despite the tragedy of what has happened, Yahweh remains sovereign over all. The capture of Jerusalem and the destruction of the temple are not due to God's impotence. Evidence of this comes in the restoration of the temple, God's earthly temple, to which Book 5 bears witness through a series of psalms known as the 'Songs of Ascents' (Pss 120 – 134). More importantly, the Davidic king does not disappear from sight. Psalms 110 and 132 are important reminders of God's commitment to David. Psalm 110 emphasizes that God will give victory to an individual whom David describes as 'my lord':[18]

> The LORD says to my lord:
> 'Sit at my right hand
>   until I make your enemies
>   a footstool for your feet.'
> The LORD will extend your mighty sceptre from Zion, saying,
>   'Rule in the midst of your enemies!'[19]

The theme of ruling from Zion recalls Psalm 2. In the light of post-exilic circumstances, this promise of victory over enemies is noteworthy. Despite the rebuilding of the temple, Jerusalem remains a city under the control of the Persians. Nevertheless, the Lord God remains omnipotent and he will fulfil his purposes on the earth.

A similar hope underpins the words of Psalm 132. Acknowledging the lack of a Davidic king, in verses 10–12 the author prays,

> For the sake of your servant David,
>   do not reject your anointed one.
> The LORD swore an oath to David,
>   a sure oath he will not revoke:
> 'One of your own descendants
>   I will place on your throne.

---

[18] For a fuller discussion of how Ps. 110 is used in the New Testament, see chapter 18.
[19] Ps. 110:1–2.

If your sons keep my covenant
    and the statutes I teach them,
then their sons shall sit
    on your throne for ever and ever.'

Observing God's choice of Zion as his dwelling-place (13–16), in verses 17–18 the psalmist looks in faith for Yahweh to restore a Davidic king to the throne as he promised:

Here I will make a horn grow for David
    and set up a lamp for my anointed one.
I will clothe his enemies with shame,
    but his head shall be adorned with a radiant crown.

On a note of optimism regarding the future, the Psalter concludes with a series of hallelujah songs (Pss 146 – 150). In praising the Lord, these celebratory songs contain echoes of the Psalter's opening psalms. Psalm 148 ends with remarks that focus on the divine provision of a king:

Let them praise the name of the LORD,
    for his name alone is exalted;
    his splendour is above the earth and the heavens.
And he has raised up for his people a horn,
    the praise of all his faithful servants,
    of Israel, the people close to his heart.
Praise the LORD.[20]

The author speaks of God raising up a 'horn', words that recall God's commitment in Psalm 132:17:

Here I will make a horn grow for David
    and set up a lamp for my anointed one.

Building on this, the author of Psalm 149 exhorts others to praise the Lord with these words:

May the praise of God be in their mouths
    and a double-edged sword in their hands,

---

[20] Ps. 148:13–14.

> to inflict vengeance on the nations
>   and punishment on the peoples,
> to bind their kings with fetters,
>   their nobles with shackles of iron,
> to carry out the sentence written against them –
>   this is the glory of all his faithful people.
> Praise the LORD.[21]

With the references to 'nations', 'peoples', 'kings' and 'nobles', these verses echo the start of Psalm 2. The mention of 'fetters' and 'shackles of iron' recalls the rebellious words of those who set themselves against Yahweh and his anointed, saying,

> *Let us break their chains*
>   *and throw off their shackles.*
> (3)

Framing the Psalter, the opening and closing psalms create the expectation that the Lord God will overcome those who are hostile to his rule on earth. Central to this is the role of Yahweh's anointed king.

7. Conclusion

By structuring the Psalter into five books, its compiler(s) traces God's commitment to establish his kingdom on earth by placing his anointed on the throne in Zion. Against the historical background of Yahweh's temple being reconstructed in Jerusalem after its destruction by the Babylonians, the hope survives that God will restore his king to the throne in Zion. This prospect, which rests on God's prior promises beginning in Genesis 3:15, comes to fruition in Jesus Christ. As we shall see in subsequent chapters, he is the promised king, the perfect vicegerent, who will establish God's kingdom throughout the whole earth.

---

[21] Ps. 149:6–9.

Daniel 7:1–28

13. A kingdom to end all kingdoms

Some years ago, during a visit to our local museum, my young son became fascinated by a large sword that was on display. As he drew my attention to it, I noticed that a few Latin words had been engraved on it. I was surprised to see the inscription SOLI DEO GLORIA, meaning 'Glory to God alone', carefully carved on a weapon that was intended to injure and kill people. It seemed incongruous to me that anyone could consider this appropriate. How could a sword be used for the glory of God? Jesus' reaction to the use of a sword in the garden of Gethsemane suggests that he would not approve of this inscription (Matt. 26:51–52; John 18:10–11). The sword in the museum is a clear example of a misguided understanding of how God's kingdom is to be created.

The Old Testament story of God's kingdom being established on earth reaches an important pinnacle with the inauguration of the Davidic dynasty and Solomon's construction of the temple in Jerusalem. These interrelated developments are indicative of progress towards God's ultimate goal. Yet subsequent events give the appearance of reversing all that has been achieved. This reaches a climax when the Babylonians capture Jerusalem in 586 BC and destroy the temple that was erected centuries earlier in the reign of Solomon. With the razing of Jerusalem's walls, it appears that Babylon, the symbol of humanity's opposition to God, has won the day and God's plan of redemption has been reduced to nothing. To add to this sense of reversal, Davidic kings no longer reign over Jerusalem and Judah.

Despite the reality of the Babylonian conquest, the hope is not extinguished that God will yet establish his kingdom on earth. This expectation permeates the book of Daniel, which ironically reflects, perhaps more than any other Old Testament book, the effect of the Babylonian assault on Jerusalem. Although the principal characters of the book are natives of Jerusalem, they have all been deported to Babylon. Not only is the city of Babylon the setting for almost all the events narrated in Daniel, but Babylonian kings figure prominently in the narratives that come in Daniel 1 – 5. In addition, half of the book is penned in Aramaic, the language promoted by the Babylonians as the lingua franca of the Middle East. In the light of these factors that give prominence to Babylon, it is all the more noteworthy that the book of Daniel proclaims as loudly as any Old Testament book the expectation that God's eternal kingdom will one day be established on earth, replacing every human kingdom that stands in opposition to God. While the entire book of Daniel announces the coming of God's kingdom, chapter 7 provides a helpful window into understanding the book's message.

1. Daniel, faithful to God (7:1)

The narrative of Daniel 7 focuses on a night-time dream that Daniel has in *the first year of Belshazzar king of Babylon*. This dates the *dream* to 552 BC. This is the year in which Belshazzar became the de facto ruler of the Babylonian Empire. His father, King Nabonidus, left Babylon to live in Arabia, where he remained for ten years, moving around various cities. During this period away from Babylon, Nabonidus entrusted the throne to Belshazzar. Belshazzar's status as regent probably explains why he offers to make the one who can interpret the writing on the wall 'the third highest ruler in the kingdom'.[1]

Read in the light of other chronological notices in the book of Daniel, this *dream* occurs approximately fifty years after Daniel's deportation from Jerusalem to Babylon. According to Daniel 1:1, Nebuchadnezzar king of Babylon besieged Jerusalem in the third year of Jehoiakim's reign. Expressed in terms of Babylonian chronology,[2] this is the year 605 BC.

---

[1] Dan. 5:7, 16, 29. Although Belshazzar's feast is recorded in Dan. 5 it took place chronologically after Daniel's dream in chapter 7. As S. R. Miller, *Daniel*, NAC 18 (Nashville: Broadman & Holman, 1994), p. 194, remarks, 'Chronologically . . . Daniel's first vision occurred many years before the events of chaps. 5 and 6.'

[2] Jer. 25:1 refers to 'the first year of Nebuchadnezzar king of Babylon', but, according to Judean chronological practices, dates it to the fourth year of Jehoiakim. The difference between the two systems is due to the inclusion or exclusion of the first months after accession to the throne prior to the start of a new calendar year.

At this time, Daniel and some other young men, most likely from influential families, are deported to Babylon where they are subjected to a process of re-education and indoctrination designed to prepare them for service within the royal administration of Babylon.[3]

Despite their relocation to Babylon, Daniel and his friends remain at heart citizens of Jerusalem and loyal worshippers of Yahweh. As the early chapters of Daniel reveal, the young Judeans stay faithful to their religious convictions, even when intimidated with the threat of death. Shadrach, Meshach and Abednego refuse to bow before a massive statue of Nebuchadnezzar, despite the threat of being burned alive (3:1–30). Many years later when the Persian king Darius takes control of Babylon in 539 BC, Daniel's commitment to the worship of Yahweh is such that his enemies use his religious devotion to entrap him, hoping to have him put to death by being thrown into a den of lions (6:1–28).

From his deportation in 605 BC through to his dream in 552 BC, Daniel knew from the inside the workings of the Babylonian court and witnessed the growth and consolidation of the Babylonian Empire under Nebuchadnezzar. Later known as Nebuchadnezzar the Great, he was the most powerful and longest-reigning monarch of the Neo-Babylonian Empire, ruling from 605 to 562 BC. Apart from his military successes, he oversaw major construction projects in Babylon, his capital. Daniel also knew of the siege of Jerusalem in 587–586 BC and the subsequent deportation of other Judeans to Babylon. From Daniel's perspective, it must have appeared that Babylon held all the aces. The wealth of defeated nations flowed to Babylon and the architecture of the city was a testimony to its pre-eminence among the nations. This was an empire that appeared unassailable.

Against such a background, Daniel's faith in God rests not on what he sees around him, but in the traditions that he imbibed as a young man prior to his deportation. Living within an alien culture for almost all his adult life, Daniel has good reason to question the validity of his inherited beliefs. He knows the challenge of social pressure to conform to the religious beliefs and values of the Babylonians.

Nevertheless, Daniel remains faithful to God and his faith is rewarded by a unique experience. God speaks to him through a dream, revealing that the kingdom of Babylon and other human kingdoms will ultimately

---

[3] This process of assimilation into Babylonian culture involved changing their names.

be replaced by the kingdom of God. Daniel's dream gives him confidence to believe that, despite his exile in Babylon, God's kingdom will prevail. His dream, which consists of various scenes (or 'visions'[4]) that jump from one subject to another, provides reassurance that God will achieve his goal despite the existence of powerful earthly kingdoms that appear invincible. Given its importance, Daniel records *the substance of his dream.*

2. The four great beasts (7:2–8)

Four beasts emerge from the churning waters of *the great sea.*[5] This is no scene of tranquil waters. Daniel's reference to *the four winds of heaven* implies that the waters are being churned up by winds from all directions. There is something frightening and sinister about the imagery of four creatures emerging from the waters. All four are large predators, but some have unexpected features that transform them from ordinary animals into supernatural beasts: a lion with the wings of an eagle; a flesh-eating bear; a leopard with four wings and four heads; and a terrifying fourth beast with iron teeth and ten horns. As Joyce Baldwin notes, 'The reader is meant to register terror before these fearsome beasts, especially in view of their supernatural features, and not regard them merely as signs, satisfactorily interpreted by reason alone.'[6]

From Daniel's brief description of the beasts, it seems likely that they symbolize human kings or kingdoms. The lion-like beast stands upright like *a human being* and has *the mind of a human* given to it. The leopard-like creature is *given authority to rule.* The other two creatures prey on their victims, displaying horrifying power. In the light of these factors it comes as no surprise when later Daniel is told that the four beasts represent four kings (17) and four kingdoms (23).

Daniel's vision of four frightening creatures recalls the vision that Nebuchadnezzar has regarding an image of a man that comprises four different types of material. Drawing on the interpretation of Daniel 2,

---

[4] The idea of 'visions' is conveyed through the repetition of the term *ḥāzē* 'seeing/watching' in verses 2, 4, 6, 7, 9, 11 (x2) and 13.

[5] Although the expression 'great sea' sometimes refers in the Old Testament to the Mediterranean Sea (e.g. Num. 34:6; Josh. 1:4), this need not be the case here, especially in the context of this being a dream.

[6] J. G. Baldwin, *Daniel: An Introduction and Commentary*, Tyndale Old Testament Commentaries (Downers Grove: InterVarsity Press, 1978), p. 154.

most scholars view the four creatures as representing either the kingdoms of Babylon, Medo-Persia, Greece and Rome or the kingdoms of Babylon, Media, Persia and Greece. Advocates of each position attempt to correlate the visions of Daniel 2 and 7 with historical events that begin with the reign of Nebuchadnezzar.[7]

The kingdoms of Daniel 2 are represented by different parts of a human statue – head; chest and arms; belly and thighs; legs and feet – each part made of different materials.[8] The imagery of the statue implies that these kingdoms are unified in some manner, although it is noteworthy that the fourth kingdom is described as 'a divided kingdom' (41). In 2:43 Daniel tells Nebuchadnezzar: 'And just as you saw the iron mixed with baked clay, so the people will be a mixture and will not remain united, any more than iron mixes with clay.' The imagery of Daniel 2 conveys a picture of great empires and also lesser, fragmented kingdoms that display remarkable strength, symbolized by iron.

To some degree the creatures of Daniel 7 parallel the four kingdoms of Daniel 2. As in chapter 2, the fourth kingdom has its own distinctive features. As Daniel observes, the fourth beast *was different from all the former beasts, and it had ten horns.* As Daniel focuses on the ten horns, another horn appears, uprooting *three of the first horns.* This new horn has human eyes and is boastful. The existence of these different horns suggests that the fourth kingdom is less unified than the other kingdoms. Horns are often associated with rulers and their presence suggests that this fourth beast does not represent one unified kingdom, but numerous kingdoms that share something in common. Like the fourth kingdom of Daniel 2, this kingdom is associated with iron, an indication of great strength.

The four creatures emerging from the sea produce ominous feelings of dread. Their origin suggests that they are evil powers. God's earthly presence is associated most often with the summit of mountains (e.g. Mount Sinai; Mount Zion). The depths of the sea symbolize distance from God.[9]

---

[7] See, for example, R. J. M. Gurney, 'The Four Kingdoms of Daniel 2 and 7', *Themelios* 2 (1977), pp. 42–45; J. H. Walton, 'The Four Kingdoms of Daniel', *JETS* 29 (1986), pp. 25–36; J. M. Hamilton, *With the Clouds of Heaven: The Book of Daniel in Biblical Theology,* New Studies in Biblical Theology 32 (Nottingham: Apollos; Downers Grove: InterVarsity Press, 2014), pp. 85–104.

[8] It should be noted that the legs are of iron, but the feet are a mixture of iron and clay.

[9] We see this movement away from God in the story of Jonah, as the fleeing prophet goes downward at each stage, looking to evade his calling from God. He eventually arrives at the 'roots of the mountains' in the depths of the sea (Jon. 2:5–6).

While it is natural to look for correspondences between the dream and later historical events, we should perhaps exercise restraint when attempting to pin everything down. The primary purpose behind the dream is not to reveal in detail historical events that have yet to occur. From Daniel's perspective the outworking of the precise details is irrelevant. Rather, these graphic scenes are meant to reassure Daniel that despite the reality of powerful, hostile rulers in the world, God's kingdom will prevail over all. This becomes evident as we move to the next scene in Daniel's dream.

3. The Ancient of Days (7:9–10)

Daniel's dream suddenly switches away from the predatory creatures emerging from the churning sea to a scene of tranquillity and order. The prose account of the chaotic imagery of verses 2–8 is replaced by a poetic description of *the Ancient of Days* taking his seat upon his throne as judge. As Joyce Baldwin remarks, 'The balanced poetry conveys the order and beauty which surround the divine judge as opposed to the chaos of the sea and its beasts.'[10] The four beasts are now replaced by a vision of God. Daniel's description highlights the importance of the one seated on the throne:

> *His clothing was as white as snow;*
> *the hair of his head was white like wool.*
> (9)[11]

The *throne* itself stands apart, *flaming with fire*, with its wheels *all ablaze*. Adding to the awesome splendour of the vision, a *river of fire* flows out from the throne. Elsewhere in the Old Testament, fire is often associated with God's presence, from the burning bush where God appears to Moses (Exod. 3:2), to the pillar of cloud and fire which accompanies the Israelites in their journey from Egypt to the Promised Land (e.g. Exod. 14:24; 40:36–38).

The visual impact of what Daniel sees conveys a sense of power and purity. Enhancing this majestic vision of God, *thousands upon thousands*

---

[10] Baldwin, *Daniel*, p. 57.

[11] Miller, *Daniel*, p. 204, comments, 'White hair is a sign of old age and an apt symbol of God's eternal nature, already emphasized in this passage by the title "Ancient of Days". The figure may delineate the holiness of God as well.'

and *ten thousand times ten thousand* are stationed before the throne. The brightness of the scene, the references to fire and the enormous assembly of attendants make it abundantly clear that this is a vision of the divine court, with God sitting as judge.[12] Although the NIV in verse 10 speaks of *books* being opened, Daniel is probably referring to scrolls. Daniel's vision is a reminder that we shall all appear before the judgment throne of God (see Rev. 20:11–15).

4. The boastful horn (7:11–12)

Daniel's dream then takes him back to the *little horn* that is introduced in verse 8. Daniel noted previously that it had *a mouth that spoke boastfully*. We are given no indication of what the horn says, but Daniel keeps watching it. He then sees the entire beast, of which the little horn is only a part, being *slain and its body destroyed and thrown into the blazing fire*. The incineration of the beast's body implies that it can never exist again. It is totally and permanently destroyed. As for the other beasts, which continue to survive for *a period of time*, they are *stripped of their authority*. Their loss of authority provides a link to the next scene in Daniel's dream, where we witness authority being given to *one like a son of man*.

5. One like a son of man (7:13–14)

Verses 13–14 introduce a new scene that jumps back to the vision of the *Ancient of Days* in verses 9–10. *One like a son of man* comes into God's presence. This individual has the appearance of a human. He comes *with the clouds of heaven*, an indication that the location of the divine court is not on earth. Importantly, the events described in this scene contrast sharply with those recorded in verses 11–12 concerning the four beasts. Whereas the beasts are *stripped of their authority*, God gives *authority, glory and sovereign power* to this human-like figure. This bestows on him *everlasting dominion*. His kingdom will never be destroyed, unlike those of the four beasts. Acknowledging his royal status, *all nations and peoples of every language* serve him.

---

12 For a fuller discussion of the divine court in the Old Testament, see M. Z. Brettler, *God Is King: Understanding an Israelite Metaphor*, JSOTSup 76 (Sheffield: JSOT Press, 1989), pp. 100–109.

The contrast between the one who looks like a human and the four beasts is striking. While the latter are viewed as evil, bringing devastation and death, the one enthroned by God enjoys the service of nations and peoples. Daniel does not comment on the identity of this human-like figure, but there is good reason to believe that he is the long-promised vicegerent, who will establish God's kingdom on earth, bringing blessing to the nations.

As we observe the beasts being stripped of their authority and everlasting dominion being given to one who looks human, we should recall that similar imagery is found in Daniel 2. The statue representing earthly kingdoms is destroyed by a rock that becomes an enormous mountain, filling the whole earth (2:31–35). Interpreting Nebuchadnezzar's dream, Daniel states in 2:44:

> In the time of those kings, the God of heaven will set up a kingdom that will never be destroyed, nor will it be left to another people. It will crush all those kingdoms and bring them to an end, but it will itself endure for ever.

The brief description of one like a son of man coming on the clouds of heaven to the Ancient of Days is unique in the Old Testament. The closest parallel comes in Psalm 110, which speaks of God instructing David's 'Lord' to sit at his right hand until he subdues his enemies. This psalm speaks of how God 'will judge nations', crushing 'kings' and 'the rulers of the whole earth'.[13] While the language of Psalm 110 does not echo that of Daniel 7, the psalmist speaks of dominion being taken from earthly rulers and given to the one seated at Yahweh's right hand.

Various New Testament passages have been associated with Daniel's description of this human-like figure coming with the clouds of heaven (e.g. Matt. 26:64; Mark 8:38; 13:26; 14:62). However, the details are sufficiently different to suggest that the New Testament passages are not describing how the Ancient of Days bestows authority on this unique figure. They refer to events that picture 'the Son of Man' coming to earth 'in clouds with great power and glory'.[14] Only in an indirect way do these

---

[13] See Ps. 110:1, 5–6.

[14] Matt. 24:30; Mark 13:26; Luke 21:27. See E. Adams, 'The Coming of the Son of Man in Mark's Gospel', *Tyndale Bulletin* 56 (2005), pp. 39–61.

passages allude to Daniel 7. The closest parallel to Daniel 7 comes in Luke 22:69: 'But from now on, the Son of Man will be seated at the right hand of the mighty God.'

In the Gospels, Jesus often uses the expression 'the Son of Man' to refer to himself, but others rarely do. It comes eighty-two times in the Gospels, almost always from the lips of Jesus. Many scholars assume that this usage is connected in some way to Daniel 7:13–14, but this is not necessarily the case because Daniel 7:13 refers to *one like a son of man*. Jesus may have adopted the expression 'Son of Man' to avoid using other titles that could have been misunderstood by his hearers. While many New Testament scholars suggest that the expression 'Son of Man' was used by Jesus as an allusion to Daniel 7,[15] it is noteworthy that, except for Stephen's words in Acts 7:56, the expression 'Son of Man' never becomes a Christological title for Jesus in the early church. The apostle Paul, for example, never uses 'Son of Man' to designate Jesus. It seems more likely that on most occasions Jesus adopted the expression 'Son of Man' because it did not convey mistaken messianic connotations.

6. The dream's interpretation (7:15–28)

Daniel's mind is *disturbed* by what he has seen. Unsure of the significance of all that he has witnessed in the dream, Daniel asks for clarification from *one of those standing there*.

a. The four beasts (7:17–18)

The initial response to Daniel is brief: *The four great beasts are four kings that will rise from the earth. But the holy people of the Most High will receive the kingdom and will possess it for ever – yes, for ever and ever* (17–18). The mention of *kings* and *kingdom* draws attention to a subtle, but important, contrast. Whereas the four beasts represent kings who will exercise authority over others in an oppressive manner for a period of time, *the holy people of the Most High* will possess the kingdom *for ever – yes, for ever and ever*. For Daniel, exiled in Babylon, the explanation of his dream offers hope regarding the establishment of God's everlasting kingdom. However, this will not happen in the immediate

---

15 See D. L. Bock, 'Son of Man', in J. B. Green et al. (eds.), *Dictionary of Jesus and the Gospels*, 2nd edn (Nottingham: Inter-Varsity Press, 2013), pp. 894–900.

future. Daniel himself will witness the overthrow of the Babylonians by Cyrus, but this represents only a fraction of what is revealed in his dream.

b. The fourth beast and its horns (7:19–27)

Daniel's curiosity prompts him to ask for more information regarding the fourth beast and its horns. He recalls in verses 19–20 its main features, most of which have already been described in verses 7–8. An interesting addition is Daniel's remark that the beast has *bronze claws*, an observation that increases our sense of its ferocity. Expanding upon the earlier report, Daniel describes how *the other horn that came up* attacks and defeats *the holy people* until *the Ancient of Days* intervenes to judge and punish the boastful horn. At this stage *the holy people of the Most High* take possession of *the kingdom.*

Daniel then receives an *explanation* concerning the fourth kingdom and its horns. This emphasizes how the beast *will devour the whole earth*, a point not previously made. Differing from the kingdoms symbolized by the other beasts, this universal kingdom will initially be controlled by ten kings. There will then arise another king who *will speak against the Most High*, oppressing *the holy people of the Most High*. He will also attempt *to change the set times and the laws.* What these actions entail is not entirely clear. It probably implies some restriction on how and when God may be worshipped. As Stephen Miller briefly remarks, 'Denying religious liberty is characteristic of dictators (e.g. Antiochus IV, Nero, Domitian, Stalin, Hitler, and others).'[16] God's people will be forced to live under the constraints imposed by the boastful horn. This will be necessary for a period of time. While many scholars attempt to identify this horn with a particular historical person, we should perhaps view it as symbolizing every tyrant who attempts to create a kingdom by suppressing the true worship of God.[17] As Dale Ralph Davis remarks,

> The one Daniel calls the little horn here in chapter 7 is the one Paul calls the 'man of lawlessness' in 2 Thessalonians 2:1–12 and whom John would

---

[16] Miller, *Daniel*, p. 214.

[17] On the complexity of identifying the little horn, see, for example, M. A. Hassler, 'The Identity of the Little Horn in Daniel 8: Antiochus IV Epiphanes, Rome, or the Antichrist?', *The Master's Seminary Journal* 27 (2016), pp. 33–44; J. M. Sprinkle, *Daniel*, Evangelical Biblical Theology Commentary (Bellingham: Lexham Academic, 2020), pp. 193–197.

call the Antichrist (1 John 2:18) . . . Even now across the world, various little-horn-types mash and mangle Jesus' people.[18]

Daniel's dream, however, does not end by focusing on the horn's oppression of God's loyal worshippers. The boastful horn will be punished. This will end all inhumane governments. With this outcome, *the holy people of the Most High* will participate in an *everlasting kingdom* that will surpass in *sovereignty, power and greatness* all previous kingdoms. Recalling what Daniel records in verses 13–14, this kingdom will be governed by *one like a son of man* who will receive the worship and obedience rightly due to him.

7. Conclusion

Daniel's dream focuses on earthly kingdoms that elevate themselves through the exploitation and oppression of others. Daniel himself has experienced the impact of such actions through being deported from Jerusalem to Babylon. Importantly, however, his dream underlines that all such aggressive kingdoms will ultimately be judged by God and punished.

In the year that Belshazzar is appointed regent by his father, King Nabonidus, Daniel's dream gives prominence to one like a son of man who is received by the Ancient of Days as his vicegerent. The inclusion of this distinctive event within the dream is a reminder to Daniel that despite the destruction of Jerusalem and the ousting of Davidic kings from the city, God has not forgotten his commitment to overthrow the serpent, the father of all earthly empires, through one of Eve's offspring. Rich in dramatic symbolism, Daniel's vision reaffirms truths that he would have known from his childhood. Importantly, it asserts that ultimately God's kingdom will prevail over all others and be established for ever and ever. Yet, before this happens, the holy ones of the Most High will face opposition in a world dominated by hostile empires. Understandably, the dream leaves Daniel *deeply troubled* (28).

---

18 D. R. Davis, *The Message of Daniel: His Kingdom Cannot Fail*, The Bible Speaks Today (Nottingham: Inter-Varsity Press, 2013), p. 104.

Part 4
The kingdom of God in the New Testament

Matthew 3:13 – 4:17

14. The coming of the king

Some years ago, as a family we decided to take a holiday on the west coast of Ireland on Achill Island. It was not our first visit to Achill, but on this occasion we decided to book self-catering accommodation that was advertised on a holiday website. The description of the cottage and the accompanying photographs suggested that the holiday home would more than serve our needs. Unfortunately, our hopes were dashed when we arrived on the island. The cottage was poorly maintained and the rooms were filthy. Almost everything failed to meet our expectations. We felt cheated. A deep sense of disappointment hung over us as we began our holiday with mops and cleaning cloths.

As we have traced the story of God's redemptive activity in the Old Testament, it has created expectations regarding the establishment of God's kingdom on the earth. From God's earliest promise that one of Eve's descendants will overcome the serpent, through to the establishment of the Davidic dynasty, there is an ever-developing hope that God will raise up a future vicegerent who will establish his kingdom throughout the world.

As we jump to the New Testament, will these expectations come to fruition? How will God's promises be fulfilled? Will we feel disappointed and cheated by what happens? In this chapter we focus on the arrival of the king.

The Gospel according to Matthew may not have been the first account of the life of Jesus to be penned, but in the early church it was consistently listed as the first of the four canonical Gospels. With good reason it stands at the start of the New Testament because it creates a natural bridge back to the Old Testament Scriptures. Every Gospel alludes to and quotes from the Old Testament, all of which was viewed as authoritative by Jesus. Matthew stands apart from the other Gospels by giving special attention to how Jesus fulfils Old Testament expectations concerning the Davidic dynasty. In its opening sentence Matthew's Gospel affirms Jesus' connection to the Davidic dynasty: 'This is the genealogy of Jesus the Messiah the son of David, the son of Abraham.' Matthew's account then reinforces this claim by providing a genealogy that begins with Abraham, mentions David and ends in 1:16 with 'Joseph, the husband of Mary . . . the mother of Jesus'.

Remarkably, Matthew recognizes that Joseph is not the biological father of Jesus. His wording in 1:16 speaks of Joseph as Mary's husband and avoids stating that he is Jesus' father. Matthew subsequently states in 1:18 that Mary conceives Jesus through the activity of the Holy Spirit. While Joseph initially considers divorcing Mary, an angel persuades him to remain engaged to her. Consequently, he adopts Jesus as his son, legitimizing the claim that Jesus is heir to the Davidic throne.[1] Taken as a whole, the contents of chapter 1 confirm Matthew's opening statement that Jesus is the 'son of David'.

Matthew then proceeds in chapter 2 to record the search of the Magi for the recently born 'king of the Jews' (2). This episode, which is unique to Matthew's Gospel, reinforces the theme of Jesus' kingship. Jesus' royal status is highlighted through the frequent references to 'King Herod' and his reaction to the birth of a possible rival. The focus on Bethlehem recalls Old Testament expectations about the Davidic dynasty recorded in Micah 5:2–4, quoted in Matthew 2:6:

> But you, Bethlehem, in the land of Judah,
>   are by no means least among the rulers of Judah;
> for out of you will come a ruler
>   who will shepherd my people Israel.

By the end of chapter 2, Matthew has prefaced his account of Jesus' adult life by recording unique material that centres on the theme of Jesus being

---

[1] C. S. Keener, *Matthew*, The IVP New Testament Commentary Series (Downers Grove: InterVarsity Press, 1997), p. 57, writes, 'If the genealogy indicates that Joseph descended from King David, this narrative explains in what sense this son of David (1:20) became Jesus' legal father by adoption.' C. L. Quarles, *Matthew*, Evangelical Biblical Theology Commentary (Bellingham: Lexham Academic, 2022), p. 118, states, 'The act of naming the child served to identify Joseph as the boy's legal father.'

the promised Davidic king. With these expectations in view, Matthew proceeds to focus on Jesus' baptism in the River Jordan by John the Baptist.[2]

To set the scene, Matthew describes briefly something of John's ministry. In keeping with Matthew's emphasis on Jesus as the promised king, he highlights how John's message is a call to repentance because God's kingdom is coming. In Matthew 3:2 John proclaims, 'Repent, for the kingdom of heaven has come near.'

In the New Testament the Greek term *basileia* sometimes means territory (4:8), but more often it means 'reign'. Matthew predominantly uses the expression 'kingdom of heaven' in preference to 'kingdom of God', which he does use in 12:28; 19:24; 21:31, 43. The two expressions denote the same entity. Matthew does not have in mind something different from the other Gospel writers (compare Matt. 19:23–24 and Mark 10:23–25). Possibly Matthew uses the expression 'kingdom of heaven' to avoid causing offence to Jewish readers. 'Heaven' is used as a circumlocution for 'God'. Perhaps, by employing 'heaven' in place of 'God', Matthew can suggest more easily that Jesus is the king (cf. 16:28; 25:31, 34, 40; 27:42). It is the kingdom of God the Father (26:29) and of the Son, Jesus Christ. More likely, Matthew opts for the expression 'kingdom of heaven' to convey the idea that this kingdom is unlike all other, earthly kingdoms. As Jonathan Pennington remarks, 'God's kingdom is not like earthly kingdoms, stands over against them, and will eschatologically replace them (on earth).'[3] Regarding Matthew's use of the term 'kingdom' when associated with God, it refers either to 'God's rule through the messianic king or to the realm over which the Messiah rules'.[4]

According to Matthew 3:5, John's ministry has an impact on people 'from Jerusalem and all Judea and the whole region of the Jordan'. To signal their repentance, the people come to John to be baptized in the River Jordan. Importantly, as John baptizes the people, he contrasts his actions with those of another who will come after him. He states,

> I baptise you with water for repentance. But after me comes one who is more powerful than I, whose sandals I am not worthy to carry. He will baptise you with the Holy Spirit and fire. His winnowing fork is in his

---

2 This is the point where Mark begins his account of the life of Jesus.

3 J. T. Pennington, *Heaven and Earth in the Gospel of Matthew*, NovTSup 126 (Leiden: Brill, 2007), p. 321.

4 Quarles, *Matthew*, p. 79.

hand, and he will clear his threshing-floor, gathering his wheat into the barn and burning up the chaff with unquenchable fire.[5]

John's words create an expectation that the coming one will reward the righteous but punish the wicked. Not surprisingly, John is reluctant to baptize Jesus, viewing him as the promised king.

1. This is my Son (3:13–17)

In the context of Matthew's Gospel, the baptism of Jesus can be interpreted as displaying strong royal imagery in the light of various Old Testament passages. The coming of the Spirit recalls how both judges and kings were empowered by the Spirit of God to undertake their duties. This is noteworthy, for example, when David is anointed by Samuel. First Samuel 16:13 states, 'So Samuel took the horn of oil and anointed [David] in the presence of his brothers, and from that day on the Spirit of the LORD came powerfully upon David.' In a similar fashion, the Spirit descends upon Jesus and subsequently leads him out into the wilderness to confront the devil.

God's declaration that Jesus is his Son with whom he is pleased recalls how God speaks of his relationship with the descendants of King David using father–son terminology. God says in 2 Samuel 7:12–14:

> When your days are over and you rest with your ancestors, I will raise
> up your offspring to succeed you, your own flesh and blood, and I will
> establish his kingdom. He is the one who will build a house for my Name,
> and I will establish the throne of his kingdom for ever. I will be his father,
> and he shall be my son.

The same imagery appears in Psalm 2:7. While the New Testament proclamation of Jesus as the Son of God is not restricted to royal imagery, in the context of Matthew's account of Jesus' baptism and his subsequent temptations it makes good sense to view Jesus as the human vicegerent through whom God's kingdom will be established on earth.[6]

---

[5] Matt. 3:11–12.

[6] Interestingly, Mark's Gospel offers a different perspective on Jesus' baptism by John, focusing on Jesus' divine nature. Mark first speaks of Jesus being the 'Son of David' in 10:47.

The baptism of Jesus marks his anointing to be king. There is no enthronement at this stage. In line with this, it is interesting to observe that the Gospels associate John's baptism of people in the Jordan with the coming of a 'Joshua' who looks to repossess the land for God.[7] As Tremper Longman and Dan Reid observe, 'From an eschatological perspective, Jesus was carrying out a new Exodus and Conquest, routing the enemy that had occupied the land and held individuals in his thrall.'[8]

2. A sign of his sonship (4:1–4)

In the light of John's comments regarding 'one who is more powerful than I' and God's acknowledgment of Jesus as his beloved Son, it comes as something of a surprise that the Spirit should lead Jesus into the wilderness, a barren, uninhabited region. This lifeless location would have been viewed as God-forsaken. Here, on what might be perceived as hostile territory, Jesus will confront his greatest enemy, variously called in this passage the devil, the tempter and Satan.[9]

Matthew records three temptations. Mark merely mentions briefly that Jesus was tempted in the wilderness (Mark 1:12–13). Luke records the same temptations as Matthew, but in a different order (Luke 4:1–13). There is no obvious explanation for the differing orders in Matthew and Luke, although with his particular interest in Jesus as the 'son of David' Matthew possibly views the devil's offer of the kingdoms of this world as a climax to the temptations.

The temptations address what it means for Jesus to be the Son of God.[10] Will Jesus selfishly use his God-given authority to provide for his own needs? Will Jesus draw on his special relationship with God to protect himself, avoiding the dangers of normal human life? Will Jesus seize the opportunity to rule over the world by abandoning God to serve the devil? In different ways Satan subtly seeks to undermine Jesus' status as God's human vicegerent. He comes not merely to test Jesus, but to defeat him. As Heinrich Seesemann remarks, the devil 'attempts to turn Jesus from

---

[7] The Greek name for Joshua is *Iēsous* 'Jesus'.

[8] T. Longman III and D. G. Reid, *God Is a Warrior*, Studies in Old Testament Biblical Theology (Grand Rapids: Zondervan, 1995), p. 109.

[9] The name Satan means 'adversary'.

[10] L. Morris, *The Gospel According to Matthew*, The Pillar New Testament Commentary (Grand Rapids: Eerdmans, 1992), p. 72, comments, 'The Spirit . . . leads him into the place where some important truths about the nature of that sonship would become clear through the process of resisting temptation.'

the task which God has laid upon Him in His baptism, and therewith to render His mission impossible. He exerts himself in every possible way to deflect Jesus from obedience to God.'[11]

Exploiting Jesus' hunger, the devil encourages him to turn stones into bread.[12] This challenge focuses on Jesus' own ability to perform such a miracle. It would have been easy for Jesus to show the devil his miraculous power, but Jesus resists, signalling that he will not use his power for personal benefit to impress his adversary. He refuses to take instructions from the devil.

Responding to Satan's temptation, Jesus quotes from the Book of the Law that is preserved in Deuteronomy 5 – 26. Jesus displays his familiarity with this portion of the Old Testament by recalling the words of Deuteronomy 8:3: *Man shall not live on bread alone, but on every word that comes from the mouth of God* (4). His use of this quotation, and two others from Deuteronomy, is possibly influenced by the instructions given in Deuteronomy 17:18–20 that the king is to 'follow carefully all the words of this law and these decrees'. By selecting quotations from Deuteronomy, Jesus signals his royal status.

3. Putting God to the test (4:5–7)

Adopting a different tactic, the devil tempts Jesus to demonstrate how much God loves him. If Jesus is truly his Son, God will watch over him in a special way. Quoting Psalm 91:11–12, the devil encourages Jesus to substantiate God's promise of protection. However, as Leon Morris ably demonstrates, it would be entirely inappropriate for Jesus to place himself deliberately in danger:

> The servants of God cannot demand that God should keep on intervening with miraculous provision for their needs. To jump from a height and then look to God to avert the natural consequences of such an act is just such an offense . . . It is a temptation to manipulate God, to create a situation not of God's choosing in which God would be required to act as Jesus dictated.[13]

---

[11] H. Seesemann, 'πειρα', *TDNT* 6:34.

[12] Satan's use of food recalls how the serpent tempted Adam and Eve to disobey God by eating the fruit from the tree of the knowledge of good and evil, despite having an abundance of food from all the other trees in the garden of Eden.

[13] Morris, *Gospel According to Matthew*, p. 76.

Cunningly, the devil's temptation reverses the roles expected of Jesus and God. God is expected to serve Jesus, but as his faithful vicegerent Jesus is expected to serve God.

In response to the devil, Jesus quotes once more from the Book of the Law (Deut. 6:16): *Do not put the Lord your God to the test.* By rejecting the devil's request, Jesus displays his confidence in God. He has no need to test God's willingness to rescue him from harm.

4. Serving the devil (4:8–11)

The devil's initial temptations have focused on Jesus' own power to perform miracles and on God's power to protect Jesus. In both cases, Jesus has rejected the devil's promptings. He is not prepared to do what the tempter asks. The devil now adopts another tactic that focuses on his own power. Conscious that Jesus' mission is to establish God's kingdom on the earth, the devil offers Jesus *all the kingdoms of the world and their splendour*, on the condition that Jesus will worship him. This is a bribe on the grandest scale and it highlights the magnitude of the challenge that Jesus faces if he is to rule over the world. As Luke's version of this temptation records (Luke 4:6), the devil can legitimately claim with reference to the kingdoms of the world that 'all their authority and splendour' has been given to him. He is, to quote the apostle John, 'the prince of this world'.[14] The devil controls the earth's kingdoms and in an instance he can make Jesus ruler of the world, governor of all its kingdoms. However, to serve the devil would destroy Jesus' unique father–son relationship with God; Jesus would become the devil's vicegerent.[15] Fittingly, Jesus rejects the devil's offer, quoting Deuteronomy 6:13: *Worship the Lord your God, and serve him only.*

The devil's temptations come at the start of Jesus' ministry and reveal his opposition to Jesus as the 'son of David' and to the kingdom that he will establish. This conflict with the devil reappears in the Gospels in a distinctive way when Jesus exorcises evil or unclean spirits.[16] The

---

14 John 12:31; 14:30; 16:11.

15 Morris, *Gospel According to Matthew*, p. 77, writes, 'If Jesus was to obtain these kingdoms he would have to accord to the evil one the place that belongs to God alone. Jesus would obtain the mighty empire only by doing what Satan wanted.'

16 For a fuller discussion, see G. H. Twelftree, *Jesus the Exorcist: A Contribution to the Study of the Historical Jesus* (Eugene: Wipf & Stock, 2010); C. A. Evans, 'Inaugurating the Kingdom of God and Defeating the Kingdom of Satan', *Bulletin for Biblical Research* 15 (2005), pp. 49–75.

exorcisms performed by Jesus are evidence of his assault on the demonic world. Importantly for the Gospel writers, Jesus' attack on the powers of evil provides evidence that the kingdom of God has come.[17] We see this reflected in Matthew 12:22–29 (cf. Luke 11:14–20). Jesus heals a 'demon-possessed man who was blind and mute'. Those watching are astonished and ask, 'Could this be the Son of David?' In response the Pharisees claim, 'It is only by Beelzebul, the prince of demons, that this fellow drives out demons.' To this false claim Jesus replies,

> Every kingdom divided against itself will be ruined, and every city or household divided against itself will not stand. If Satan drives out Satan, he is divided against himself. How then can his kingdom stand? And if I drive out demons by Beelzebul, by whom do your people drive them out? So then, they will be your judges. But if it is by the Spirit of God that I drive out demons, then the kingdom of God has come upon you.[18]

Given Jesus' ability to heal a demon-possessed man, his opponents attempt to undermine his action by attributing his power to Beelzebul, the prince of demons. Jesus, however, highlights the fallacy of their argument. Why would 'Satan' drive out 'Satan'? Contradicting the Pharisees, Jesus attributes his power to the Spirit of God, stating that 'the kingdom of God has come upon you'. Commenting on this expression, Dan McCartney writes, 'This is one of the clearest statements by Jesus that the kingdom has already arrived (ἔφθασεν [ephthasen] rather than the more usual ἤγγικεν [ēngiken 'is arriving']).'[19] For Jesus to establish the reign of God on earth he must defeat the evil one and those siding with him.

While Matthew and Luke record three temptations, this is not the limit of the devil's assault on Jesus. Later, Matthew will recount how Jesus associates Peter's words with Satan (16:23). The continuing existence of evil, despite Jesus' coming, will be a significant theme in Jesus' teaching on the kingdom, as we shall see in our next chapter.

---

[17] Evans, 'Inaugurating the Kingdom of God', p. 75, states, 'For Jesus and his following, the exorcisms offered dramatic proof of the defeat and retreat of Satan's kingdom in the face of the advancing rule of God.'

[18] Matt. 12:25–28.

[19] D. G. McCartney, 'Ecce Homo: The Coming of the Kingdom as the Restoration of Human Vicegerency', WTJ 56 (1994), pp. 9–10. He goes on to say, 'When Jesus as man, empowered by the Spirit, exercises authority over the demons, the proper vicegerency of man under God is restored. Jesus did what Adam should have done; he cast the serpent out of the garden.'

To be tempted is not in itself a sin. What matters is our response. Jesus draws on quotations from Deuteronomy not simply to underscore his royal calling but to provide authoritative reasons for not yielding to the devil's temptations. For us, the memorization of Scripture may offer helpful protection when the devil looks to influence our lives.

5. The dawning of the promised light (4:12–17)

From events that occur in the wilderness – probably the Judean wilderness to the south-east of Jerusalem – Matthew's account of Jesus' life moves northward to the region of Galilee. This location plays an important role in Jesus' ministry. While Matthew recounts in detail Jesus' death and resurrection in Jerusalem, he concludes his Gospel account by returning to Galilee, where Jesus encounters his disciples on a mountain (28:16–20). This final location is possibly the mountain that Matthew mentions in 5:1.

To explain the significance of Jesus' residence in Galilee, Matthew observes that Jesus' presence there fulfils what was said by the prophet Isaiah centuries earlier in Isaiah 9:1–2:

> Land of Zebulun and land of Naphtali,
>   the Way of the Sea, beyond the Jordan,
>   Galilee of the Gentiles –
> the people living in darkness
>   have seen a great light;
> on those living in the land of the shadow of death
>   a light has dawned.
> (15–16)

Three aspects of this quotation stand out. First, Isaiah speaks of the light dawning. There is a new beginning as darkness gives way to daylight. Importantly, light dawns *on those living in the land of the shadow of death*. This is especially so when the resurrected Jesus appears to his disciple in Galilee.[20] Out of death comes life.

Second, Isaiah associates Galilee with the nations. Although Jesus is the 'son of David', his kingdom will not be restricted to the nation of Israel; he is not simply the 'king of the Jews'. Even in his opening chapters,

---

[20] It is worth noting that the apostle John in his account of the life of Jesus introduces the theme of Jesus being 'the light of the world' in the prologue to his Gospel (see John 1:4–9; cf. 8:12; 9:5).

Matthew hints at Jesus' universal kingship. The four women referenced in the genealogy of Jesus prior to Mary are either Gentiles or married to Gentiles. They are Tamar, Rahab, Ruth and Uriah's wife (that is, Bathsheba). The Magi who come looking for Jesus are most likely foreigners of non-Jewish descent associated with Persia.[21] As he sends his eleven disciples out into the world to 'make disciples of all nations', Jesus' reign will be universal (28:18–20). Strikingly, while the devil offered Jesus all the kingdoms of this world, Jesus tells his followers that he has been given 'all authority in heaven and on earth'.[22] Remarkably, his reign is not limited to the earth itself.

Third, the quotation from Isaiah is closely linked to the promise of a future Davidic king who will govern with justice and righteousness. Those familiar with the book of Isaiah will immediately recall that chapter 9 speaks of a future king who will stand apart from all other monarchs:

> For to us a child is born,
>> to us a son is given,
>> and the government will be on his shoulders.
> And he will be called
>> Wonderful Counsellor, Mighty God,
>> Everlasting Father, Prince of Peace.
> Of the greatness of his government and peace
>> there will be no end.
> He will reign on David's throne
>> and over his kingdom,
> establishing and upholding it
>> with justice and righteousness
>> from that time on and for ever.
> The zeal of the Lord Almighty
>> will accomplish this.[23]

While Matthew limits his quotation to Isaiah 9:1–2, he undoubtedly intended his readers to take into account Isaiah's subsequent words. The

---

[21] According to Keener, *Matthew*, p. 65, 'Magi were astrologers from the royal court of the king of Persia.'

[22] Morris, *Gospel According to Matthew*, p. 78, writes, 'It is worth reflecting that, while Satan offered Jesus sovereignty over all the earth if he would but worship him, Jesus worshipped God only and all power in heaven and on earth was given him (28:18).'

[23] Isa. 9:6–7.

dawning of the light is intimately connected to the coming of an heir to the Davidic throne.

As the light dawns in Galilee, Matthew focuses on how Jesus' mission continues that of John the Baptist who has been imprisoned. Jesus' teaching echoes that of John with its emphasis upon repentance and the coming of the kingdom: *Repent, for the kingdom of heaven has come near* (17; cf. 3:2).

6. Conclusion

The opening chapters of the Gospel according to Matthew firmly anchor his account of Jesus' life within Old Testament expectations regarding a Davidic king who will be God's perfect vicegerent. As the 'son of David', Jesus is presented as heir to the Davidic throne. From his birth, there are those who recognize him as the promised king and come to worship him. In anticipation of his reign, John the Baptist warns his listeners to prepare themselves for his coming, for he will reward the righteous and punish the wicked. At Jesus' baptism, God announces his approval of his beloved Son, a further indication of Jesus' royal status in the light of Old Testament passages that use father–son imagery to describe God's relationship with the Davidic king. Against the background of God's commendation of Jesus, the devil cunningly attempts to undermine this relationship. Given Jesus' mission to establish God's kingdom on earth, the devil attempts to buy Jesus' loyalty by offering him all the kingdoms of the world. Jesus, however, remains steadfast in his commitment to being God's perfect human vicegerent. Satan may control the kingdoms of this world, but Jesus is wholeheartedly determined to establish God's kingdom on earth. To this end, like John the Baptist, he summons people to repent *for the kingdom of heaven has come near.*

As we shall see in subsequent chapters, the arrival of Jesus as king is not welcomed by everyone. God's kingdom will not be established without opposition. Nevertheless, Jesus remains committed to his mission. Throughout his ministry, he presents his hearers with a life-changing decision. Will they embrace him as their king, taking to heart his teaching on the kingdom, or will they continue to live in opposition to God, subject to the powers of evil? The challenge that Jesus issued then remains relevant today. Where do my loyalties rest? Who is my king – Christ or the devil?

Matthew 5:1–12

15. The shared values of the kingdom

Early in my career, I sought advice from a Christian friend before being interviewed for a permanent job. Her advice was exceptionally helpful, but I suspect that only one part of it has remained with me. My brain is too much of a sieve to retain everything that I hear, no matter how helpful. The part that stuck with me concerns the importance of shared values. As we chatted, my mentor commented on how most conflicts in the workplace and elsewhere are ultimately due to a lack of shared values. This truth has stayed with me and has often helped me better understand situations of conflict.

As we shall see, at the heart of Jesus' teaching are fundamental values that are designed to shape the lives of his followers. Not only do these values define the nature of the kingdom that Jesus has come to establish, but often they stand in conflict with the values of others. With good reason, John Stott adopted the expression 'Christian counter-culture' to describe these values.[1] And Jesus himself recognizes that the values of the kingdom will lead to hostility and persecution.

1. The good news of the kingdom

The opening chapters of the Gospel according to Matthew are dominated by the idea that Jesus Christ is heir to the Davidic dynasty. Matthew emphasizes that Jesus is the promised king, the son of David. To introduce Jesus' mission, Matthew highlights how John the Baptist calls people to prepare for the coming of God's kingdom. They are to repent, for

---

[1] J. R. W. Stott, *The Message of the Sermon on the Mount: Christian Counter-Culture*, The Bible Speaks Today, rev. edn (London: Inter-Varsity Press, 2020).

participation in the kingdom can be experienced only by those who sense their own failure to live with wholehearted integrity.

Jesus, like John the Baptist, also proclaims the coming of the kingdom and urges his listeners to become part of it. As Matthew observes in 4:23, Jesus 'went throughout Galilee, teaching in their synagogues, proclaiming the good news of the kingdom, and healing every disease and sickness among the people'. Given this emphasis on Jesus' proclamation of the good news of the kingdom, Matthew devotes major sections of his Gospel to recording Jesus' teaching on the kingdom. One of the noteworthy features of his Gospel is the way in which Matthew incorporates into his account five blocks of material that summarize Jesus' message.[2]

The first major section of Jesus' teaching in Matthew's Gospel comes in chapters 5–7 and is commonly known as the Sermon on the Mount. Since Matthew mentions briefly in 4:23 (and 4:17) that Jesus was teaching the good news of the kingdom, it is hardly surprising that the overarching theme of this sermon is the kingdom of heaven. As Don Carson observes,

> The unifying theme of the sermon is the kingdom of heaven . . . This is established, not by counting how many times the expression occurs, but by noting where it occurs. It envelops the Beatitudes (5:3, 10) and appears in 5:17–20, which details the relation between the OT and the kingdom, a subject that leads to another literary envelope around the body of the sermon (5:17; 7:12). It returns at the heart of the Lord's Prayer (6:10), climaxes the section on kingdom perspectives (6:33), and is presented as what must finally be entered (7:21–23).[3]

As part of Jesus' teaching on the kingdom, the Sermon on the Mount focuses on how life is to be lived within the kingdom. Jesus presents here his lifestyle manifesto, outlining the characteristics and behaviour that ought to be displayed by kingdom people.[4] This is immediately apparent

---

[2] The five main sections of Jesus' teaching are 5:3 – 7:27; 10:5–42; 13:3–52; 18:3–35; 24:4 – 25:46. See R. T. France, *Matthew: An Introduction and Commentary* (Nottingham: Inter-Varsity Press, 1985), p. 63. Each of the five sections concludes with a similar statement: 'When Jesus had finished saying these things . . .' (7:28; compare 11:1; 13:53; 19:1; 26:1).

[3] D. A. Carson, W. W. Wessel and M. L. Strauss, *The Expositor's Bible Commentary: Matthew–Mark*, rev. edn. (Grand Rapids: Zondervan, 2010), p. 157.

[4] The characteristics of kingdom people are expounded by John Stott in his exposition of the Sermon on the Mount, *Message of the Sermon on the Mount*. See also D. A. Carson, *The Sermon on the Mount: An Evangelical Exposition of Matthew 5 – 7* (Grand Rapids: Baker, 1982); J. T. Pennington, *The Sermon on the Mount and Human Flourishing: A Theological Commentary* (Grand Rapids: Baker Academic, 2017).

at the start of the sermon in a short section of sayings known as the Beatitudes.[5]

2. The Beatitudes (5:3–10)

Each saying in verses 3–10 begins with the Greek term *makarioi* (the plural of the adjective *makarios*, which is usually translated 'blessed').[6] Jonathan Pennington presents a strong case for interpreting the term *makarios* as 'flourishing'.[7] He contends that *makarios* (and its Hebrew equivalent *'ašrê*) 'describes one in a state of human flourishing'.[8] This needs to be carefully distinguished from *eulogētos* (and its Hebrew equivalent *brk*), which denotes the divine action of blessing. He writes,

> They [the Beatitudes] are Jesus' macarisms, declaring with authority what is the true way of being that will result in happiness and human flourishing. They are Jesus's answer to the universal philosophical and religious questions, how can one be truly happy?[9]

The Beatitudes listed in verses 3–10 each consist of an initial statement followed by a reward. The eight sayings are framed by verses 3 and 10, which have identical rewards: *theirs is the kingdom of heaven*. The other sayings list different rewards, but in common these rewards are placed in the future: *they will . . .* Whereas the kingdom of heaven is a present reward, the same is not true for everything else that is promised. This encompasses being comforted; inheriting the earth; being filled (with justice and righteousness); being shown mercy; seeing God; and being called children of God.

The difference between present and future rewards is noteworthy. Jesus' teaching on the kingdom draws a crucial distinction between the *arrival* of the kingdom and the *consummation* of the kingdom. Whereas the former is linked to this present age, the latter is associated with the age to come. This distinction is important to note for Jesus is not claiming in the Beatitudes that all the rewards listed are immediately available to

---

[5] The term Beatitudes is derived from the Latin word *beatus*, which translates the Greek term *makarios*. *Beatus* means 'happy, blissful, fortunate, or flourishing'.

[6] Whereas verses 3–10 are addressed in the third person plural, verse 11 switches to the second person plural.

[7] See Pennington, *Sermon on the Mount*, pp. 41–67.

[8] Ibid., p. 49.

[9] Ibid., p. 54; see also his exposition of the Beatitudes on pp. 143–161.

his followers. He is not saying that those who are now mourning will be comforted straight away. Nor is he claiming that those who are meek will immediately inherit the earth. Rather, Jesus is saying that those who now are part of the kingdom will at a later stage experience astonishing benefits. This distinction between the 'present' and the 'future' runs throughout the teaching of Jesus regarding the kingdom. We shall explore this more fully in our next chapter.

As Jesus sets out the characteristics of those who will flourish as members of the kingdom, he highlights a range of distinctive virtues. Some of these would not normally be associated with human well-being and happiness. To be *poor in spirit* (3) is to acknowledge spiritual bankruptcy; it is to feel that you are lacking spiritually and in need of help. The term for *poor* conveys a sense of destitution and a need to be dependent on others. In the light of this, it is noteworthy that in the rest of Matthew's Gospel we witness Jesus responding positively to those who are viewed as being on the margins of community life. Jesus reaches out to those who are ostracized because they are considered to be ritually unclean (e.g. those with skin diseases [8:1–4]). His association with 'tax collectors and sinners' engenders criticism from those who view themselves as zealously religious (9:10–11; 11:19). Jesus highlights their hypocrisy and condemns them because of their pride. Those who are *poor in spirit* are more likely to be truly dependent on God.

Jesus speaks next of *those who mourn* (4). Such people sense their own personal guilt and their despair regarding the current state of human affairs. The message of John and of Jesus, that the kingdom was near, was intended to produce tears of repentance, not shouts of joy. A helpful illustration of this comes in Jesus' parable about the Pharisee and the tax collector going to the temple to pray (Luke 18:9–14). To those listening, the religious status of the two men could hardly be more different. Whereas the Pharisee arrogantly considers himself worthy of God's commendation and boasts of his religious achievements, the tax collector's demeanour is altogether different. Describing himself as a sinner, he begs God for mercy. Highlighting their differing attitudes, Jesus comments at the end of the parable, 'I tell you that this man [the tax collector], rather than the other, went home justified before God. For all those who exalt themselves will be humbled, and those who humble themselves will be exalted.'[10]

---

[10] Luke 18:14.

In his next beatitude Jesus commends the importance of being *meek* (5). This implies the absence of an assertive spirit. It is to be gentle and respectful. Contrary to what is commonly believed, the aggressive will not inherit the earth. Jesus picks up on this theme a little later in the Sermon on the Mount in 5:38–42 when he addresses the issue of how we should respond to the demands of others. He says,

> You have heard that it was said, 'Eye for eye, and tooth for tooth.' But I tell you, do not resist an evil person. If anyone slaps you on the right cheek, turn to them the other cheek also. And if anyone wants to sue you and take your shirt, hand over your coat as well. If anyone forces you to go one mile, go with them two miles. Give to the one who asks you, and do not turn away from the one who wants to borrow from you.

Turning the other cheek and going the extra mile illustrate well what it is to be meek. Such actions are not generally viewed as the key to success in a world where those with power exercise control over others. To be meek is to be truly counter-cultural.

In his fourth beatitude, Jesus highlights the importance of hungering and thirsting for righteousness. He commends those who have a longing for both personal and social justice. Such people desire that all evil and tyranny will be banished. This deep-hearted longing for justice is not limited to punishing criminals for the harm they perpetrate against their victims. It is equally concerned with social injustices that are deeply embedded within human cultures and societies. It stands against every form of bigotry that is fuelled by hatred of others because they are perceived as inferior.

Next, Jesus commends the importance of showing mercy (7). To be *merciful* is to have compassion for others. It is to respond graciously to the failings of others, conscious that we too need mercy because of our own shortcomings. The importance of showing mercy is illustrated by Jesus in his parable of the unforgiving servant (18:23–35). Set in the context of Peter's questions 'Lord, how many times shall I forgive my brother or sister who sins against me? Up to seven times?', Jesus compares the kingdom of heaven to 'a king who wanted to settle accounts with his servants'.[11] One of his servants owed his master the king 'ten thousand

---

[11] Matt. 18:21, 23.

talents' (ESV), an exceptionally large sum of money. A talent was worth approximately 6,000 denarii, and a denarius was the wage that a labourer received for a day's work. Working as a labourer, it would have taken the servant around 200,000 years to pay off his debt to the king. The king's generosity in forgoing this debt is extraordinary. Jesus then contrasts the king's incredible munificence with that of the servant, who refuses to cancel a debt of 100 denarii owed by one of his debtors. For failing to pay back 100 denarii, the servant has the man thrown into prison. When the king learns of the servant's actions, he is filled with anger and has him imprisoned. Jesus ends by saying in 18:35: 'This is how my heavenly Father will treat each of you unless you forgive your brother or sister from your heart.' Everyone who hopes to receive divine mercy must show mercy to others (cf. 6:12).

In his sixth beatitude, Jesus focuses on the need to be *pure in heart* (8). By speaking of purity of heart Jesus emphasizes inner moral purity in contrast to external piety or ceremonial cleanness. Jesus is especially critical of Jewish religious leaders who give the appearance of being righteous but are inwardly lacking in moral integrity. Most noteworthy are his comments about the teachers of the law and the Pharisees resembling whitewashed tombs. As one of a series of woes, Jesus states in 23:27–28:

> Woe to you, teachers of the law and Pharisees, you hypocrites! You are like whitewashed tombs, which look beautiful on the outside but on the inside are full of the bones of the dead and everything unclean. In the same way, on the outside you appear to people as righteous but on the inside you are full of hypocrisy and wickedness.

Strikingly, in the first of the woes recorded by Matthew, in 23:13, Jesus speaks of how the teachers of the law and the Pharisees 'shut the door of the kingdom of heaven in people's faces'. He then adds with reference to the kingdom of heaven, 'You yourselves do not enter, nor will you let those enter who are trying to.' For Jesus, purity of heart is a vital characteristic of those who belong to God's kingdom.[12]

When Jesus states, *Blessed are the peacemakers* (9), he encourages his followers to be those who reconcile people to God and others. As Jesus

---

12 See Matt. 15:1–20; Mark 7:1–23.

illustrates in the rest of the Sermon on the Mount, peacemakers actively promote reconciliation especially with those who are alienated from them. As Jesus remarks in 5:23–24:

> Therefore, if you are offering your gift at the altar and there remember that your brother or sister has something against you, leave your gift there in front of the altar. First go and be reconciled to them; then come and offer your gift.

He subsequently speaks in 5:43–48 of the necessity of loving our enemies and praying for those who persecute us:

> You have heard that it was said, 'Love your neighbour and hate your enemy.' But I tell you, love your enemies and pray for those who persecute you, that you may be children of your Father in heaven. He causes his sun to rise on the evil and the good, and sends rain on the righteous and the unrighteous. If you love those who love you, what reward will you get? Are not even the tax collectors doing that? And if you greet only your own people, what are you doing more than others? Do not even pagans do that? Be perfect, therefore, as your heavenly Father is perfect.

Drawing on God's willingness to show kindness towards the wicked in this life, Jesus commands his followers to do likewise. In this way, they may serve as peacemakers in a world where alienation from others is ubiquitous.

Bringing the main section of Beatitudes to a conclusion, Jesus describes as blessed those *who are persecuted because of righteousness* (10). In the minds of most people, this beatitude appears ridiculous. Why should someone feel blessed when others persecute them? Most people look to avoid persecution at the hands of others. Jesus, however, realizes that those who are citizens of God's kingdom will be ostracized and attacked because of the values they hold. Because the kingdom of this world is evil, its citizens hate and persecute those who seek to be righteous. Jesus himself is not put to death because he is a wicked person. On the contrary, he is executed because his righteousness exposes the evil of others. Persecution is normal for the follower of Jesus. However, if we are to consider ourselves blessed, we must always ensure that persecution is the result of righteousness and not for other reasons.

3. Further comments on persecution (5:11–12)

Jesus expands upon the theme of persecution in verses 11–12. Although these verses have the appearance of being a further beatitude, Jesus now addresses his listeners in a more direction way, saying, *Blessed are you when people insult you, persecute you and falsely say all kinds of evil against you because of me* (11). Previously, Jesus had spoken of being persecuted because of righteousness. He now speaks of opposition that arises because of him. This should be no surprise. As the king who comes to establish God's kingdom on earth, Jesus is acutely aware of the opposition that confronts him. Matthew records later further remarks by Jesus about opposition to the coming of God's kingdom. In 11:12 Jesus says, 'From the days of John the Baptist until now, the kingdom of heaven has been subjected to violence, and violent people have been raiding it.' The coming of God's kingdom on earth will be greeted with violent hostility. John the Baptist has already experienced this and Jesus will soon be executed. As Charles Quarles observes, 'John's martyrdom and especially Jesus's crucifixion show that even the future kingdom's king and his herald were victims of violent and unscrupulous men.'[13] However, Quarles goes on to observe, 'But in the eschatological kingdom, the so-called victims would become victors. God would crush all evil and sentence violent men like the murderers of John and Jesus to the punishment they deserved.'[14] Focusing on this future outcome, Jesus says to his followers, *Rejoice and be glad, because great is your reward in heaven, for in the same way they persecuted the prophets who were before you* (12).

4. Conclusion

The counter-cultural characteristics revealed in the Beatitudes are the hallmark of those who are in the kingdom of heaven. With these values running against the grain of innate human expectations, those who display them are presently within the kingdom of heaven and will eventually enjoy life in all its fullness as God intended. For the present, however, they must be kingdom people in a world that is hostile to the reign of God. Commenting on the Beatitudes, John Calvin observed,

---

[13] C. L. Quarles, *Matthew*, Evangelical Biblical Theology Commentary (Bellingham: Lexham Academic, 2022), p. 272.

[14] Ibid., p. 272.

We know that not only the great body of the people, but even the learned themselves, hold this error, that he is the happy man who is free from annoyance, attains all his wishes, and leads a joyful and easy life. At least it is the general opinion, that happiness ought to be estimated from the present state.[15]

According to Calvin, Jesus Christ teaches his followers that 'true happiness' should not be judged by 'the present state, because the distresses of the godly will soon be changed for the better'.[16] This leads us on to consider the timeline that Jesus gives for the establishment of God's kingdom in all its glorious fullness.

---

[15] J. Calvin, *Commentary on a Harmony of the Evangelists, Matthew, Mark, and Luke*, vol. 1 (Edinburgh: Calvin Translation Society, 1845), p. 259.

[16] Ibid., p. 260.

Matthew 13:1–50

16. The timeline of the kingdom

Like many others, our family has high expectations when it comes to celebrating Christmas with a special meal. Much thought goes into deciding the menu and gathering all the ingredients. When it comes to the cooking of the meal, a timeline is set out on paper to ensure that everything is ready at the appropriate time. While my children enjoy making fun of the complex timeline that sits on the countertop, they recognize its usefulness. And for those doing the cooking, it offers a sense of reassurance that nothing has been overlooked. We can be sure that all is going to plan. In a similar way, Jesus presented to his disciples a broad timeline regarding the coming of the kingdom. It too was intended to offer reassurance that all was going according to God's plan.

1. Parables of the kingdom of heaven

As we have observed, Matthew's Gospel consolidates most of Jesus' teaching into five main blocks. The third of these (13:1–52) consists of a series of seven parables that shed light on the kingdom of heaven. In this instance, unlike the Sermon on the Mount, the focus is not primarily on the behaviour and characteristics of those who will be citizens of the kingdom, but on the process by which God's kingdom will be established on earth.

These parables are placed in chapter 13 of Matthew's account of Jesus because they address questions that have been raised by the events narrated in chapters 11–12. These events begin with John the Baptist expressing doubts about Jesus' status as the promised king and conclude with the Pharisees' claim that Jesus heals and exorcises evil spirits through demonic power. Underlying John's doubts and the Pharisees' opposition is Jesus' apparent failure to meet their expectations regarding the impact that the promised 'son of David' would have on the world.

John's doubts surface due to his unjust imprisonment. If Jesus is the king who will establish a universal kingdom of justice and righteousness, why is John incarcerated? Why does Jesus not act to release him, preventing his subsequent execution? If God's kingdom has come, why does evil still exist in the world? Why do bad things happen to good people? In his parables on the kingdom Jesus addresses these important questions.

From a different perspective, Jesus' credentials as the promised 'son of David' do not match the expectations of the Pharisees. David Bauer highlights the hopes of the Pharisees as they are expressed in the Psalms of Solomon, a short anthology of psalms that was compiled in the middle of the first century BC. Importantly, these non-biblical psalms reflect Pharisaic beliefs. Analysing how the 'son of David' is described in the Psalms of Solomon, Bauer writes,

> According to this description the 'Son of David' (the title appears here for the first time) will (1) violently cast out the foreign nations occupying Jerusalem (17:15, 24–25, 33); (2) judge all the nations of the earth (17:4, 31, 38–39, 47) and cause these nations to 'serve him under his yoke' (17:32); (3) reign over Israel in wisdom (17:23, 31, 42) and righteousness (17:23, 28, 31, 35, 41; 18:8), which involves removing all foreigners from the land (17:31) and purging the land of unrighteous Israelites (17:29, 33, 41) in order to eliminate all oppression (17:46) and gather to himself a holy people (17:28, 36; 18:9).[1]

With such expectations, it is easy to understand why the Pharisees are uncomfortable with the idea that Jesus is the promised 'son of David'. Among Jesus' failings in the eyes of the Pharisees are his mixing with unrighteous Israelites and his disregard for purity and Sabbath regulations.

---

[1] D. R. Bauer, 'Son of David', in J. B. Green, I. H. Marshall and S. McKnight (eds.), *Dictionary of Jesus and the Gospels* (Downers Grove: InterVarsity Press, 1992), p. 767. In the Psalms of Solomon/Salomon the future king is described as 'the anointed of the Lord' (Pss Sol. 17:32; cf. Luke 2:26). The author of the non-biblical Psalm 17 asks God to raise up 'their king, the son of David' 'to rule over Israel' (Pss Sol. 17:21). The king is to 'drive out sinners from the inheritance' (Pss Sol. 17:23) and 'not allow injustice to lodge in their midst any longer' (Pss Sol. 17:27).

After highlighting concerns that Jesus does not meet the expectations of both supporters and opponents, Matthew uses Jesus' own parables to explain indirectly why these expectations are mistaken. He begins, however, by introducing a parable that emphasizes how and why Jesus' message of the kingdom evokes differing responses from his contemporaries.

2. Four types of soil (13:1–23)

Jesus tells a story that reflects farming practice in ancient Palestine. He describes briefly how a farmer sows seeds and how the seeds grow in different ways depending on the nature of the soil where they are planted. Jesus' story is often referred to as 'the parable of the sower'. More accurately it is 'the parable of the soils'. The focus of attention is not on the sower but on the different types of soil: hard; shallow; overcrowded; good.

Jesus subsequently explains the parable of the soils, revealing how people will respond to the message of the kingdom. Some, due to the hardness of their hearts, will remain oblivious to the message. Satan does not permit the good news of the kingdom to take root in their lives. It will never have any impact on them. Others will hear the message and initially respond positively. However, due to different factors the message will make no lasting impact. For some the cost of following Jesus will prove too much. When opposition arises, they wilt under pressure because their commitment is essentially shallow. For yet other people the message will get crowded out as other concerns dominate their lives. Only the good soil produces a crop. Importantly, Jesus' explanation emphasizes that the good soil represents *someone who hears the word and understands it* (23). This has not been said of other soils where at best people only hear the message. The good soil represents those who comprehend the truth of the message. This emphasis on understanding is noteworthy, especially given what Jesus says to his disciples in verses 11–17.[2]

Before explaining the parable of the soils (18–23), Jesus speaks of how people may hear but not understand, or see but not perceive (13). To reinforce this idea, in verses 14–15 Jesus quotes from Isaiah 6:9–10:

---

[2] It is noteworthy that after recounting the parables of the kingdom of heaven Jesus asked his disciples, 'Have you understood all these things?' (51).

You will be ever hearing but never understanding;
you will be ever seeing but never perceiving.
For this people's heart has become calloused;
they hardly hear with their ears,
and they have closed their eyes.
Otherwise they might see with their eyes,
hear with their ears,
understand with their hearts
and turn, and I would heal them.

Jesus' remarks about not understanding shed light on the hostile response of the Pharisees and others. Because their hearts are hard, like the hard soil, they are unreceptive to the message of the kingdom. The Pharisees lack perception. They are unable to see themselves for who they are. They have no sense of regret or shame regarding how they live. Their self-righteousness masks their inner corruption. Their hardness of heart blinds them to the good news of the kingdom. They fail to see Jesus as the 'son of David'. His message of the kingdom cannot take root in their lives.

By drawing attention to the different ways in which people respond to the message of the kingdom, Jesus challenges his hearers to examine themselves. Which type of soil are they? Are their hearts hard, over-crowded, shallow or good?

3. Two types of seed (13:24–30, 34–43)

After explaining the parable of the soils, Jesus proceeds to describe how a farmer sows wheat in his field. During the night, his enemy comes and sows weeds.[3] When the farm labourers see the weeds starting to grow alongside the wheat, they think to pull them out, but the farmer stops them. He decides to let the wheat and the weeds grow side by side until harvest-time.

Some verses later, Matthew describes how Jesus' disciples ask him to explain the parable of the weeds in the field. In verses 37–43 Jesus states,

The one who sowed the good seed is the Son of Man. The field is the world, and the good seed stands for the people of the kingdom. The weeds are the

---

[3] The *weeds* in the story, possibly bearded darnel, may have resembled wheat. The sowing of darnel among wheat was not unknown; it was punishable in Roman law.

people of the evil one, and the enemy who sows them is the devil. The
harvest is the end of the age, and the harvesters are angels.

As the weeds are pulled up and burned in the fire, so it will be at the
end of the age. The Son of Man will send out his angels, and they will
weed out of his kingdom everything that causes sin and all who do evil.
They will throw them into the blazing furnace, where there will be
weeping and gnashing of teeth. Then the righteous will shine like the
sun in the kingdom of their Father. Whoever has ears, let them hear.

In some detail, Jesus indicates that the initial coming of the kingdom does
not result in the immediate punishment of the wicked. While the kingdom
is growing, good and evil people will live side by side. Only at the end of the
age will they finally be separated.

Undoubtedly, many Jews in the time of Jesus, if not all, associated the
coming of the promised king with a time of judgment when the wicked
would be punished and the righteous rewarded. Jesus, however, reveals
that he has not come at this time to judge the wicked. This will happen
eventually, but much later. For the present, good and evil people will
co-exist, like the wheat and the weeds in the farmer's field. Only at the end
of the age will the children of the kingdom be separated from those who
are not its citizens.

Contrary to what most Jews expected, Jesus teaches that the coming of
the kingdom will not bring an immediate end to all evil. The devil will
actively seek to hinder the kingdom's expansion. Those who become
members of the kingdom will face persecution from Satan and those who
knowingly or unknowingly side with him.[4]

4. A kingdom that grows (13:31–33)

Closely linked to the parable of the wheat and weeds are two other short
parables that Jesus tells. These contribute in a different way to his teaching
on the kingdom. The parables of the mustard seed (31–32) and yeast (33)
both focus on growth. They reveal that although the kingdom starts out
as something small, it will grow to become much larger.

In these parables, Jesus challenges a popular misconception about the
kingdom. Most Jews expected the kingdom of God to be ushered in with

---

[4] See Jesus' comments in Matt. 5:11–12.

spectacular happenings that would be highly visible to everyone. The arrival of God's kingdom would make a profound impact on human history.[5] However, the parables of the mustard seed and yeast contradict the common expectation in Jesus' day regarding the arrival of the kingdom of God.

To unsettle his listeners, Jesus uses two images that would have been exceptionally offensive to them. The mustard seed was proverbial among the Jewish rabbis for its smallness. Yeast or leaven was normally associated with evil due to the use of unleavened bread in religious rituals (e.g. Passover). No respectable rabbi would ever have imagined comparing God's kingdom to a mustard seed or yeast. How could anyone possibly equate God's kingdom with the smallest of garden seeds, or compare the kingdom to yeast with its negative connotations?

Jesus deliberately chooses these images to shock his listeners. As in many of his parables, he encourages his hearers to re-evaluate their current beliefs. In the parables of the mustard seed and yeast, Jesus points to the gradual growth of the kingdom, beginning with something very small. This growth, as with yeast in dough, may be difficult to perceive. This image of a slowly growing kingdom did not conform to popular expectations. Jesus' listeners expected God's kingdom to come fully formed with highly visible earth-shattering events. In marked contrast, Jesus paints a picture of slow, gradual, almost imperceptible growth.

5. A kingdom to treasure (13:44–45)

After a brief narrative comment by Matthew in verses 34–35 about Jesus' use of parables, Matthew records two more parables: the parables of the hidden treasure (44) and the expensive pearl (45–46). The central message of these two short stories is not hard to grasp. The picture of a man selling everything that he has in order to buy either a field with hidden treasure or an exceptionally valuable pearl is not difficult to interpret. Using these

---

[5] In the Psalms of Solomon/Salomon, a Pharisaic composition dated about 50 BC, we read, 'See, O Lord, and raise up for them their king, the son of Dauid, at the time which you chose, O God, to rule over Israel your servant. / And gird him with strength to shatter in pieces unrighteous rulers, to purify Ierousalem from nations that trample her down in destruction, / in wisdom of righteousness, to drive out sinners from the inheritance, to smash the arrogance of the sinner like a potter's vessel, / to shatter all their substance with an iron rod, to destroy the lawless nations by the word of his mouth, / that, by his threat, nations flee from his presence, and to reprove sinners with the thought of their hearts' (Pss Sol. 17:21–25, NETS).

images Jesus teaches that possessing the kingdom of heaven is worth everything. If you appreciate the kingdom's value, you will want to have it at any price. It is worth giving up everything to own it.

6. Two types of fish (13:47–50)

Jesus' final parable in this chapter is about two types of fish, good and bad. Drawing on an everyday practice that his hearers would have easily understood, Jesus once more illustrates the idea that for the present good and evil will co-exist on earth. This parable reinforces what has already been stated in the parable of the wheat and the weeds. Ultimately, there will be a process of judgment whereby those classified as good and evil will be separated, like the fish, with tragic consequences for those judged to be evil.

Later in his Gospel account, Matthew records further comments by Jesus about a final judgment that will divide people into two categories (see 25:31–46). Using the illustration of a shepherd separating his sheep from his goats, Jesus describes how 'the Son of Man' will come in his glory and 'sit on his glorious throne' as king. After judging the people, the king then announces to those on his right:

> Come, you who are blessed by my Father; take your inheritance, the kingdom prepared for you since the creation of the world. For I was hungry and you gave me something to eat, I was thirsty and you gave me something to drink, I was a stranger and you invited me in, I needed clothes and you clothed me, I was ill and you looked after me, I was in prison and you came to visit me.[6]

Significantly, Jesus tells those on his right that they are to inherit 'the kingdom prepared for you since the creation of the world'. He later associates this kingdom with 'eternal life'. In marked contrast, those on his left are condemned to the 'eternal fire prepared for the devil and his angels'.[7] As in the parables of the wheat and the weeds and of the fish, the consummation of the kingdom, after a final judgment, is the goal towards which God's timeline points.

---

[6] Matt. 25:34–36.
[7] Matt. 25:34, 46, 41.

7. Conclusion

Through the parables of Matthew 13, Jesus reveals that the continued presence of evil in the world is not because God is powerless to make things otherwise. Rather, Jesus expects that God's kingdom will be established through a process of growth that takes time to achieve. Starting small, the kingdom will expand as news of it is told to others in the hope that they will submit to Jesus as king. For the present, people have a choice to make. They can side with Jesus or remain under Satan's control. Eventually, at the end of this growing phase, Jesus as universal judge will separate the righteous from the wicked. This will have disastrous consequences for those who have not become part of God's kingdom.

To establish the reign of God on the earth Jesus must defeat the evil one and those siding with him. Although Jesus' exorcisms indicate that the kingdom of God has come, it is equally apparent from his teaching that Jesus does not anticipate that the kingdom of Satan will soon be annihilated. On the contrary, he teaches that the two kingdoms will co-exist for some time to come.

One day, the messianic kingdom will be established in all its glory under Jesus' rule, but during the period of growth evil continues to make its ugly presence felt upon the earth. Nonetheless, God's kingdom has already come. As George Ladd helpfully observes, 'The Kingdom which is to come finally in apocalyptic power, as foreseen by Daniel, has in fact entered into the world in advance in a hidden form to work secretly within and among human beings.'[8]

The continued presence of evil in the world, as God's kingdom grows gradually, is not something that Jesus' contemporaries would have expected. However, the co-existence of the two kingdoms provides an opportunity for those who respond positively to the message of the kingdom to escape Satan's control. For Jesus, the coming of the kingdom of God offers hope to those who are the downtrodden in society. The good news is for the poor, the blind, the lame, the leper and the demon-possessed. God is establishing a new community.

> The bliss that is associated with the age to come is already being experienced, and this bliss is not just for the people who think they are

---

[8] G. E. Ladd, *A Theology of the New Testament*, rev. edn (Grand Rapids: Eerdmans, 1993), p. 92.

entitled to it by virtue of their religious orthodoxy and adherence to the Jewish law.[9]

Jesus speaks positively about the benefits of kingdom membership. Nothing is more important. To possess the kingdom is worth everything that a person owns. Jesus, however, reminds his listeners that not everyone who initially responds positively will remain submissive to his authority as king. And regrettably others will claim kingdom membership but their actions will reveal otherwise (see 7:21–23).

While Jesus announces that the kingdom has come and calls on people to enter it, he clearly states that the consummation of the kingdom lies in the future. Jesus anticipates a time when all that is evil will be brought to an end. As we shall see in subsequent chapters, the timeline of the kingdom will eventually lead to the creation of a new earth where God will reign in all his glory as he presently does in heaven. For the present, however, God's earthly kingdom continues to grow despite intense opposition from the evil one.

---

[9] I. H. Marshall, 'The Hope of a New Age: The Kingdom of God in the New Testament', in *Jesus the Saviour: Studies in New Testament Theology* (London: SPCK, 1990), pp. 221–222.

Mark 15:16–39

17. The execution of the king

A poor boy becomes king! It is the stuff of fairy tales. Real life is not like this. Yet this theme lies at the heart of all four Gospels, which in multiple ways associate Jesus with kingship. We see this most clearly in Matthew's account of Jesus. From its opening words to its concluding sentence, Matthew's Gospel affirms that Jesus, the adopted son of Joseph, a carpenter from Nazareth, becomes a king who claims to have received all authority in heaven and on earth.

In penning his account, Matthew wants his readers to embrace Jesus as a unique king, a king they should faithfully serve. This royal dimension is vital for understanding Matthew's portrayal of Jesus. Intentionally, Matthew ends his account of Jesus with the resurrected king announcing to his closest disciples:

> All authority in heaven and on earth has been given to me. Therefore go and make disciples of all nations, baptizing them in the name of the Father and of the Son and of the Holy Spirit, and teaching them to obey everything I have commanded you. And surely I am with you always, to the very end of the age.[1]

Matthew's royal portrait of Jesus is quite astounding. Jesus grew up as the son of a carpenter in a relatively insignificant town. Matthew records in 13:55 how some people, surprised by Jesus' actions, asked, 'Isn't this the carpenter's son? Isn't his mother's name Mary, and aren't his brothers

---

[1] Matt. 28:18–20.

James, Joseph, Simon and Judas?' In the ancient world, a son typically followed in his father's footsteps. If Joseph was a carpenter, Jesus himself would have been trained in the same occupation. How did a carpenter's son come to be viewed as a king? More astonishingly, how did Jesus of Nazareth come to be viewed as an extraordinary king sent by God to establish the kingdom of heaven on earth? Why did his earliest followers believe that Jesus was God's perfect human vicegerent, sent to achieve all that Adam and Eve failed to do? Such questions demand careful consideration.

But there is considerably more to the story of Jesus beyond his remarkable rise from obscurity to kingship. Within days of the crowds welcoming Jesus into Jerusalem and hailing him as the 'son of David', he is put to death by Roman soldiers. The descriptions of Jesus' execution in the Gospels abound in royal motifs. All record how a sign is placed on his cross declaring him to be 'the king of the Jews'. In all four Gospels, his horrific death is intimately linked to God's kingdom being established on earth. This appears to be counter-intuitive. How can the king's death have a positive outcome? How can Jesus' execution be of vital significance for the fulfilment of God's redemptive plan? And, adding to the drama of this extraordinary story, after being crucified to death and placed in a tomb, the king is restored to life again. All this would beggar belief, but for the profound sense that behind everything that happens lies the plan of an awesome God who is establishing his kingdom on the earth. Jesus does not defeat the powers of evil through military power. He deliberately shuns such an approach, becoming the victim of an unjustified execution. As the Gospels graphically reveal, this alternative, self-giving, sacrificial death of the king is vital for the creation of the God-orientated kingdom that Jesus comes to establish.

We pick up the story after Pilate the Roman governor sentences Jesus to be crucified and hands him over to soldiers who will oversee his execution. We shall focus on Mark's account in 15:16–39, drawing occasionally on the parallel versions in Matthew 27:27–54, Luke 23:26–47 and John 19:1–37.

1. The king is mocked (15:16–20)

The theme of Jesus as a king permeates the account of his execution. When Pilate asks him, 'Are you the king of the Jews?', Jesus replies, 'You have said so.'[2] While Pilate is not convinced that Jesus should be put to death, he concedes in the face of opposition from the chief priests. In the end, Pilate hands Jesus over to the Roman soldiers stationed in the *Praetorium*.[3]

Seizing the opportunity, *the whole company of soldiers* mocks Jesus, dressing him in a *purple robe*, a sign of nobility, and placing on his head a pretend crown fashioned from thorns. Making fun of him as the king of the Jews, they strike him repeatedly on the head with a staff and *spat on him*. They even go down on their knees, pretending to pay *homage to him*. As the occupying force in Palestine, these foreign soldiers take morbid delight in mocking a supposedly Jewish king.

Their vindictive actions call to mind how the servant of the Lord is portrayed in the book of Isaiah. The servant will be abused and insulted. Describing his experience, he declares,

> I offered my back to those who beat me,
>   my cheeks to those who pulled out my beard;
> I did not hide my face
>   from mocking and spitting.[4]

Isaiah later describes how the servant will suffer, silently bearing the punishment that should have fallen on others (see Isa. 53:3–8).

When the time comes for Jesus to be executed by crucifixion, the soldiers prepare him for the journey to Golgotha, a location outside the city that appears to have been used for executions.

2. The king is crucified (15:21–25)

After humiliating Jesus by mocking him as a king, the soldiers force him to carry the cross on which he will be executed. With Jesus already weakened by the torture that he has endured, the soldiers conscript a passer-by called Simon to carry the cross. When they arrive at *Golgotha* (*which means 'the place of the skull'*), they nail Jesus to the cross.

Adding to the significance of what is happening, Mark, like the other Gospel writers, includes various details that underline the reality of what

---

[2] Mark 15:2; cf. Matt. 27:11; Luke 23:3; John 18:33.
[3] Mark 15:15–20; cf. Matt. 27:27–31; John 19:2–3.
[4] Isa. 50:6.

is taking place. Possibly to lessen the pain of crucifixion, the soldiers offer Jesus *wine mixed with myrrh*, but he refuses to take it. Emphasizing the finality of the execution, the soldiers share out among themselves Jesus' clothes, casting lots to see what each will get. Mark even notes the time at which the crucifixion begins; it is *nine in the morning*. Death comes slowly. It will be three in the afternoon when Jesus eventually dies.

3. The king is insulted (15:26–32)

As Jesus endures the agonizing pain of hanging on the cross, he must also contend with the taunts of those who come to witness the execution. Their cutting remarks are probably fuelled by the sign that is placed upon the cross: THE KING OF THE JEWS (26).[5] According to John, 'the sign was written in Aramaic, Latin and Greek'.[6] John also records that the chief priests protested to Pilate regarding the sign, wanting the wording to state that 'this man claimed to be king of the Jews'.[7] Pilate, however, dismisses their request.

As *the chief priests and the teachers of the law* witness the execution, they scoff at the possibility of Jesus being the king of the Jews. There is no place in their preconceived view of God's kingdom for a king who will suffer and die at the hands of Gentile soldiers. With ridicule the chief priests and the teachers of the law refer to Jesus as *this Messiah, this king of Israel* (32). Some translations read 'the Christ, the King of Israel' (e.g. ESV; NET; NJB). The English words 'Christ' and 'Messiah' are derived from the Greek terms *christos* and *messias* respectively, both of which mean 'one who has been anointed'.[8] *Christos* is the term used in Mark 15:32, which NIV translates as *Messiah*.

The Greek word *christos* comes over five hundred times in the New Testament, mostly with reference to Jesus of Nazareth. In its original context, *christos* is used as a title. This is evident from the expressions *iēsous christos* and *christos iēsous*, which come 139 and 88 times respectively in the New Testament. These expressions would have been understood as meaning 'Jesus the anointed' or 'the anointed Jesus'. Since

---

[5] Cf. Matt. 27:37; Luke 23:38; John 19:19.

[6] John 19:20.

[7] John 19:21.

[8] The word *messias* is used only twice in the New Testament because it would have been meaningless to most non-Aramaic speakers. See John 1:41; 4:25. Greek *messias* is used to transliterate the Aramaic word *mešîḥā'*, which corresponds to the Hebrew term *māšîaḥ*. Both words mean 'anointed one'.

Jewish or Roman names were never reversed, the term *christos* must be understood as a title.[9] The frequent usage of *christos* in the New Testament emphasizes how Jesus is perceived as the 'anointed one', a title that carries royal connotations.[10]

Historically, the concept of anointing is strongly associated with kingship. The prophet Samuel anoints with oil both Saul and David to signal their divine appointment as kings (1 Sam. 9:16; 10:1; 16:3, 6, 12–13). After the creation of the monarchy in ancient Israel, the Hebrew term *māšîaḥ* 'anointed' usually denotes a king. This royal connection is underlined by the words of the chief priests and the teachers of the law when they speak of *this Messiah, this king of Israel* (32).

The use of the term *Messiah* (Greek *christos*) by Jesus' opponents draws attention to the expectations that existed among his contemporaries concerning the coming of a unique king who would establish God's kingdom on earth. These expectations took various forms and in the time of Jesus there was no uniform Jewish belief regarding the promised Messiah.[11] However, the idea of a crucified king was not part of these expectations. Even Peter objects to such a possibility and Jesus of necessity has to teach the disciples that he will suffer and die (see Matt. 16:13–23; Mark 8:27–33).

Jesus is not the only one to be executed by the Roman soldiers on this occasion. Two others, described as *rebels*, are crucified on either side of him. Despite experiencing the same horrendous treatment, they join with those who hurl insults at Jesus. Mark captures the irony of the verbal abuse directed at Jesus. Those watching mock Jesus for his inability to save himself, not realizing that he willingly suffers to save others. Jesus is not powerless to come down from the cross. Nor does he view his death as futile. Rather, as he has indicated previously, he sacrificially gives 'his life as a ransom for many'.[12] 'Jesus reveals his kingship not by coming down from the cross to save himself, but by staying on the cross to save others. Jesus reigns by saving, and he saves by giving his life.'[13]

---

[9] See M. F. Bird, *Jesus Is the Christ: The Messianic Testimony of the Gospels* (Milton Keynes: Paternoster, 2012), p. 16.

[10] See J. W. Jipp, *Christ Is King: Paul's Royal Ideology* (Minneapolis: Fortress, 2015).

[11] See J. Neusner, W. S. Green and E. S. Frerichs (eds.), *Judaisms and Their Messiahs at the Turn of the Christian Era* (Cambridge: Cambridge University Press, 1987), pp. ix–xxiii, 1–16.

[12] Mark 10:45. For a fuller discussion, see J. R. Treat, *The Crucified King: Atonement and Kingdom in Biblical and Systematic Theology* (Grand Rapids: Zondervan, 2014).

[13] Treat, *Crucified King*, p. 107.

To those who understand Christ's statements concerning the kingdom, his death on the cross comes as no surprise. But to those who have not grasped the significance of his teaching, the cross is inexplicable. As Joel Marcus observes, Jesus' mockers are blind 'to the upside-down way in which God's purposes work themselves out in a world where a cross may truly become a throne'.[14] Highlighting the paradox of what happens at Golgotha, Michael Bird writes,

> Crucifixion was an evocative symbol of Roman power that declared the sovereignty of Caesar over the world. Yet Jesus submits to it with a view to establishing once for all the kingdom of God. The crucifixion that expresses the zenith of disempowerment, degradation, and death becomes the vehicle for the expression of the kingdom's salvific power. It is by renouncing power to save oneself that the power to save others is unleashed with formidable force.[15]

Luke's account of the crucifixion highlights this cross–throne connection. Luke describes how one of the criminals executed alongside Jesus perceives something special about Jesus. Responding to the insults hurled at Jesus by the other rebel, he states, 'Don't you fear God . . . since you are under the same sentence? We are punished justly, for we are getting what our deeds deserve. But this man has done nothing wrong.' Then, addressing Jesus, he adds, 'Jesus, remember me when you come into your kingdom.'[16] Given the circumstances this is an astonishing statement. With good reason, Jeremy Treat asks the question, 'How could this thief view a beaten, bloodied, and crucified criminal as one who rules over a kingdom?'[17] Answering his own question, he continues,

> Maybe he was confused by the title 'King of the Jews' on Jesus' cross or by the crown of thorns on his head. Or perhaps, as Jesus' response indicates, this man rightly saw the kingdom of God in the *crucified* Christ.[18]

---

[14] J. Marcus, *Mark 8 – 16: A New Translation with Introduction and Commentary*, The Anchor Yale Bible 27A (New Haven: Yale University Press, 2009), p. 1052. Elsewhere Marcus states, 'The central irony in the passion narratives of the Gospels is that Jesus' crucifixion turns out to be his elevation to kingship' (J. Marcus, 'Crucifixion as Parodic Exaltation', *JBL* 125 [2006], p. 73).

[15] M. F. Bird, 'The Crucifixion of Jesus as the Fulfillment of Mark 9:1', *Trinity Journal* 24 (2003), p. 31. Bird also writes, 'The power*ful* one of his own accord became power*less* for the sake of others (cf. John 10:11–18; 2 Cor 8:6; Phil 2:5–11)' (p. 31).

[16] Luke 23:40–42.

[17] Treat, *Crucified King*, p. 25.

[18] Ibid.

As he witnesses Christ's execution, the rebel's attitude towards him changes. Despite his own ordeal he sees and believes that Jesus is the king. Others, however, demand that Jesus come down from the cross, that they *may see and believe* (32). Their words are full of irony. When we recall how Jesus taught his disciples that some will see but not perceive (Mark 4:12), the mockers' lack of perception reflects their inability to understand the significance of Christ's sacrificial death. They fail to appreciate how the cross 'constitutes the very axis upon which the kingdom hinges'.[19] As Treat perceptively writes,

> The kingdom is the ultimate goal of the cross, and the cross is the means by which the kingdom comes. Jesus' death is neither the failure of his messianic ministry nor simply the prelude to his royal glory. His death is the apex of his kingdom mission.[20]

4. The king is the Son of God (15:33–39)

Mark's account of the crucifixion moves swiftly towards the report of Jesus' death. Adding to the drama, Mark records that *darkness came over the whole land* from noon *until three in the afternoon*. No explanation is offered to explain this phenomenon, but it ends with Jesus' loud cry in Aramaic *'Eloi, Eloi, lema sabachthani?' (which means 'My God, my God, why have you forsaken me?')*. By preserving Jesus' final words in their original language of Aramaic, Mark's testimony graphically portrays the reality of what took place. Perhaps mishearing Jesus' words, some of those standing nearby assume that Jesus is summoning the Old Testament prophet Elijah to rescue him from the cross. The hope of a dramatic intervention is possibly fuelled by a recognition that this is no ordinary execution. However, no supernatural deliverance occurs. Despite being offered *wine vinegar* to lessen his pain, Jesus dies.

Unexpectedly, Mark's account suddenly jumps from Golgotha to the temple. In a short sentence, Mark records that *the curtain of the temple was torn in two from top to bottom* (38). Mark offers no explanation, but his earliest readers would have understood that this curtain stood as a barrier separating God from people. The tearing of the temple curtain in

---

[19] Bird, 'Crucifixion of Jesus', p. 36.
[20] Treat, *Crucified King*, p. 247.

two *from top to bottom* implies that something significant has occurred as regards the relationship between God and humans. Importantly, the impact of Christ's death on the cross reaches to the earthly throne of God in the temple.

Mark's other observation about the death of Jesus focuses on the words of a Roman centurion who is overseeing the execution. In the light of Mark's entire biography of Jesus, the centurion's remarks take on extra significance. As Michael Bird remarks, 'The confession of Jesus as υἱός θεοῦ [*uios theou*] ("Son of God") by the centurion is the climax of Mark's Christology and points to Jesus' kingship.'[21]

Even when Jesus appears most powerless, on the cross, Mark records how a Gentile recognizes that Jesus truly is the Son of God. For Mark the cross is not a denial of Jesus' divine sonship. On the contrary, it is in keeping with who Jesus is. As David Bauer notes,

> By bringing his Gospel to a climax with the christological confession at the cross, Mark indicates that Jesus is first and foremost Son of God, and that Jesus is Son of God as one who suffers and dies in obedience to God (cf. Mk 14:36).[22]

From start to finish, Mark's Gospel emphasizes the theme of Jesus as God's Son. God himself speaks of Jesus as his Son when Jesus is baptized (Mark 1:9–11; cf. Matt. 3:13–17; Luke 3:21–22; John 1:32–34) and at the transfiguration (Mark 9:2–8; cf. Matt. 17:1–8; Luke 9:28–36). Mark even records how unclean spirits speak of Jesus as the Son of God (Mark 3:11; 5:7).[23] Importantly, this filial relationship has, among other things, royal significance when viewed in the light of Old Testament passages that describe God's relationship to the Davidic king. We have seen how in 2 Samuel 7:14 God speaks of being father to the Davidic king, and similar sentiments are expressed in Psalms 2:7 and 89:26–27.

---

[21] Bird, 'Crucifixion of Jesus', pp. 29–30.

[22] D. R. Bauer, 'Son of God', in J. B. Green, I. H. Marshall and S. McKnight (eds.), *Dictionary of Jesus and the Gospels* (Downers Grove: InterVarsity Press, 1992), p. 773. In a similar fashion, P. Schreiner, *The Kingdom of God and the Glory of the Cross*, Short Studies in Biblical Theology (Wheaton: Crossway, 2018), p. 91, remarks, 'Mark's first words identify Jesus as the King who acts for the Father upon the earth. Yet clarity comes for readers only when they see the centurion confessing Jesus as the Son of God on the cross. The power of the King is manifested in suffering.'

[23] On the first of these occasions, Mark records that after the unclean spirits spoke, Jesus 'gave them strict orders not to tell others about him' (Mark 3:12). Bauer, 'Son of God', p. 773, writes, 'The Markan Jesus does not wish to be proclaimed as Son of God until it is clear his divine sonship involves not spectacular miracles but suffering and death. Hence, the secret of Jesus' divine sonship is revealed only gradually.'

It has been argued that the centurion's assessment of Jesus as *the Son of God* does not convey the full Christological meaning that Mark assigns to this expression. Some scholars suggest that the Greek expression *huios theou* means 'a son of God', implying that Jesus was 'one of the many extraordinary heroes known to the ancient world rather than *the* Son of God in an ontological sense'.[24] However, as James Edwards indicates, this conclusion is not sustained by grammatical considerations. Mark undoubtedly sees in this comment a recognition that Jesus is much more than an ordinary, if remarkable, man. Even in death Jesus stands apart from others. Observing the contrast between the centurion and those who mocked Jesus, Jeremy Treat remarks, 'Whereas the mockers looked at Jesus and thought his kingship was laughable, the centurion saw "truly" (15:39) that Jesus' kingship is laudable.'[25] Contrasting two types of seeing, 'the seeing of unbelief, which remains wedded to human notions of rule and power, and the seeing of faith, which perceives in apparent powerlessness the hidden, saving power of God', Christopher Marshall comments,

> Faith alone can penetrate the ultimate paradox of the gospel: that the kingly power of God is manifest in the suffering and death of Jesus on the pagan cross, transforming the cross into a power that is infinitely greater than any human power.[26]

This contrast between two types of seeing draws attention to an important contrast between two types of power. To those with perception, Christ's death on the cross demonstrates a divine power that transcends all earthly powers. Jesus exemplifies a different type of power. His power is demonstrated in weakness. Through his death on the cross he triumphs over the powers of evil, giving his life to ransom others. His suffering and death bring freedom to those who trust in him. As Sigurd Grindheim helpfully observes,

> Jesus's power is the power that truly transforms the world. It is the power that brings the new creation, the kingly rule of God, because it is the

---

[24] J. R. Edwards, *The Gospel According to Mark*, The Pillar New Testament Commentary (Grand Rapids: Eerdmans, 2002), p. 480.

[25] Treat, *Crucified King*, p. 109.

[26] C. D. Marshall, *Faith as a Theme in Mark's Narrative*, SNTSMS 64 (Cambridge: Cambridge University Press, 1989), pp. 207–208.

power that brings the rule of love, not the rule of coercion. Jesus triumphs over evil by thwarting its power. One does not defeat violence by escalating it. One does not put an end to violence by exacting vengeance. All that vengeance can do is to perpetuate the cycle of violence. But the cycle of violence is broken when someone has the audacity to forgive instead of taking revenge.[27]

Capturing something of this transformative power, Luke recalls Jesus' words of forgiveness on the cross: 'Father, forgive them, for they do not know what they are doing.'[28]

Many of those witnessing the crucifixion see Jesus as a defeated messianic pretender, but others see a king who sacrificially gives his life to rescue those who believe in him from Satan's kingdom, bringing them into the kingdom of God. 'For Mark, the cross is not a defeat but the divinely willed means for God to bring about his kingdom through his Messiah.'[29] To those with perception, the paradoxical nature of the cross reflects the paradoxical nature of the kingdom. As Joel Williams writes,

Mark's Gospel embraces paradox. The smallest seed produces the largest plant (4:31–32). Saving life means losing it, and losing life results in saving it (8:35). The first are last and the last, first (9:35; 10:31). Greatness comes by being a slave of all (10:43–44). The stone rejected by the builders is the chief cornerstone (12:10–11). The one who gave the least gave the most (12:41–44). The crucified Christ is the King of the Jews (15:25–26, 32). The one who cannot save himself saves others (15:31). The one forsaken by God is the Son of God (15:34, 39).[30]

While Jesus' death is not the end of the story for Mark, who proceeds to recount Jesus' burial and resurrection, he intentionally gives prominence to the cross because of its significance in establishing God's kingdom on earth. Turning everything upside down, Jesus suffers and dies to end Satan's rule over the earth and his control over human beings. To those who see Jesus as the divinely sent king, his death brings release from bondage to evil.

---

[27] S. Grindheim, *Living in the Kingdom of God: A Biblical Theology for the Life of the Church* (Grand Rapids: Baker Academic, 2018), p. 48.

[28] Luke 23:34.

[29] Treat, *Crucified King*, p. 110.

[30] J. F. Williams, 'Is Mark's Gospel an Apology for the Cross?', *Bulletin for Biblical Research* 12 (2002), p. 103.

5. Conclusion

From the outset of his Gospel narrative, Mark proclaims that Jesus is the unique Son of God, a claim that he supports in a variety of ways, including Jesus' supernatural power to restore people to wholeness. Yet, remarkably, the climax towards which Mark directs his readers is Christ's death on the cross. The great paradox of Mark's account is that, for those with eyes of faith, Jesus' divine power is supremely displayed through his sacrificial death on the cross. The inauguration of God's kingdom depends on Christ's crucifixion. Without the cross there can be no kingdom.

But the cross is not only key to understanding Jesus' kingship. It is also central to understanding the nature of discipleship. To follow Jesus is to go the way of humility, rejection and suffering, the way of the cross. Mark underlines this in 8:27 – 10:52. Three times Jesus mentions his suffering, rejection, death and resurrection.[31] However, the disciples' reaction reveals that they are slow to grasp the significance of Jesus' remarks. Mark makes this point after the second reference to Jesus' death (9:31). He writes, 'But they did not understand what he meant and were afraid to ask him about it' (32). Mark then describes how the disciples debate among themselves 'Who is the greatest?' (see verse 34). Aware of their conversation, Jesus teaches them again about the true nature of discipleship: 'Anyone who wants to be first must be the very last, and the servant of all' (35).

This pattern is repeated after Jesus' third passion prediction (10:33–34). On this occasion James and John request the privilege of sitting on either side of Jesus in his glory (35–37). Highlighting their failure to understand his teaching, Jesus responds,

> You know that those who are regarded as rulers of the Gentiles lord it over them, and their high officials exercise authority over them. Not so with you. Instead, whoever wants to become great among you must be your servant, and whoever wants to be first must be slave of all.[32]

Whereas the disciples envisage exalted honour and glory, Jesus focuses on self-denial and suffering. Reinforcing his teaching, Jesus states, 'For even the Son of Man did not come to be served, but to serve, and to give his life

---

[31] See Mark 8:31; 9:31; 10:33–34.
[32] Mark 10:42–44.

as a ransom for many' (45). Kingship for Jesus is not about being served by others, but about giving his life in service for others.

Drawing on Old Testament expectations but not fully understanding them, Jesus' contemporaries, including his closest disciples, await the coming of a powerful, triumphant king, a messiah, who will oust his enemies, bringing peace and prosperity. Jesus' disciples anticipate a triumphant life. Jesus, however, expects martyrdom.

Paradoxically, at the cross on Golgotha we witness Christ's power as the king of love who lays down his life for others. His sacrificial death has cosmic significance which will have a positive impact on the lives of those who see and believe. With good reason, Mark takes his readers on a journey to the cross to see the king broken and bloodied, yet victorious in defeating the powers of evil through sacrificial love.

Moreover, the cross provides the perfect exemplar for discipleship. Like Jesus, his disciples must walk the path of humility, suffering and even death (see Mark 8:34).[33] They must learn that messiahship and discipleship involve self-denial and cross-bearing:

> Whoever wants to be my disciple must deny themselves and take up their cross and follow me. For whoever wants to save their life will lose it, but whoever loses their life for me and for the gospel will save it.[34]

Richard Middleton captures something of this challenge when he writes,

> Christian discipleship will be cruciform, following the pattern of Christ's life, and will therefore often be characterized by suffering and sacrifice; this is because of the ethical tension between the promised kingdom of God and the powers of the present age. The cruciform pattern of the Christian life is very hard for contemporary Westerners to hear, since we (and I include myself here) typically want quick fixes, and we somehow think that our (presumed) faithfulness should make us immune to suffering. It turns out, on the contrary, that faithfulness to Christ and our love for others will often require a voluntary taking up of suffering on our part in order to live ethically in this fallen world.[35]

---

[33] Importantly, although the emphasis is clearly upon Jesus' suffering and death, three times it is stated that after three days he will rise again (8:31; 9:31; 10:34).

[34] Mark 8:34–35.

[35] J. R. Middleton, *A New Heaven and a New Earth: Reclaiming Biblical Eschatology* (Grand Rapids: Baker, 2014), p. 221.

The Message of the Kingdom of God

Christ's death on the cross has much to teach us. To those with perception, Jesus' cross is not simply a reminder of human depravity and barbarity, as an innocent man is brutally executed, but rather a testimony to the magnitude of divine love, as Christ bears the punishment due to others. The cross is also a vivid reminder of the cost of following Christ. Of the many who have attempted to capture the significance of the cross, few have bettered the sentiments of the hymn writer Isaac Watts:

> When I survey the wondrous cross
> On which the Prince of Glory died,
> My richest gain I count but loss,
> And pour contempt on all my pride.
>
> Forbid it, Lord, that I should boast,
> Save in the death of Christ my God:
> All the vain things that charm me most,
> I sacrifice them to his blood.
>
> See from his head, his hands, his feet,
> Sorrow and love flow mingled down!
> Did e'er such love and sorrow meet,
> Or thorns compose so rich a crown?
>
> Were the whole realm of nature mine,
> That were a present far too small;
> Love so amazing, so divine,
> Demands my soul, my life, my all.

Acts 2:14–41

18. The king ascends to his throne

No-one had witnessed the like of this before. The large crowd consisted of Jews and converts to Judaism who had travelled to Jerusalem to celebrate Pentecost.[1] As the people mingled together, their cosmopolitan nature was evident to all. As Luke, the author of Acts, records in Acts 2:9–11, as well as the citizens of Jerusalem there were 'Parthians, Medes and Elamites; residents of Mesopotamia, Judea and Cappadocia, Pontus and Asia, Phrygia and Pamphylia, Egypt and the parts of Libya near Cyrene; visitors from Rome (both Jews and converts to Judaism); Cretans and Arabs'. As the multilingual crowd listened, everyone could understand in their own language what the Spirit-empowered followers of Jesus were saying. No simple explanation could account for the ability of these Galilean Jews to speak using such a vast range of languages.

Forward steps Peter, one of the natural leaders among the closest disciples of Jesus. Addressing the bewildered crowd, he seizes the opportunity to explain what has happened. Jesus' followers are not drunk with wine, as some in the crowd have supposed. Rather, as the prophet Joel predicted, God has poured out his Spirit upon them.

To explain why this has happened, Peter presents to those listening an explanation for the extraordinary event that they have just witnessed. With noteworthy conciseness, he proceeds to focus his remarks on Jesus of Nazareth. Summarizing the essential details of Jesus' life, he highlights how his death on the cross is followed by his resurrection and exaltation

---

[1] The Greek term *pentēkostē*, meaning 'fiftieth', is used to denote the one-day harvest festival that the Israelites are to celebrate seven weeks, or fifty days, after Passover (see Lev. 23:15–21). It is also known as the Festival of Weeks (see Exod. 34:22; in Exod. 23:16 it is called the 'Festival of Harvest').

to the right hand of God in heaven, where God makes him both Lord and Messiah. Enthroned in heaven, Christ then sends the Holy Spirit to empower his followers as he awaits the defeat of all his enemies.

Despite its brevity, Peter's speech casts important light on the establishment of God's kingdom on the earth. It reminds us that the death of the king on the cross is not the end of the story. The subsequent resurrection and ascension of Jesus are vital to the success of his mission, as is the coming of the Holy Spirit. We shall unpack these details as we review what Peter says to the crowd.

1. God pours out his Spirit (2:14–21)

Identifying himself with his hearers, Peter begins his speech by denying the insinuation that those speaking are intoxicated with wine. It is too early in the day for this to be the case. Rather, with boldness, Peter claims that this unusual event is due to an outpouring of God's Spirit on those who are his servants. Importantly, this outpouring was predicted by the Old Testament prophet Joel, who anticipated a time when young and old, male and female, would be empowered by God's Spirit.

In anticipation of this outpouring of the Holy Spirit, Luke records at the start of the Acts of the Apostles Jesus' promise to his disciples: 'But you will receive power when the Holy Spirit comes on you; and you will be my witnesses in Jerusalem, and in all Judea and Samaria, and to the ends of the earth.'[2] What Jesus promised is now being fulfilled as the Spirit emboldens the disciples to proclaim Jesus as Lord and Messiah. Whereas in the context of the Old Testament the Spirit was given to specific individuals to empower them for particular tasks, the coming of the Holy Spirit at Pentecost is not limited to only some of God's people. As David Peterson notes, 'Whereas the Spirit especially designated and empowered the prophets and other leaders of Israel under the Old Covenant, God promises that "all" his people will be possessed by the Spirit in the last days.'[3]

Although the coming of the Spirit on the day of Pentecost stands apart as the first outpouring of the Holy Spirit, the book of Acts records further outpourings that reflect the ever-expanding nature of the early Christian

---

[2] Acts 1:8.

[3] D. G. Peterson, *The Acts of the Apostles*, The Pillar New Testament Commentary (Grand Rapids: William B. Eerdmans, 2009), pp. 140–141.

mission in the world. As Peterson remarks, 'The Spirit created and verified new communities of believers in Jesus, enabling them to enjoy the messianic salvation and minister its benefits, both inside and outside their fellowship (cf. 2:41–47; 4:31–37; 8:14–17; 10:44–48; 11:14–18; 15:8; 19:1–7).'[4] In the light of Acts 1:8, the initial outpourings of the Holy Spirit are traced from Jerusalem (2:1–4) to Samaria (8:14–17) to the house of a Gentile in Joppa (10:44–48).

2. Nailed to the cross (2:22–23)

Peter continues his speech by reminding the crowd of how Jesus performed *miracles, wonders and signs*. Importantly, Peter contends that these supernatural events are evidence that Jesus was someone *accredited by God*. Peter possibly draws parallels here between Jesus and Moses. When Moses was called by God to lead the Israelites out of Egypt, God enabled him to perform signs in order to gain the trust of the people (see Exod. 4:1–9, 29–31). Similar and additional signs and wonders were later performed before Pharaoh to confirm Moses' special status as God's representative (see Exod. 7:1–5). Like Moses, Jesus performs signs and wonders that point to his divine commissioning. While all of the Gospels record various miracles undertaken by Jesus, John's Gospel in particular highlights a series of signs that are intended to evoke faith in Jesus as the Messiah (see John 20:30–31).

Peter proceeds to state that, as God had planned, Jesus was put to death on a cross. His words emphasize two important ideas. First, Christ's death on the cross was not a tragic accident of history. It was something intended by God. It was part of *God's deliberate plan and foreknowledge*. While Peter does not unpack the details of this claim, we have observed in earlier chapters how the story of the Old Testament foresees a future king who will suffer and die at the hands of his enemies in order that he might be an atoning sacrifice for the sins of others. With this in view, God is intimately linked to all that Christ does. As David Peterson observes, 'God is shown to be the hidden actor behind Jesus' mighty works (v. 22), his death (v. 23), his resurrection (vv. 24, 32), his exaltation and giving of the Spirit (vv. 33–34), and his enthronement as Lord and Christ (v. 36).'[5]

---

4 Ibid., p. 142.
5 Ibid., p. 139.

Second, Peter implicates his hearers in the death of Jesus Christ. They, *with the help of wicked men, put him to death by nailing him to the cross.* Peter is not claiming that his hearers physically nailed Jesus to the cross themselves. This was done by Roman soldiers. Nevertheless, his hearers bear some responsibility for Jesus' execution. This is a serious indictment, given Peter's prior comment that Jesus is *a man accredited by God.* In the light of this charge, it is no surprise that those listening *were cut to the heart* (37).

Peter's emphasis upon God's plan and the people's responsibility for the execution of Jesus involves an interesting interplay between divine and human actions. According to John Polhill,

> This double dimension of divine purpose and human responsibility runs throughout Luke–Acts. On the one hand, Jesus' death follows the divine purpose: Luke 9:22; 17:25; 22:37; 24:26; 24:44, 46; Acts 17:3. On the other, guilt of the people is strongly emphasized in the passion narrative: Luke 23:2, 4–5, 20–23, 25, 51.[6]

Since Christ willingly goes to the cross to atone for the sins of every human, we all, without exception, bear responsibility for his execution. We may not have been present when Jesus was nailed to the cross, but his willingness to suffer and die was motivated by a desire to atone for our wrongdoing. The nineteenth-century hymn writer Philip Bliss captures well the substitutionary nature of Christ's atoning death when he writes,

> Bearing shame and scoffing rude,
> In my place condemned he stood;
> Sealed my pardon with his blood:
> Hallelujah, what a Saviour!

3. Raised to life (2:24–32)

After focusing on Jesus' execution and death, Peter then proceeds to speak of Jesus' resurrection: *But God raised him from the dead.* To emphasize the significance of this event, Peter quotes Psalm 16:8–11. In doing this, he presupposes that David, the psalm's author, is not speaking of his own

---

[6] J. B. Polhill, *Acts*, NAC 26 (Nashville: Broadman, 1992), p. 112.

experience. Peter reminds his listeners that *the patriarch David died and was buried, and his tomb is here to this day.* This being the case, David cannot be referring in Psalm 16 to his own deliverance from death. Additionally, Peter describes David as a *prophet.* As such, David has insight into what will happen in the future. Peter states, *Seeing what was to come, he* [David] *spoke of the resurrection of the Messiah, that he was not abandoned to the realm of the dead, nor did his body see decay.* After highlighting how David in Psalm 16 foresees *the resurrection of the Messiah,* Peter asserts that *God has raised this Jesus to life.* He then supports this claim by stating that *we are all witnesses of it.*

The importance of Jesus' resurrection cannot be overstated. It is a vital stage in the process that leads to his enthronement at the right hand of God in heaven. In marked contrast to Adam and Eve, who forfeited their vicegerent status by heeding the serpent, Jesus remains obedient to God, even to the point of dying on a cross. Yet death has no hold over him. Consequently, he ascends into the heavenly presence of God to be seated at his right hand.[7]

4. Exalted to the right hand of God (2:33–36)

Resurrection, however, is not an end in itself. As Peter proceeds to explain, the resurrection of Jesus is followed by his ascension to heaven. According to Peter, Jesus has been *exalted to the right hand of God.* Once again Peter contrasts Jesus' experience with that of King David, by quoting the opening words of another psalm associated with David, Psalm 110:

> *The Lord said to my Lord:*
> *'Sit at my right hand*
> *until I make your enemies*
> *a footstool for your feet.'*

According to Peter, King David, who did not ascend to heaven, speaks here of someone greater, who has ascended to the right hand of God. God's declaration *Sit at my right hand until I make your enemies a footstool for your feet* implies that this individual will rule as God's vicegerent. Peter views

---

[7] We shall explore further the importance of Jesus' resurrection in our next chapter.

Jesus as the one whom God honours by seating him at his right hand. Due to his resurrection and ascension Jesus is David's Lord.

Peter's use of Psalm 110 may well have been influenced by Jesus' own use of this psalm. According to Matthew 22:41–45,[8] after being questioned by his opponents on various issues in an attempt to undermine his authority as a teacher, Jesus poses a counter-question to some Pharisees: 'What do you think about the Messiah? Whose son is he?' (42). As Jesus expects, they reply by saying, 'The son of David' (42). Seizing the opportunity, Jesus questions them regarding their interpretation of the opening words of Psalm 110. He says to them:

How is it then that David, speaking by the Spirit, calls him 'Lord'?
For he says,

> 'The Lord said to my Lord:
> "Sit at my right hand
> until I put your enemies
> under your feet."'

If then David calls him 'Lord', how can he be his son?[9]
Jesus' response is not designed to contradict the answer of the Pharisees. The Messiah will be 'the son of David'. However, Jesus' probing question signals that the Pharisees' perception of the Messiah is mistaken. Their understanding of the 'son of David' is deficient.

By focusing on Psalm 110, Jesus indicates that King David's son, the promised Messiah, will have far greater authority than David himself. He is one greater than David. The Pharisees anticipate that the Messiah will create a kingdom like that of David, but Jesus indicates, based on Psalm 110, that the Messiah's kingdom will far exceed that of King David. The enthronement of David's son will not take place on earth but in heaven at the right hand of God. For this reason, King David refers to him as 'my Lord'.

Drawing on Psalm 110, Peter emphasizes that Jesus' resurrection and exaltation to heaven confirm his status as *Lord and Messiah*. In the light of the importance that Peter gives to Jesus' resurrection and ascension,

---

[8] Parallel accounts are found in Mark 12:35–37 and Luke 20:41–44.
[9] Matt. 22:43–45.

we should observe that the title *christos* (Anointed/Christ/Messiah) was rarely given to Jesus during his earthly life. Only after his death and resurrection do his followers commonly attribute this title to him. Thus, for example, *christos* comes only seven times in Mark's account of Jesus' life, but sixty-five times in the apostle Paul's letter to the believers in Rome.[10] As Peter's speech makes clear, it is only after the resurrection and ascension of Jesus that he is enthroned by God as vicegerent in heaven.

The post-resurrection timing of Jesus' enthronement explains why the title *christos* (Anointed/Christ/Messiah) is rarely used of Jesus during his earthly life. Nevertheless, all four Gospels confidently declare that Jesus is the Anointed/Christ/Messiah. As Michael Bird remarks, 'For all the diversity within the Gospels about Jesus, each of the other three evangelists, in his own way, shares Mark's contention that the Jesus-story is a messianic narrative.'[11] In the Synoptic Gospels, Matthew, Mark and Luke each highlight Simon Peter's confession 'You are the Messiah, the Son of the living God.'[12] Although the apostle John does not record Peter's confession, he incorporates a noteworthy parallel. When Jesus speaks to Martha after the death of her brother Lazarus, she responds by saying, 'Yes, Lord . . . I believe that you are the Messiah, the Son of God, who is to come into the world.'[13] Her declaration exemplifies John's purpose in writing the Gospel:

> Jesus performed many other signs in the presence of his disciples, which are not recorded in this book. But these are written that you may believe that Jesus is the Messiah, the Son of God, and that by believing you may have life in his name.[14]

For John, the raising of Lazarus to life encapsulates how Jesus, as Messiah, has come to give eternal life to those who believe in him.

As reflected in Peter's speech, it becomes evident that the earliest followers of Jesus viewed his resurrection and ascension as essential steps

---

[10] Mark 1:1; 8:29; 9:41; 12:35; 13:21; 14:61; 15:32; Rom. 1:1, 4, 6–8; 2:16; 3:22, 24; 5:1, 6, 8, 11, 15, 17, 21; 6:3–4, 8–9, 11, 23; 7:4, 25; 8:1–2, 9–11, 17, 34–35, 39; 9:1, 3, 5; 10:4, 6–7, 17; 12:5; 13:14; 14:9, 15, 18; 15:3, 5–8, 16–20, 29–30; 16:3, 5, 7, 9–10, 16, 18, 25, 27. A similar pattern is repeated when the other canonical Gospels are compared with the New Testament Epistles.

[11] M. F. Bird, *Jesus Is the Christ: The Messianic Testimony of the Gospels* (Milton Keynes: Paternoster, 2012), p. 1.

[12] Matt. 16:16; Mark 8:29. Luke 9:20 has the briefer statement, 'God's Messiah.'

[13] John 11:27.

[14] John 20:30–31.

towards his enthronement as God's vicegerent. While the concepts of Lord and Messiah are occasionally associated with Jesus prior to his ascent to the heavenly sanctuary, they become a reality when God exalts Jesus to his right hand. Enthroned by God as *Lord and Messiah*, Jesus offers forgiveness of sins and the gift of the Holy Spirit to those who repent and are baptized in his name.

We see something of the significance of Jesus' enthronement in the apostle Paul's letter to the church at Philippi. Encouraging the believers in Philippi to have the mind of Christ, Paul highlights Jesus' ascension following on from his death on the cross. He writes,

> In your relationships with one another, have the same mindset as Christ Jesus:
>
> who, being in very nature God,
>> did not consider equality with God something to be used to his
>>> own advantage;
> rather, he made himself nothing
>> by taking the very nature of a servant,
>> being made in human likeness.
> And being found in appearance as a man,
>> he humbled himself
>> by becoming obedient to death –
>>> even death on a cross!
> Therefore God exalted him to the highest place
>> and gave him the name that is above every name,
> that at the name of Jesus every knee should bow,
>> in heaven and on earth and under the earth,
> and every tongue acknowledge that Jesus Christ is Lord,
>> to the glory of God the Father.[15]

As Paul observes, only after his death and resurrection is Jesus robed in royal glory and given authority over all creation.

Peter's affirmation that the resurrected Jesus has ascended to rule at the right hand of God is accompanied by another significant event: the outpouring of the Holy Spirit on Jesus' followers in Jerusalem. As Peter

---

15 Phil. 2:5–11.

states, *Exalted to the right hand of God, he* [Jesus] *has received from the Father the promised Holy Spirit and has poured out what you now see and hear* (33). With these comments, Peter returns to the topic with which his speech started. The outpouring of the Holy Spirit enables Jesus' disciples to speak in different languages. Peter now explains that this remarkable phenomenon is a direct consequence of Jesus' being enthroned in heaven at the right hand of God. Having *received from the Father the promised Holy Spirit*, Jesus is now able to gift the Holy Spirit to others. In this way, as Max Turner comments, 'the people of Jesus continue to experience his ongoing messianic/transformative reign (and hence the Holy Spirit is now called "the Spirit of Jesus"; cf. Acts 16:7)'.[16] Empowered by the Spirit of Jesus, his followers are equipped to continue Jesus' earthly ministry.[17]

The apostle Peter makes a very direct connection between Christ's ascension and the outpouring of the Holy Spirit. A similar link is made by Paul in his letter to the church at Ephesus. In Ephesians 4:7–13 he writes,

> But to each one of us grace has been given as Christ apportioned it. This is why it says:
>
> 'When he ascended on high,
>   he took many captives
>   and gave gifts to his people.'
>
> . . . So Christ himself gave the apostles, the prophets, the evangelists, the pastors and teachers, to equip his people for works of service, so that the body of Christ may be built up until we all reach unity in the faith and in the knowledge of the Son of God and become mature, attaining to the whole measure of the fullness of Christ.

While Ephesians 4 has a short list of gifts associated with particular roles within the church, Romans 12 and 1 Corinthians 12 (and also to a lesser extent 1 Pet. 4:8–11) broaden considerably the range of gifts that may be used in the task of building up the church. Underlying Paul's view of the

---

16 M. Turner, 'Holy Spirit', in T. D. Alexander and B. S. Rosner (eds.), *New Dictionary of Biblical Theology* (Leicester: Inter-Varsity Press, 2000), p. 554.

17 Peterson, *Acts of the Apostles*, p. 153 n. 80, writes, 'The power that Jesus exercised during his earthly ministry for the benefit of a limited number of people is now to be offered to all. Only the exalted Lord is able to extend the blessing of his ministry to all Israel and the world. So the Spirit that rested on him is poured out on others for this work.'

church is the idea that all Christians receive grace-gifts[18] which they are to use for the benefit of others.

5. Repent and be baptized (2:37–41)

Peter's speech evokes a strong reaction from the listening crowd. *Cut to the heart*, they ask Peter and the other apostles for guidance: *Brothers, what shall we do?* Luke records the essence of Peter's response: *Repent and be baptised, every one of you, in the name of Jesus Christ for the forgiveness of your sins. And you will receive the gift of the Holy Spirit.*

Peter's emphasis on repentance recalls the preaching of John the Baptist, which Luke summarizes as a 'baptism of repentance for the forgiveness of sins'.[19] In similar fashion, Jesus also challenged people to repent (Matt. 4:17; Mark 1:15; Luke 13:3, 5). John the Baptist and Jesus both stress the importance of repentance. In John's case, repentance is closely tied to baptism with water. As Matthew 3:5–6 records, 'People went out to him [John the Baptist] from Jerusalem and all Judea and the whole region of the Jordan. Confessing their sins, they were baptised by him in the Jordan River.' As regards Jesus, however, John the Baptist anticipates that he will baptize not with water, but with the Holy Spirit: 'I baptise you with water for repentance. But after me comes one who is more powerful than I, whose sandals I am not worthy to carry. He will baptise you with the Holy Spirit and fire.'[20] In the light of this expectation, Peter's instructions to the people on the day of Pentecost are noteworthy. Repentance and baptism in the name of Jesus Christ are linked to both forgiveness of sin and the gift of the Holy Spirit.

Luke subsequently records that those who accepted Peter's message *were baptised, and about three thousand were added to their number that day* (41). This marks the beginning of a process that sees an astonishing expansion in the numbers of those who are followers of Jesus. Importantly, two further 'Pentecost-type' events occur that are highly significant. The first of these takes place in Samaria (Acts 8:14–17) and the second in the house of Cornelius, a centurion in the Italian Regiment (10:1). In the latter case, Luke writes in Acts 10:45–46: 'The circumcised believers who

---

[18] Paul deliberately uses the term *charismata* to denote these gifts because of its association with the word *charis* 'grace'. These gifts are not earned but are given by Christ.

[19] Luke 3:3; cf. Matt. 3:2; Mark 1:4–5.

[20] Matt. 3:11; cf. Luke 3:16.

had come with Peter were astonished that the gift of the Holy Spirit had been poured out even on Gentiles. For they heard them speaking in tongues and praising God.' This outpouring of the Holy Spirit resembles what had occurred in Jerusalem on the day of Pentecost. Importantly, on this occasion the recipients are Gentiles, not Jews. These developments involving Samaritans and Gentiles recall how the resurrected Jesus had told the disciples that they were to be his witnesses 'in Jerusalem, and in all Judea and Samaria, and to the ends of the earth'.[21]

6. Conclusion

The events that take place on the day of Pentecost are highly significant. Jesus' ascension to heaven and his enthronement at the right hand of God results in the outpouring of the Holy Spirit as the prophet Joel had predicted. This marks a new phase in the establishment of God's kingdom on the earth.

In the two New Testament books authored by Luke, Jesus' ascension enjoys prominence. It is the goal towards which Luke's account of Jesus moves. Of the four Gospel writers, only Luke records the ascension (Luke 24:51). He even refers to Jesus being taken up to heaven in 9:51, anticipating what is still to come. Complementing his Gospel, Luke presents in the book of Acts the ascension of Jesus as the event that sets in motion everything else that is recorded. Jesus' ascension is the event that hinges Luke's two books together.

Importantly, for Luke, Jesus' earthly ministry and his ascension to heaven are bound together by the activity of the Holy Spirit. Jesus himself is empowered by the Spirit (e.g. Luke 3:22; 4:1, 14, 18) and the outpouring of the Spirit transforms his followers. As Acts reveals, the gift of the Spirit, involving 'conversion-initiation', 'is fundamental to Christian life'.[22] The Holy Spirit comes upon those who repent and receive forgiveness through Jesus Christ.

Since the coming of the Holy Spirit is intimately bound to Christ's enthronement as God's vicegerent in heaven, it naturally follows that God's kingdom on earth is associated with the outpouring of the Holy Spirit. According to Sigurd Grindheim, 'The kingdom, or the kingly rule,

---

[21] Acts 1:8.
[22] Turner, 'Holy Spirit', p. 554.

of God becomes a reality through the work of the Holy Spirit. The Holy Spirit is at work in the disciples of Jesus, and in this way God's kingly rule is restored.'[23] In the light of this, it is worth observing that the kingdom of God is a recurring motif throughout the book of Acts. As Max Turner observes,

> Luke regularly (and redactionally) summarizes the content of Christian preaching in Acts in terms of 'the kingdom of God' (8.12; 14.22; 19.8; 20.25; 28.23), and his very last words (forming an *inclusio* with his opening ones) are that Paul welcomed all, 'proclaiming the kingdom of God and teaching the things about the Lord Jesus Christ . . .' (28.31).[24]

Dismissing contemporary expectations of a Messiah who will rule on earth, Peter announces on the day of Pentecost that the resurrected and ascended Jesus is enthroned at the right hand of God as the perfect vicegerent (Acts 2:34–36). As the divinely appointed king, Jesus will eventually bring the whole earth under his authority when all his enemies are subdued. In a subsequent speech Peter indicates that this will usher in a new age of universal peace and prosperity in fulfilment of Old Testament expectations: 'Heaven must receive him until the time comes for God to restore everything, as he promised long ago through his holy prophets.'[25] We shall turn to consider the fulfilment of these expectations in chapter 20.

---

[23] S. Grindheim, *Living in the Kingdom of God: A Biblical Theology for the Life of the Church* (Grand Rapids: Baker Academic, 2018), p. 154.

[24] M. Turner, *Power from on High: The Spirit in Israel's Restoration and Witness in Luke–Acts*, Journal of Pentecostal Theology Supplement Series 9 (Sheffield: Sheffield Academic, 1996), p. 296. Given its mention in both the introduction (Acts 1:3) and conclusion (Acts 28:31), it seems reasonable to assume that the entire book of Acts has a special interest in the kingdom of God.

[25] Acts 3:21.

1 Corinthians 15:1–58

19. The return of the king

In the rush and bustle of everyday life it is easy to lose sight of what really matters. Often our priorities get turned on their heads. Less important matters take over and the truly important issues of life get sidelined and ignored. We easily get distracted as something of lesser significance grabs our attention. At times we need to reorientate ourselves to what should take priority in our lives.

In our contemporary world where the Christian faith takes many forms, with different denominations and traditions, different cultural contexts and different theological emphases, it is very important to retain a clear sense of what really matters. What is at the heart of the gospel? What is, in Paul's words, *of first importance* (1 Cor. 15:3)? This is what Paul sets out to clarify in 1 Corinthians 15.

1. Good news: Christ has been raised to life (15:1–11)

In writing to the followers of Jesus in the city of Corinth, the apostle Paul wants to remind them of what matters most. Amid all the demands that are placed upon them and all of life's distractions, what is essential and fundamental to their faith? What is the gospel, the good news, that they have received and believed? What did Paul preach? What saves them? What must they centre their lives on as followers of Jesus?

For Paul, the essentials of the gospel are found in two related events: the death and resurrection of the Messiah, Jesus of Nazareth. He writes, *For what I received I passed on to you as of first importance: that Christ died for our sins according to the Scriptures, that he was buried, that he was raised on the third day according to the Scriptures* (3–4). Both events are highly significant, for each achieves something that is vitally necessary for the establishment of God's eternal kingdom on earth. And as Paul notes, both events fulfil expectations that are set out in the Scriptures.[1]

For reasons that become clearer as Paul writes, his remarks in verses 5–8 focus on the resurrection of Jesus. As subsequent sentences reveal, some at Corinth have expressed strong reservations about the possibility of anyone being raised to life again. For these doubters, *there is no resurrection of the dead* (12). Countering such sceptical thinking, Paul offers a brief list of those who saw the risen Jesus:

> *he appeared to Cephas, and then to the Twelve. After that, he appeared to more than five hundred of the brothers and sisters at the same time, most of whom are still living, though some have fallen asleep. Then he appeared to James, then to all the apostles, and last of all he appeared to me also, as to one abnormally born.*

Paul includes himself as a witness to Jesus' resurrection but views his experience as somewhat *abnormal* because it occurred later (see Acts 9:4–6). In all, Paul claims that more than five hundred people saw the resurrected Jesus.

2. The importance of Christ's resurrection (15:12–19)

Paul drives home the importance of Jesus Christ's resurrection through a series of logical arguments. If the sceptics are correct in claiming that there is no resurrection, then Christ cannot have been raised to life. If Christ experienced no resurrection, then Paul has been misleading people in his preaching. And if Paul has been spreading fake news, there is no basis for believing that Jesus Christ's death saves people from their sin. Furthermore, if Jesus has not been raised to life, there is no reason to suppose that those who have already died will be raised to experience eternal life in the consummated kingdom of God. As Paul fully recognizes, Jesus' resurrection is the linchpin that holds everything together. Deny Christ's resurrection and you destroy the apostolic gospel message with its hope of eternal life for all who believe that Jesus is the Messiah.

---

[1] Paul has in view here the Hebrew Bible, what will later be called the Old Testament.

3. In Christ all will be made alive (15:20–34)

Paul has no doubts about the reality of Jesus' being raised to life. Importantly, Jesus' resurrection prepares the way for the resurrection of others. He is *the firstfruits of those who have fallen asleep*. Paul will expand upon the concept of firstfruits, but before he does this he makes an important contrast between Jesus Christ and Adam. Alluding to the events of Genesis 3, Paul recalls how Adam's disobedience brought death to humanity, an outcome underlined by Adam's expulsion from the garden of Eden and his lack of access to the tree of life. However, if Adam brings death, according to Paul Jesus brings life. This comes through *the resurrection of the dead*.

Developing this idea, Paul emphasizes that for the present only Jesus has been resurrected. Like the firstfruits of a crop, his resurrection anticipates a greater crop to follow. The resurrection harvest of those who belong to Christ will occur only when he comes back to earth. With this reference to Jesus' coming (Greek *parousia*), Paul has in mind a particular event.

In what scholars believe to be one of his earliest letters, Paul offers a fuller description of Jesus' coming. Writing to the followers of Jesus in Thessalonica, Paul states,

> Brothers and sisters, we do not want you to be uninformed about those who sleep in death, so that you do not grieve like the rest of mankind, who have no hope. For we believe that Jesus died and rose again, and so we believe that God will bring with Jesus those who have fallen asleep in him. According to the Lord's word, we tell you that we who are still alive, who are left until the coming of the Lord, will certainly not precede those who have fallen asleep. For the Lord himself will come down from heaven, with a loud command, with the voice of the archangel and with the trumpet call of God, and the dead in Christ will rise first. After that, we who are still alive and are left will be caught up together with them in the clouds to meet the Lord in the air. And so we will be with the Lord for ever.[2]

As in 1 Corinthians 15:23, Paul associates Jesus' coming with the resurrection of those who have fallen asleep, an appropriate euphemism for those who are dead but will be resurrected. Paul's description of Christ's

---

[2] 1 Thess. 4:13–17.

coming is portrayed using language that conveys the image of an imperial visit. His mention of the archangel's voice and the sounding of God's trumpet recalls how the visit of a special dignitary is announced. Paul, however, highlights another action that occurs during such visits. He notes how those who are alive and those who are raised to life will 'meet the Lord in the air'. According to Gene Green, '*To meet* (*eis apantēsin*) was almost a technical term that described the custom of sending a delegation outside the city to receive a dignitary who was on the way to town.'[3] Luke describes such an event in Acts 28:15:

> The brothers and sisters there had heard that we were coming, and they travelled as far as the Forum of Appius and the Three Taverns to meet us. At the sight of these people Paul thanked God and was encouraged.

After going out to meet and welcome their special visitor, they escort him into the city.

In 1 Thessalonians 4, Paul describes how those who have fallen asleep will rise to greet the coming king. They will be raised to life to join those who are still alive when Christ returns. Paul stresses that believers who have already died will be among the first to welcome the returning Christ. They will greet Jesus as he descends through the clouds, with his return resembling his departure (see Acts 1:9–11). Paul does not envisage the permanent departure from the earth of those who go up to welcome Jesus. Rather, they will accompany Jesus on the final stage of his downward journey to the earth.

In contrast to the fuller picture that Paul offers in 1 Thessalonians 4, his remarks in 1 Corinthians 15 are brief. Nevertheless, he links the resurrection of the dead with Christ's coming. However, this resurrection lies in the future; it is something that Paul anticipates based on Christ's own resurrection being the firstfruits.

Filling out the picture of what will occur, Paul links Christ's second coming with *the end*. When Paul speaks here of *the end*, he is not thinking of the end of the world or of time. He has in view the end of everything evil, including death itself, and the beginning of the fully consummated kingdom of God. At this point in time, Jesus will hand *over the kingdom to*

---

[3] G. L. Green, *The Letters to the Thessalonians*, The Pillar New Testament Commentary (Grand Rapids: Eerdmans, 2002), p. 226.

God the Father after he has destroyed all dominion, authority and power. For he must reign until he has put all his enemies under his feet. The last enemy to be destroyed is death (24–26).

In Paul's construction of what will happen, Christ as king will overthrow all opposition, destroying *all dominion, authority and power*. According to Leon Morris, the verb 'to destroy' (Greek *katargeō*)

> basically means 'render null and void', 'make inoperative', and this is much in point here. Paul does not speak of battles, or of rulers being dethroned. But he does speak of all rule, other than that of Christ, as being rendered completely inoperative.[4]

After defeating all his enemies, Christ will establish his rule over all the earth as God's vicegerent. He will then hand *over the kingdom to God the Father*.

Paul's remarks recall the expectations recorded in Psalm 110, which speak of David's Lord being seated at the right hand of the Majesty in heaven until all his enemies are placed under his feet. As we have noted in the preceding chapter, Jesus Christ's ascension results in his enthronement in heaven. Seated there as the perfect human vicegerent, he oversees the growth of God's kingdom on earth, waiting for the day when he will return to bring an end to every power that stands in opposition to God.

Until Christ's return to earth, his followers are engaged in a conflict against the powers of evil that oppose the expansion of God's kingdom in the world. Paul writes of this hostility in his letter to the Ephesians, when he advises the followers of Jesus to equip themselves for a spiritual battle:

> Put on the full armour of God, so that you can take your stand against the devil's schemes. For our struggle is not against flesh and blood, but against the rulers, against the authorities, against the powers of this dark world and against the spiritual forces of evil in the heavenly realms. Therefore put on the full armour of God, so that when the day of evil comes, you may be able to stand your ground, and after you have done everything, to stand. Stand firm then, with the belt of truth buckled round your waist, with the breastplate of righteousness in place, and with your feet fitted with the readiness that comes from the gospel of

---

4 L. Morris, *1 Corinthians: An Introduction and Commentary* (Leicester: Inter-Varsity Press, 1985), p. 207.

peace. In addition to all this, take up the shield of faith, with which you can extinguish all the flaming arrows of the evil one. Take the helmet of salvation and the sword of the Spirit, which is the word of God.[5]

From Paul's perspective, Jesus' resurrection marks the start of a process that will come to completion only when Jesus returns to the earth. Paul looks forward to Christ's second coming, but for the present Christ's reign as a perfect vicegerent already has an impact on the lives of those who believe in him. They have received the Holy Spirit who equips and empowers them to be kingdom builders. Yet they continue to live in a world where sin and death are constant realities and they themselves experience the challenge of a human nature that draws them away from living truly spiritual lives. Salvation is both an 'already' and a 'not yet' experience. All this will change when Jesus Christ returns to bring to completion the establishment of God's kingdom on a new earth.

4. Raised imperishable to inherit the kingdom of God (15:35–49)

As Paul continues his letter, he addresses two more related questions: *How are the dead raised? With what kind of body will they come?* (35). In response, Paul states that the resurrected body will not be identical to the one that dies. Using the image of a seed, Paul notes that the plant which grows does not resemble the seed that is placed in the ground. Building on this, Paul observes that in the world there are many different types of bodies. Humans, animals, birds and fish have bodies that differ. With such a variety of bodies in existence, we should not be surprised that the resurrection body may differ from our present bodies.

Using the image of a seed becoming a plant, Paul lists some of the ways in which the resurrected body differs from the body that dies:

The body that is sown is perishable, it is raised imperishable; it is sown in dishonour, it is raised in glory; it is sown in weakness, it is raised in power; it is sown a natural body, it is raised a spiritual body. If there is a natural body, there is also a spiritual body.
(42–44)

---

5 Eph. 6:11–17.

Observing the repetition that comes in verse 44, Mark Taylor comments,

> The last pair, the natural body/spiritual body, is a summary description
> of the contrasting bodies; that is, the natural body is the human body of
> this creation, which is corruptible, dishonorable, and weak; and the
> spiritual body is the resurrected body of new creation, which is
> incorruptible, glorious, and powerful.[6]

Acknowledging that our present fragile bodies are prone to decay, Paul
states that the resurrected body will be imperishable. Unlike our present
human bodies, resurrected bodies will be designed to be immortal. As Paul
later states, *When the perishable has been clothed with the imperishable,
and the mortal with immortality, then the saying that is written will come
true: 'Death has been swallowed up in victory'* (54).[7] Death will have no
impact on the bodies of those who are raised to life.

Paul also contrasts the dishonour and weakness of our present bodies
with the glory and power of future resurrection bodies. He develops the
concept of future glorious bodies elsewhere in his writings. In his letter
to the church at Philippi, Paul remarks,

> But our citizenship is in heaven. And we eagerly await a Saviour from
> there, the Lord Jesus Christ, who, by the power that enables him to bring
> everything under his control, will transform our lowly bodies so that
> they will be like his glorious body.[8]

In Romans 8:18, Paul writes, 'I consider that our present sufferings are not
worth comparing with the glory that will be revealed in us.' Looking to
encourage his readers to persevere through trials, Paul contrasts 'present
sufferings' with 'future glory'. The next few verses explain what Paul has in
mind. In 8:19 he writes, 'For the creation waits in eager expectation for the
children of God to be revealed.' Looking to the future, Paul anticipates
a time when those who are God's children will become evident to the
whole of creation. Importantly, Paul associates this with the resurrection of
the dead.

---

[6] M. Taylor, *1 Corinthians*, NAC 28 (Nashville: B&H, 2014), p. 405.

[7] P. R. Williamson, *Death and the Afterlife: Biblical Perspectives on Ultimate Questions*, New Studies in Biblical Theology 44 (London: Apollos, 2017), p. 92, comments, 'Our present physical constitution is unsuited to our eternal inheritance.'

[8] Phil. 3:20–21.

We know that the whole creation has been groaning as in the pains of childbirth right up to the present time. Not only so, but we ourselves, who have the firstfruits of the Spirit, groan inwardly as we wait eagerly for our adoption to sonship, the redemption of our bodies.[9]

Paul uses the metaphor of pregnancy. The present world is like a pregnant woman. Eventually, creation will give birth to the children of God when the resurrection of the dead takes place. When this happens, God's children will be revealed in all their glory.

The apostle Paul recognizes that this world is not as God intended it to be. It is a world in bondage to decay and death, a world marked by frustration. Paul speaks of creation being liberated, set free. Paul has in view the renewing of the earth that will occur following the return of Jesus Christ. And he associates this with the glory that will be revealed in those who have been redeemed by Jesus Christ. This glory will be evident in those who are resurrected to eternal life; it will be a feature of their resurrected bodies.

As we have noted, Paul contrasts how the body that dies is *natural*, but the resurrected body is *spiritual* (44). It needs to be repeated that Paul is not distinguishing a physical body from a non-physical body. Paul speaks of a *spiritual body*, but this does not imply a non-corporeal body. According to Anthony Thiselton, Paul's 'spiritual body . . . implies a self which is recognizable and identifiable publicly, but animated and characterized by the Holy Spirit'.[10] He goes on to say, 'Paul is addressing the problem of moral transformation as the raised Christian enters God's immediate presence, rather than a change into a non-material mode of existence.'[11] In similar fashion, Gordon Fee remarks, 'The transformed body . . . is not composed of "spirit"; it is a *body* adapted to the eschatological existence that is under the ultimate domination of the Spirit.'[12] This emphasis upon the Holy Spirit is noteworthy. As Mark Taylor notes,

---

[9] Rom. 8:22–23.

[10] A. C. Thiselton, *The Living Paul: An Introduction to the Apostle and His Thought* (London: SPCK, 2009), p. 72.

[11] Ibid., p. 72.

[12] G. D. Fee, *The First Epistle to the Corinthians*, The New International Commentary on the New Testament (Grand Rapids: W. B. Eerdmans, 1987), p. 786. A. F. Johnson, *1 Corinthians* (Downers Grove: IVP Academic, 2004), p. 305, writes, 'The proper distinction between the two types of embodiments is not material or physical versus immaterial or nonphysical but a body suited for the mere functioning of the *psychē*, the life principle, a body destined because of sin to die and to corrupt (Gen 3:19), in contrast to a body suited for the full functioning of the Holy Spirit, the imperishable resurrection body.'

'In principle, all believers are "spiritual" by virtue of their reception of the Holy Spirit (cf. 12:1–3, 13), but what becomes clear in the present argument (15:44–49) is that believers have not yet received a "spiritual" body.'[13]

Paul's use of the term *spiritual* does not mean that those raised to life will have no physical body. Resurrection bodies will take tangible form, designed for life on a renewed earth. Just as people on earth resemble Adam, bearing all the hallmarks of those who have been alienated from God, those who will be resurrected will resemble Jesus Christ, who has ascended into God's presence. Whereas Adam is associated with the earth, Jesus Christ is *the heavenly man*. Envisaging the transformation that comes through the resurrection, Paul states, *And just as we have borne the image of the earthly man, so shall we bear the image of the heavenly man* (49).

5. At the last trumpet (15:50–58)

In countering the claims of those who say that there is no resurrection, Paul describes how our human bodies will be radically transformed when those who belong to Christ are resurrected to eternal life. To reinforce the importance of this transformation, Paul writes, *I declare to you, brothers and sisters, that flesh and blood cannot inherit the kingdom of God, nor does the perishable inherit the imperishable* (50). Importantly, Paul is not stating here that the eternal *kingdom of God* will be inherited only by people with non-material bodies. His previous remarks exclude such an interpretation. Rather, Paul is making the point that 'the present human body is radically incompatible with God's imperishable kingdom'.[14]

Paul's reference to inheriting the kingdom of God (50) recalls Jesus' affirmation that the meek shall inherit the earth (Matt. 5:5). Set in the context of the Beatitudes,[15] Jesus' words foresee that God's kingdom will be fully established on earth. As we shall see in our next chapter, the earth itself will be renewed to become an appropriate inheritance for those whose bodies have become imperishable, glorious and powerful.

---

13 Taylor, *1 Corinthians*, p. 406.
14 Ibid., p. 411.
15 See chapter 15.

While Paul has focused primarily on the concept of resurrection, he also observes that not everyone will die before being transformed:

We will not all sleep, but we will all be changed – in a flash, in the twinkling of an eye, at the last trumpet. For the trumpet will sound, the dead will be raised imperishable, and we will be changed. For the perishable must clothe itself with the imperishable, and the mortal with immortality.

(51–53)

Paul adopts the metaphor of sleep to describe death. This is a common euphemism for death in the New Testament, conveying well the idea that death is not the end of existence. Paul has argued that those who are resurrected will have transformed bodies. He now states that the same will be true for those who are alive when Christ returns. Paul's brief reference to the sound of a *trumpet* recalls the fuller description that he gives in 1 Thessalonians 4:13–17. There, as here, Paul assumes that Christ's return will be greeted by those who are alive at his coming and by those who will be resurrected to life.

Paul's belief in Jesus' return reflects what the disciples were told when Jesus ascended to heaven. Acts 1:9–11 records how two men dressed in white spoke to the disciples: 'Men of Galilee . . . why do you stand here looking into the sky? This same Jesus, who has been taken from you into heaven, will come back in the same way you have seen him go into heaven.' Christ's coming, coinciding with the defeat of all his enemies, marks the beginning of the next stage in the establishment of God's kingdom on the earth. The kingdom of God is inaugurated with Christ's first coming, but its full consummation awaits his second coming.

6. Conclusion

As we trace the outworking of God's redemption of humanity and the earth, Jesus Christ's resurrection foreshadows the future resurrection of those who belong to him. Linked to Christ's return to earth, this resurrection of believers will coincide with the end of all opposition to Jesus' reign as God's vicegerent. The bodies of those who are raised to life will be imperishable, glorious and powerful, differing significantly from those that died. In keeping with this transformation, the whole earth will also undergo a transformation, resulting in the creation of new heavens and a new earth. With this, the kingdom of God reaches a glorious peak and becomes the inheritance of those who have been raised to life. This goal is evident when we consider John's vision of New Jerusalem in Revelation 21 – 22. We turn to this in our next chapter.

Revelation 21:1 – 22:5

20. An unshakeable kingdom

One of the great ironies of Christian history is that John Bunyan's twelve-year imprisonment for holding religious services outside the established Church of England resulted in the publication of *The Pilgrim's Progress*, or to give the book its full title, *The Pilgrim's Progress from This World, to That Which Is to Come*. With good reason Bunyan's masterpiece has been described as one of the most significant works of English literature. Published first in 1678, *The Pilgrim's Progress* is a remarkable allegory of the Christian life. In the form of a dream, the whole allegory is based around a journey which the book's main character, Christian, makes from his home town, the City of Destruction, to the Celestial City. At the end of his journey, Christian, helped by his companion Hopeful, struggles across the River of Death, hoping to be welcomed into the Celestial City, the heavenly Jerusalem, that stands atop Mount Zion.

The inspiration for Bunyan's Celestial City undoubtedly comes from the Bible. Bunyan was especially influenced by the final chapters of Revelation, to which we shall turn shortly. However, he also took ideas from the book of Hebrews. Unlike Revelation, which in large measure is composed of dream-like visions witnessed by the apostle John, Hebrews is a pastoral letter sent to Christians who were in danger of giving up and reverting to their prior, probably Jewish, beliefs. Towards the end of his letter the author of Hebrews writes the following: 'For here we do not have an enduring city, but we are looking for the city that is to come.'[1] The author of Hebrews orientates the hopes of his readers towards a future city. They

---

[1] Heb. 13:14.

are to see themselves as citizens of an integrated and harmonious community that has yet to become a reality.

The concept of a future city is first introduced in Hebrews 11 in connection with the patriarch Abraham. According to the author of Hebrews, Abraham's faith is evident in the fact that he looked forward to a 'city with foundations, whose architect and builder is God'.[2] Importantly, the author of Hebrews views this God-constructed city as a place that will be inhabited beyond this present life. He notes in 11:13 that the patriarchs Abraham, Isaac and Jacob 'were still living by faith when they died. They did not receive the things promised; they only saw them and welcomed them from a distance, admitting that they were foreigners and strangers on earth.' Referring to Abraham and those who have lived by faith, Hebrews 11 ends with these words: 'These were all commended for their faith, yet none of them received what had been promised, since God had planned something better for us so that only together with us would they be made perfect.'[3] According to Donald Hagner, in this context, to 'be made perfect' means 'arriving at the goal of God's saving purposes'.[4] The author of Hebrews expects that both he and his readers will join all those previously mentioned, including Abraham, to receive what was promised. When this happens, they will be made perfect. Since Abraham, Isaac and Jacob have already died, the author of Hebrews expects that they will be raised to life to dwell in the city created and governed by God.

When we picture this God-created city, it is difficult not to recall the vision that the apostle John describes in Revelation 21 – 22. At the start of Revelation 21 John speaks of seeing *the Holy City, the new Jerusalem, coming down out of heaven from God* (2). He then describes the city in some detail, drawing attention to its enormous size and splendour (9–21). This is no ordinary metropolis. For John, this exceptional city is the goal towards which everything in creation is moving.[5] Importantly for our understanding of the kingdom of God, at the heart of this resplendent city sits the throne of God and of the Lamb (22:1, 3; cf. 21:3, 5). The creation of New Jerusalem marks the fulfilment of God's plan to establish his kingdom on the earth.

---

[2] Heb. 11:10.

[3] Heb. 11:39–40.

[4] D. A. Hagner, *Hebrews*, New International Biblical Commentary (Peabody: Hendrickson, 1983), p. 210.

[5] Similar eschatological expectations regarding a new Jerusalem are found in the Old Testament. See D. E. Gowan, *Eschatology in the Old Testament* (Philadelphia: Fortress, 1986); T. D. Alexander, *The City of God and the Goal of Creation*, Short Studies in Biblical Theology (Wheaton: Crossway, 2018).

1. A new heaven and a new earth (21:1–4)

As John continues his description of the various visions that he has on the island of Patmos, he witnesses *a new heaven and a new earth* (1). These replace *the first heaven and the first earth*, which pass away. John also observes that *there was no longer any sea*. This latter remark reflects a general biblical understanding that the sea, often associated with evil, poses a threat to human existence. The absence of sea conveys a sense of safety and security.[6]

Coinciding with John's vision of *a new heaven and a new earth*, John sees *the Holy City, the new Jerusalem, coming down out of heaven from God, prepared as a bride beautifully dressed for her husband* (2). The city resembles a bride, a comparison that recalls how the city of Babylon is described as a garishly dressed harlot in Revelation 17:3–4. Unlike Babylon, the antithesis of the Holy City, New Jerusalem has one lover, with whom she will have an exclusive relationship as husband and wife. Her husband has already been introduced in Revelation 19, where John records,

> Then I heard what sounded like a great multitude, like the roar of rushing waters and like loud peals of thunder, shouting:
>
> 'Hallelujah!
>> For our Lord God Almighty reigns.
> Let us rejoice and be glad
>> and give him glory!
> For the wedding of the Lamb has come,
>> and his bride has made herself ready.
> Fine linen, bright and clean,
>> was given her to wear.'

(Fine linen stands for the righteous acts of God's holy people.)

Then the angel said to me, 'Write this: Blessed are those who are invited to the wedding supper of the Lamb!' And he added, 'These are the true words of God.'[7]

---

[6] We should recall that in Dan. 7 the sea is the location from which the four frightening beasts emerge. See also Rev. 13:1.

[7] Rev. 19:6–9.

As this passage intimates, Jesus Christ, the Lamb, will wed his bride, later to be revealed as *the new Jerusalem*. The use of marital imagery strongly implies the existence of an intimate relationship of mutual love between Jesus Christ and the citizens of the city.

As John watches the Holy City descend from heaven, he hears *a loud voice from the throne*, which announces,

> *Look! God's dwelling-place is now among the people, and he will dwell*
> *with them. They will be his people, and God himself will be with them*
> *and be their God. 'He will wipe every tear from their eyes. There will be*
> *no more death' or mourning or crying or pain, for the old order of things*
> *has passed away.*
>
> (3–4)

The picture of the Holy City descending from heaven is closely tied to the concept of God's coming to live with his people on earth. Through coming to dwell with humanity, God no longer resides in heaven. With this development heaven comes to earth, bringing to completion God's creation plan that his kingdom should be established on earth.[8] Since there no longer remain any barriers to God's glorious presence filling the whole earth, heaven and earth are merged. As Leon Morris remarks, 'After the new Jerusalem descends there appears to be no difference between heaven and earth.'[9]

John's visual and auditory experience is rich in allusions to the book of Isaiah, especially Isaiah 65:17–19. John's vision appears to be the fulfilment of what God had promised in the past when he said,

> See, I will create
>   new heavens and a new earth.
> The former things will not be remembered,
>   nor will they come to mind.
> But be glad and rejoice for ever
>   in what I will create,
> for I will create Jerusalem to be a delight
>   and its people a joy.

---

[8] See D. W. H. Thomas, *Heaven on Earth: What the Bible Teaches about Life to Come* (Fearn: Christian Focus, 2018).

[9] L. Morris, *Revelation: An Introduction and Commentary*, Tyndale New Testament Commentaries 20 (Leicester: Inter-Varsity Press; Downers Grove: InterVarsity Press, 1987), p. 233.

> I will rejoice over Jerusalem
> > and take delight in my people;
> the sound of weeping and of crying
> > will be heard in it no more.

The same elements and outcomes are present in both passages. The divine creation of new heavens and a new earth is closely bound to the creation of Jerusalem, a city where, due to the absence of death, weeping and crying will be no more. Elsewhere in Isaiah, in another passage that is echoed in Revelation 21, the prophet describes how God will destroy death for ever:

> On this mountain the LORD Almighty will prepare
> > a feast of rich food for all peoples,
> a banquet of aged wine –
> > the best of meats and the finest of wines.
> On this mountain he will destroy
> > the shroud that enfolds all peoples,
> the sheet that covers all nations;
> > he will swallow up death for ever.
> The Sovereign LORD will wipe away the tears
> > from all faces;
> he will remove his people's disgrace
> > from all the earth.
> > > The LORD has spoken.[10]

John's vision has every appearance of fulfilling Old Testament prophetic expectations that focus on the theme of God's residing with his people on the earth. This resembles the outcome hoped for by those whom God rescued from Egypt when they sang,

> You will bring them in and plant them
> > on the mountain of your inheritance –
> the place, LORD, you made for your dwelling,
> > the sanctuary, Lord, your hands established.
> 'The LORD reigns
> > for ever and ever.'[11]

---

[10] Isa. 25:6–8.
[11] Exod. 15:17–18.

Subsequently, at Mount Sinai, God instructed the Israelites to construct a portable sanctuary that would enable him to dwell in their midst: 'Let them make a sanctuary for me, and I will dwell among them.'[12] When David eventually captures Jerusalem, the city becomes God's earthly dwelling-place, resulting in the construction of the temple by Solomon. Yet, as we have observed, the waywardness of the people of Jerusalem causes God to abandon the city. As the book of Isaiah highlights, Jerusalem will be destroyed by the Babylonians. Yet, against this background, God promises the creation of a new Jerusalem, linked to the creation of new heavens and a new earth, where he will dwell with his people, drawn from all the nations of the world.[13]

2. The children of God (21:5–8)

A different voice addresses John in 21:5. On this occasion God speaks to him, reminding him that the one on the throne is *the Alpha and the Omega, the Beginning and the End*. This is only the second time in Revelation that God speaks directly to John. Remarkably, on the first occasion, God declared, 'I am the Alpha and the Omega . . . who is, and who was, and who is to come, the Almighty.'[14] The repetition of this description, which draws on the first and last letters of the Greek alphabet, emphasizes God's sovereignty over all of history. From beginning to end God is king. Implicit in this reference to Alpha and Omega is the idea that God will bring to completion all that he initiated at the first creation. The world that God set in motion in Genesis 1 comes to completion in Revelation 21 – 22. The meta-story that unfolds throughout the Bible moves coherently from beginning to end. As John's vision of the city reveals, New Jerusalem draws on the past by incorporating into its structure *the names of the twelve tribes of Israel* (12) and *the names of the twelve apostles of the Lamb* (14).

Highlighting the significance of God's reference to making all things new (5), Greg Beale writes, 'The destiny of God's people is to live with resurrected physical bodies in the newly transformed physical environment of the eternal new earth and heavens.'[15] Yet, although Revelation 21

---

[12] Exod. 25:8; cf. 29:45–46; Lev. 26:11–12.

[13] G. Goldsworthy, *Christ-Centred Biblical Theology: Hermeneutical Foundations and Principles* (Nottingham: Apollos, 2012) develops in more detail the way in which God's dealings with Israel up to the time of King Solomon provide a paradigm for understanding later prophetic expectations regarding the future.

[14] Rev. 1:8.

[15] G. K. Beale, *Revelation: A Shorter Commentary* (Grand Rapids: William B. Eerdmans, 2015), p. 475.

emphasizes the newness of what is being created, this does not rule out some degree of continuity with what has already taken place. Anthony Hoekema helpfully underlines this point when he suggests that in 'his redemptive activity, God does not destroy the works of his hands, but cleanses them from sin and perfects them, so that they may finally reach the goal for which he created them'.[16] With this premise in view, he goes on to say, 'This principle means that the new earth to which we look forward will not be totally different from the present one, but will be a renewal and glorification of the earth on which we now live.'[17]

This expectation is reinforced by the way in which New Jerusalem shares distinctive features with the garden of Eden, especially with reference to a river and the tree of life (Rev. 22:1–2; cf. Gen. 2:9–10).

In speaking about the citizens of the Holy City, God describes how he will be a source of life to *those who are victorious* (7). Others, described as *the cowardly, the unbelieving, the vile, the murderers, the sexually immoral, those who practise magic arts, the idolaters and all liars* (8), will experience a *second death*, in *the fiery lake of burning sulphur* (8). God's words are a serious reminder that only those who remain faithful to Christ will experience the joy of dwelling in the new Jerusalem. There is no place in the kingdom of God for anyone or anything associated with evil. Only those who have been redeemed and consecrated can reside with God in the Holy City.

3. The Holy City (21:9–27)

John's vision of the Holy City descending from heaven in 21:1–8 is complemented by a further description in 21:9 – 22:5. As Greg Beale comments, 'Rev. 21:9 – 22:5 recapitulates 21:1–8 and amplifies the picture there of God's consummate communion with His people and their consummate safety in the new creation.'[18] In 21:9 – 22:5, John is taken to a great, high mountain, possibly Mount Zion mentioned in 14:1, where the city itself is located after it descends from heaven. Its elevated location is in keeping with biblical imagery that associates God's presence with mountains (e.g. Ps. 48). In marked contrast, Babylon, the symbol of

---

[16] A. A. Hoekema, *The Bible and the Future* (Grand Rapids: Eerdmans, 1979), p. 73.

[17] Ibid., p. 73.

[18] Beale, *Revelation*, p. 476.

human opposition to God, is in a wilderness, signalling its unclean nature (Rev. 17:3–5).

John's detailed description of the city's construction is in keeping with other visions in Revelation that are in part symbolic in nature. Constructed of precious materials, the city radiates God's glory. As regards the enormous dimensions of the city, these signal that it far exceeds any metropolis constructed by humans. Twelve thousand stadia is equivalent to about 1,500 miles, roughly the distance from Paris to Istanbul. Nothing in the ancient world, or in the modern world, comes close to resembling the city that John witnesses.

As John surveys the resplendent city, he observes that there is no temple. By this he means a distinctive complex where God might live, set apart from the rest of the city's population. No such building is needed, because *the Lord God Almighty and the Lamb are its temple* (21:22).[19] Then, echoing statements from the book of Isaiah, John notes that God's presence gives light to the city (see Isa. 60:19–20) and *the nations will walk by its light, and the kings of the earth will bring their splendour into it* (24; see Isa. 60:3). The mention of nations and kings recalls how elsewhere in Revelation John speaks of people from every nation, tribe, people and language standing before the throne of God (7:9). New Jerusalem is a cosmopolitan city, filled with the glory and honour of the nations. Importantly, however, in keeping with its holy nature, only those whose names are recorded in *the Lamb's book of life* have access to God's presence.

4. The river of the water of life (22:1–5)

After highlighting the grandeur and splendour of the city's architecture, John turns to describe other features of significance. He observes *the river of the water of life* that flows from *the throne of God and of the Lamb*. Associated with this river, with its life-giving power, is *the tree of life*. John's description recalls what the Old Testament prophet Ezekiel records in his vision of a future city in which he sees a river flowing out of the temple towards the Dead Sea (Ezek. 47:1–12). As the river flows eastward, with trees lining its banks, the ever-increasing waters transform all that they touch. Wherever the river flows swarms of living creatures flourish. The

---

19 The image of the city as an enormous golden cube is reminiscent of how the holy of holies in Solomon's temple was also a golden cube.

life-giving nature of the river is such that the salty waters of the Dead Sea become fresh and abound in fish. As he concludes his description, Ezekiel writes,

> Fruit trees of all kinds will grow on both banks of the river. Their leaves will not wither, nor will their fruit fail. Every month they will bear fruit, because the water from the sanctuary flows to them. Their fruit will serve for food and their leaves for healing.[20]

The parallels with John's vision suggest that they are both describing the same situation. John states, *On each side of the river stood the tree of life, bearing twelve crops of fruit, yielding its fruit every month. And the leaves of the tree are for the healing of the nations* (2). By specifically referring to *the tree of life*, John associates his vision with the garden of Eden, which also had a river flowing from it (Gen. 2:8–14).

After describing the river that flows from the throne of God and of the Lamb, John focuses on the significance of the throne itself. Its presence in the city underlines that this city is God's kingdom in all its glory. To reinforce the idea that God reigns supreme and unchallenged, John states, *No longer will there be any curse* (3). The Greek term *katathema*, translated *curse*, means 'accursed thing', that is, something subject to destruction.[21] Nothing within the city stands in opposition to God or is incongruous with his reign.

The picture given here contrasts sharply with that recorded in Genesis 3. All that went wrong because of Adam and Eve's disobedience in the garden of Eden has now been reversed. The barriers to the creation of God's kingdom on earth have been removed, the earth itself has been renewed, and resurrected humans can now enjoy life in all its fullness in God's glorious presence. With the descent of the new Jerusalem from heaven, God's kingdom is established on the earth in all its splendour and glory. Whereas Adam and Eve failed to obey God as his specially commissioned vicegerents, in the new Jerusalem God's throne will be set up and *his servants will serve him* (3). The failures of the past have been addressed and a new beginning takes place.

Building on this, John notes that people will experience an intimacy with God that enables them to see his face. In the past, even Moses, the

---

[20] Ezek. 47:12.

[21] Morris, *Revelation*, p. 243.

great servant of the Lord, could not see God's face. Everything is now different as people serve God faithfully. Their right to be in God's presence is signalled by the fact that his servants have God's name on their foreheads, a possible allusion to the golden sign that the Aaronic high priest wore on his forehead, proclaiming that he was holy to the Lord (see Exod. 28:36–38).

As John concludes his description of the city, he draws attention once more to how God's presence is a source of light and, because his presence is permanent, there is no need for light from other sources. Finally, John states that *they will reign for ever and ever*. While this remark may be taken to suggest that all those who serve God in the city participate in reigning, it is more likely a reference to the reign of God and the Lamb. They will govern the city for ever, bringing permanence and stability for all those who are citizens of New Jerusalem.

5. Conclusion

The books of Hebrews and Revelation draw attention to a city that is to come, a Holy City, a new Jerusalem, a city that is very obviously different from every other city. The city displays the hallmarks of a utopia, a paradise. Here we see the consummated kingdom of God. As John notes, all evil and suffering is banished from this metropolis. As a holy city under the absolute control of a perfect deity, New Jerusalem provides an exceptional environment for its inhabitants to experience life to the full. While John, like the prophet Isaiah, links the city with new heavens and a new earth, it is not difficult to imagine that he has in view a renewed earth, rather than an entirely different type of earth.

John's vision of New Jerusalem majors on only some aspects of the city, but there is good reason to believe that the kingdom rewards listed by Jesus in the Beatitudes of Matthew 5:3–10 become a reality within this city. Those who mourn are comforted; the meek inherit the earth; those who hunger and thirst for righteousness are filled; the merciful are shown mercy; the pure in heart see God; the peacemakers are called children of God.

While we still await the coming of this utopian city, Paul views the resurrection of Jesus Christ as inaugurating a 'new age'. This is consistent with his belief that the followers of Jesus become citizens of the heavenly Jerusalem. In Galatians 4:21–31 Paul contrasts the 'present city of Jerusalem', which he associates with slavery to the law, with the 'Jerusalem that is above', which brings freedom. In Philippians 3:20 he remarks, 'Our citizenship is in heaven. And we eagerly await a Saviour from there, the Lord Jesus Christ.' While Jesus' followers have the privilege of being citizens of the heavenly Jerusalem and of possessing the kingdom of God, they must await the return of Jesus before this royal city is established on a renewed earth, bringing to fulfilment God's purpose in creating this world. The whole of history is moving towards a great, unending climax that marks the consummation of the kingdom that Jesus Christ came to establish.

Conclusion

Tracing the story of God's kingdom has taken us from the opening chapters of Genesis to the final chapters of Revelation. From our perspective, we still await the completion of the story, when God will reign from the Holy City, the new Jerusalem, on a renewed earth surrounded by an innumerable multitude of people from every nation, tribe, people and language. This is the goal towards which he has been redemptively working ever since Adam and Eve rejected their commission to rule over this world on God's behalf. In response, God announced to the seditious serpent in the garden of Eden that for deceiving the woman he would be defeated by one of her offspring. As the biblical story reveals, Jesus Christ is the promised vicegerent, whom God enthrones in the heavenly sanctuary, as he waits for all his enemies to be subdued. When Christ returns to earth, those who have died believing in him will be raised to life. Adopting the words of the prophet Isaiah in Isaiah 35:10:

> They will enter Zion with singing;
>   everlasting joy will crown their heads.
> Gladness and joy will overtake them,
>   and sorrow and sighing will flee away.

Although we await in faith the coming of God's kingdom in all its splendour, we have confidence to do so because of all that God has already done. Jesus Christ does not suddenly appear from nowhere to announce the arrival of the kingdom. God has prepared for this, promising the patriarch Abraham centuries earlier that all the nations of the earth would be blessed through one of his offspring (Gen. 22:18).

As we follow the outworking of this promise, we witness God's remarkable redemption of the Israelites from brutal slavery in Egypt and his subsequent invitation for the Israelites to become his treasured possession. With the establishment of a unique covenant relationship at Mount Sinai, God comes to dwell among the Israelites, offering them a foretaste of what life will be like when his kingdom is fully established on earth. While the Israelites are especially privileged to be God's people, having him dwell in their midst, all is not perfect. Due to their sinful nature the people struggle to remain loyal and obedient to their divine king. Their shortcomings eventually result in judgment and exile. Against this background, the Old Testament prophets anticipate a greater exodus and a new covenant that will centre on the reign of a future son of David, who will rule over the whole earth (Ps. 72).

With Christ's coming we witness the inbreaking of God's kingdom into a world dominated by a devil who controls all earthly kingdoms. Remarkably, Christ's defeat of the powers of evil comes through his sacrificial death on a cross where the power of love overcomes the power of violence. Raised to life again, Christ ascends into the heavenly sanctuary to present his self-offering to God the Father to atone for the sins of humanity.

Christ's death, resurrection and ascension are important developments in the process by which God's kingdom will become a reality on earth. He is the promised perfect vicegerent, who demonstrates his perfect obedience to the Father by suffering and dying on the cross. Importantly, through his ascension, the good news of the kingdom becomes a life-transforming message as his disciples are empowered through the Holy Spirit to live in this world as citizens of God's kingdom.

In several passages, the apostle Paul contrasts his present transient experience of life with the eternal life to come. To comfort and encourage Christ's followers in the city of Corinth, he writes,

> Therefore we do not lose heart. Though outwardly we are wasting away, yet inwardly we are being renewed day by day. For our light and momentary troubles are achieving for us an eternal glory that far outweighs them all. So we fix our eyes not on what is seen, but on what is unseen, since what is seen is temporary, but what is unseen is eternal.[1]

Paul contrasts the visible with the unseen. What we see today will pass away. What we do not see presently, will last for ever. Paul understands well how

---

[1] 2 Cor. 4:16–18.

a vibrant faith in the world to come can influence our lives in the present. We can better cope with the hardships of life here and now when we know that our present suffering will give way to future glory.

Focusing on the city to come also prevents us from being captivated by the ephemeral attractions of this present world. With good reason, Jesus warns his followers:

Do not store up for yourselves treasures on earth, where moths and vermin destroy, and where thieves break in and steal. But store up for yourselves treasures in heaven, where moths and vermin do not destroy, and where thieves do not break in and steal. For where your treasure is, there your heart will be also.[2]

The social pressure to be successful in this present world may easily prevent us from being true to our citizenship of the Holy City.

Christians are sometimes ridiculed for promoting a 'pie in the sky when you die' mentality, especially when we speak of a future, eternal city, a new Jerusalem. Yet such hope need not mean that we do not care about the present. The opposite is the case. Focusing on the world to come shapes how we live in the present. For those who submit to Jesus Christ as their king, eternal life begins here and now in this world. Jesus challenges us to pray and work for the spread of God's rule in the present, constantly looking forward in faith for the coming of God's kingdom in all its glory.[3]

- We are to embrace Jesus Christ as our sole Lord and Saviour, holding fast to his teaching.
- We are to live in the present as citizens of the world to come, influenced by its values and virtues.
- We are to exercise sincere humility, constantly recalling that we have been redeemed from evil solely by the grace of God and not by our own achievements or piety.
- We are to witness to an alternative worldview that promotes belief in a creator God, highlighting the inadequacy of a purely materialistic view of human existence.

---

[2] Matt. 6:19–21.

[3] The observations that follow are drawn on a paragraph that I wrote in T. D. Alexander, *The City of God and the Goal of Creation*, Short Studies in Biblical Theology (Wheaton: Crossway, 2018), p. 163.

- We are to be peacemakers, reconciling those who are alienated, especially from God.
- We are to invite others to become disciples of Jesus Christ, extending God's kingdom throughout the world through sacrificial love.
- We are to yearn after righteousness, caring for the oppressed and promoting social justice for the benefit of the marginalized.
- We are to resist the powers of evil, arming ourselves for the spiritual battle that continues to rage until Christ returns.
- We are to live holy lives, striving for personal moral integrity and purity.
- We are to love others wholeheartedly, including our enemies, as an expression and outworking of our sincere love for God.
- We are to fulfil our creative capacity as home and city builders, while ever recognizing the temporary nature of this present world.
- We are to consider ourselves exiles and pilgrims in 'Babylon', holding lightly to this life but living in this absurd and evil world in confident anticipation of all that God will yet do.

Jesus Christ calls us to be kingdom builders here and now. We do this with the confident assurance that Christ will return as universal judge to address every injustice, vindicating and punishing as appropriate. Finally, with the overthrow and removal of all that is evil, God will establish his eternal city on a renewed earth.

With certainty in the resurrection life promised by Jesus Christ, we should approach death, not with a sense of defeat in the face of the inescapable, but with an expectation of something supremely better to come. We may struggle with the many and varied frustrations of our present lives, but in the world to come we shall experience abundant, unending life on a renewed earth in the glorious presence of our Creator and Saviour. Then we shall no longer pray, 'Your kingdom come, your will be done on earth.' Rather, in the words of Revelation 5:13, we shall join with 'every creature in heaven and on earth and under the earth and on the sea, and all that is in them', to proclaim,

> To him who sits on the throne and to the Lamb
>   be praise and honour and glory and power,
> for ever and ever!

Study guide

Introduction

The theme of 'the kingdom of God' is one that seems familiar, yet it is easy for that familiarity to prevent us from seeing and savouring the full depth and richness of this topic.

The purpose of this study guide is to enable you as a group (or an individual) to study carefully the full breadth of biblical texts from both the Old and the New Testaments, to appreciate more greatly *The Message of the Kingdom of God*, by using Desi's book as an aid. Desi Alexander makes his own view on the passages clear. The aim is that his understanding will enrich the discussion of the Bible texts, rather than pushing the discussion into a debate over whether or not he has got it right!

The guidelines expect the leader to have read this book and that a few copies will be available for reference in the discussion time. The more discussion/small-group members who have read the book, the richer the discussion will probably be, and it is recommended that all members come prepared for the study, having read the relevant Bible passages.

The hope is that, after engaging with these studies, each member will have a much better appreciation of the kingdom of God, and all hearts will be turned to praise the king. Do pray that this work will take place in your group's hearts and minds.

PART 1: THE SCENE IS SET

Ⓠ Genesis 1:1 – 2:3
1. The creator king (pp. 9–20)

1 Have you considered before the particular claims of Genesis outlined here, over and against contemporary texts?

2 You're probably familiar with the phrase 'made in the image of God'. How does this kingly/vicegerent perspective on it chime with what you've heard before?

3 These early chapters of Genesis emphasize the creator and the creation. Do you think we make enough of the distinction between the two?

4 Desi writes that humanity will be God's 'kingdom builders'. Based solely on the text of Genesis 1:1 – 2:3, what activities do you think that implies for us today?

Ⓠ Genesis 3:1–24
2. The royal betrayal (pp. 21–32)

1 We zoom from Genesis 1, and a real distinction between creator and creation, into Genesis 3, and God intimately relating to creation. Which picture of God do you find easier to reconcile with your life?

2 Compare Adam and Eve's betrayal with Jesus' rejection of the devil's betrayal (Matt. 4:8–10, Luke 4:5–7). What can you learn for your walk with God?

3 The focus narrows from all creation, and thus all humanity, to a single family line. The God of all creation turns his attention to a seemingly small detail. How do you respond to God's holding such different scales of reality in view at the same time?

4 Read through this passage again, familiar though it may be. What jumps out at you, with the above questions in mind?

Ⓠ Genesis 17:1–27
3. A saviour king is promised (pp. 33–47)

1 Whether you've acknowledged it before or not, these texts make up a part of our family history. Christians are by faith the children of Abraham. Do you think about this historical reality and what it might mean for you today?

2 The language of 'blessing' is one that can easily mean different things to different people. What does this passage teach us about 'blessing', as an aspect of God's rule and reign?

3 This passage introduces us to God's covenant with Abraham –.a covenant that Jesus fulfils and we walk in. Have you engaged with this before? How could it affect your prayer life?

4 Look at Genesis 49:8–12. Aspects of this passage are fulfilled in David, others in the life of Jesus. What qualities of this king could you ask for and cultivate in your own life? How does this passage contribute to your understanding of God's kingdom?

PART 2: THE KINGDOM OF GOD IN THE OLD TESTAMENT

Ⓠ Exodus 15:1–21
4. The divine redeemer king (pp. 51–66)

1 This passage contains a song of celebration and of acknowledgment of God's kingship. Do you see our singing as being linked to the kingdom of God? Why/how?

2 Miriam's song balances both personal concerns, and wider, more cosmic themes. Do the worship songs at your church do this?

3 Consider the two New Testament examples of redemption (John 8:31–36 and Galatians 4:3–8). How do these two passages inform each other, and what do they add to our Old Testament picture of 'the divine redeemer king'?

4 Consider the closing words of chapter 4, and the priority of a harmonious relationship of God with God's people. What world situations could you intercede about today, where the powers of evil seem to hold sway?

Ⓠ Exodus 24:1–11
5. The divine king and his chosen people (pp. 67–78)

1 'All who are subjects of God's kingdom enter into a covenant relationship with their king' (p. 67). How has this language of covenant relationship affected your understanding of the kingdom of God?

2 Did you notice that the Ten Commandments are not formulated as laws – no punishments are given. How do they point towards the kind of behaviour that God desires?

3 Following the Ten Commandments, God gives further instruction with the intention of creating a compassionate society (Exod. 22:21 – 23:9). Can you see links between these and the Ten Commandments?

4 Have you ever considered God's commandments and covenant to be a gracious gift? How does thinking about them in that way change your view of them?

(Q) Leviticus 9:1 – 10:11
6. The holy king and his high priest (pp. 79–93)

1 God's glory is often referred to, but when did you last consider it? Exodus 40:34–35 invites us to ponder again what it means.

2 From atonement flow glory and blessing. There is a contrast between Aaron (the high priest) and Nadab and Abihu (his sons). How do their deaths underline the unique role of the high priest in presenting atoning offerings to God?

3 'Holiness and life go together' (p. 91). Do you see holiness as a life-giving thing, or something that stops you from living? Ask God's Spirit, who is Holy, to help you become holy, to enjoy life in all its abundance.

4 The Levitical high priest mirrors the ministry of Jesus. How does the activity of Jesus Christ as our high priest give us hope and certainty about our place in the kingdom of God?

(Q) Joshua 1:1–18
7. A royal inheritance (pp. 94–106)

1 How is Moses different from those whom our culture sees as 'great leaders' (p. 94)?

2 God's speech to Joshua (Josh. 1:2–6) is a powerful blend of promise and challenge. Do you see echoes of it in the Great Commission?

3 Joshua's success as a leader depends upon his diligence in obeying God (Josh. 1:7–8). How does obedience change when we see it as a response to God's 'instruction' rather than God's 'law' (p. 102)?

4 Joshua is a rare old Testament example of a leader who leads like Jesus. How important do you think rest (Josh. 1:12–15) was to this successful leadership? How important is rest in your own life?

5 Running behind the themes of inheritance, leadership and instruction is also the theme of land, earth and place. How does thinking about land, earth and place affect your reading of these passages and your pursuit of rest?

ⓠ Judges 2:6–23
8. Conflicting loyalties (pp. 107–118)

1 How does Judges 2:10 shed light on how faith can be transmitted across generations? What is essential to communicate, and how could you play your part in that in your church family?

2 The chiasm on p. 110, and the provocative fact behind Baal, show how easy it is for God's people to get distracted. Are we, his people today, easily distracted away from worship by similar things?

3 The cyclical pattern of sin–punishment–deliverance–sin seems depressing. We cannot lift ourselves from the spiral without God's empowering presence. Do you call on the name of the Lord to help you, or is it easier to continue as you are?

4 As the narrative of the kingdom of God turns to anticipate the king, reflect on the need to obey the promised king rather than doing your own thing.

PART 3: ANTICIPATING THE SAVIOUR KING

ⓠ 1 Samuel 2:1–10
9. The divine king who raises up and brings down (pp. 121–135)

1 How do we choose our leaders? Whether in churches, countries or other 'institutions', leaders are chosen in a variety of ways. What ways have you experienced?

2 In the midst of the epoch-marking changes that come with the coming of a king, 1 Samuel 1:1–20 focuses on a childless woman. What might this tell us about the king to come, and the kingdom of God?

3 Saul and David offer us two different models of leadership, and two different ways of approaching humility. How do their examples strike you as models of relying on God (pp. 125–127)?

4 There are wonderful echoes of Hannah's prayer (1 Samuel 2:1–10) in Mary's song (Luke 1:46–55). What connections do you see? How might they inform your worship and prayer?

5 Recall the ways you've experienced leaders being chosen. How does God's 'counter-cultural' approach speak into those different situations?

ⓠ 1 Kings 3:1–28
10. Royal wisdom (pp. 136–146)

1 Solomon is imperfect, but we remember him as a wise king. How does his story echo some of the conflicting loyalties we saw in Judges 2:6–23?

2 1 Kings 3:6–9 records something that Solomon asked of God, and verses 10–14 reveal God's response. How could you shape the requests you make of your heavenly Father to echo the 'pleasing request' of Solomon?

3 Solomon's reign did not end well – God is gracious in punishment, and Solomon's story and wisdom survive in the Old Testament texts. It appears that pride was a key part of his fall. Perhaps on your own, not as a group, consider where pride needs to be confronted in your own life, and replaced with wisdom.

4 The books of the Kings can seem strange – but, as Desi writes, they are 'theological history'. How does it change your approach to these books to remember that they 'confirm God's pledge to establish the Davidic dynasty as the lineage that will lead to the perfect vicegerent' (pp. 145–146)?

ⓠ Isaiah 52:13 – 53:12
11. The servant king (pp. 147–158)

1 The book of Isaiah offers in some ways a microcosm of the biblical story, centring, as Desi notes, 'on the transformation of a corrupt Jerusalem into a resplendent, holy city' (p. 148). How does that image resonate with you and your own testimony?

2 The words of Isaiah 60:19–20 are a hopeful and sure promise. Do any of the words or imagery resonate with you, or might they resonate with someone you know who is struggling?

3 At the heart of God's plans for restorative transformation is the servant introduced in 52:13 – 53:1. What sets him apart? How does he, despised, differ from those held in honour?

4 The book and message of Isaiah are a sobering reminder of human sin and divine intervention. In the person of Jesus, we see the glorious paradox of the incarnation come to make all things new – transforming the corrupt into the holy. Pause and thank God for the marvellous work of his Son!

Psalm 2:1–12
12. The Lord's anointed (pp. 159–172)

1 The Psalms may be more or less familiar to you – but have you pondered the concept of 'royal psalms' before? How do these, with their specificity about a coming king, contrast with your favourite psalm? (If you don't have a favourite psalm, why not compare it with mine, Psalm 139.)

2 The Psalter was probably composed and compiled at a time when God's people were under threat. How does Psalm 2 read and sound in the light of that?

3 Psalm 2:7 offers a clear and intimate portrait of the coming king. Do you see the echoes at Jesus' baptism (Matt. 3:17; 17:5, 2 Pet. 1:17)?

4 'Hope comes through focusing on the divine king' (p. 170). How can Psalms 110 and 132 inform and infuse your hope?

Daniel 7:1–28
13. A kingdom to end all kingdoms (pp. 173–183)

1 Did you know that Daniel was half written in Aramaic, the language of the Babylonians? How can it, as a book set in the context of God's people being in exile, be encouraging to you as God's people in your context?

2 'Daniel's faith in God rests not on what he sees around him, but in the traditions that he had imbibed as a young man prior to his deportation' (p. 175). If you grew up in a Christian home, are there any traditions or patterns that have remained helpful? If you didn't, what patterns and traditions would you want children (in your church or nuclear family) to grow up with?

3 The terrifying and strange beasts in our passage seem overwhelming – but they are fatally flawed, and God's kingdom will prevail overall. What world events or more personal things can seem overwhelming? How can the frailty of the beasts of Daniel 7 give you hope for your own situation?

4 Consider the fate of 'the boastful horn' (7:11–12). Contrast that with the humility of Joshua and David as examples. How could you emulate them rather than that boastful horn?

5 At one point in this chapter, Desi alludes again to Psalm 110. Why not read that, alone or together, and give thanks to God for sending his Son, the king.

PART 4: THE KINGDOM OF GOD IN THE NEW TESTAMENT

Q **Matthew 3:13 – 4:17**
14. The coming of the king (pp. 187–197)

1 In Matthew, we are in the New Testament, but there are important echoes of the Old. How does Desi's unpacking of the Greek term *basileia* (p. 189) affect your understanding of 'kingdom'? What continuity with Old Testament themes and ideas does it provoke for you?

2 Part of Jesus' unique calling and vocation can be seen in his ability to resist temptation. Have you considered how Jesus' quotes from Deuteronomy in response to Satan provide clues to his kingship (p. 192)? How does Jesus' example here inform your own engagement with temptation?

3 Read Isaiah 9:1–2 and, instead of getting distracted by thoughts of Christmas, consider the resonance between place, story, history and hope that echo between those words from Isaiah, the present focus on Matthew, and the wider Old Testament that we've explored.

Q **Matthew 5:1–12**
15. The shared values of the kingdom (pp. 198–206)

1 Perhaps echoing the Ten Commmandments and other Old Testament instruction, we meet now the 'lifestyle manifesto' of the kingdom of God. Which elements do you find easiest to embody? Which do you find harder?

2 You may hear the phrase 'now-and-not-yet' in relation to the kingdom of God. Does Desi's explanation of the difference between *arrival* and *consummation* (pp. 200–201) help to unpack that more, particularly with reference to our living in the way of the kingdom now?

3 Purity and meekness seem particularly counter-cultural – why do you think this is?

4 Persecution is a terrible thing, and yet Jesus directly addresses the topic in 5:11–12. How do his direct words sound to you? How do the promises of reward (for example, possession of the earth for the meek) inform how we might hear and respond to Jesus' words here?

Matthew 13:1–50
16. The timeline of the kingdom (pp. 207–215)

1 How does the parable of the four types of soil (13:1–23) reassure us that 'everything is going to plan'?

2 How does the parable of the two seeds (13:24–30; 34–43) help to explain the messy, good-and-bad nature of the present time as we await Christ's return?

3 The mustard seed and yeast (13:31–33) are powerful symbols of the unstoppable growth of the kingdom of God. Does the slow (even if inexorable!) transformation these two parables point to frustrate you?

4 Inherent in these parables is the reality that, when the time comes, Jesus will be the universal judge separating the righteous from the wicked. Why not ask God to draw to your heart and mind those people who need to hear about the reality of the kingdom of God, and meet the king for themselves?

Mark 15:16–39
17. The execution of the king (pp. 216–228)

1 The counter-intuitive cross. Jesus has confounded expectation, again. How does the execution of the king (Mark 15:16–39) echo and remind you of what we saw about the timeline of the kingdom in Jesus' teaching in Matthew?

2 The rebel/thief on the cross who asks Jesus to remember him is a challenge to our thoughts that there are people who are too tough for the gospel. Why not take a moment to share about and pray for those who seem beyond grace?

3 Desi talks about two kinds of 'seeing' going on at the cross (p. 224). Which do you find easier? How does Luke 23:34 resonate when seen in the two ways?

4 The cross is not the end of the story, but it is incredibly important. 'Without the cross there can be no kingdom' (p. 226). Why do you think this is?

(Q) Acts 2:14–41
18. The king ascends to his throne (pp. 229–240)

1 Do you tend to see the cross as more important than the resurrection and/or ascension? Why do you think we often focus on one rather than the whole?

2 Throughout the Old Testament, the issue of land, earth and place has been rumbling. Now, in Acts 1:8, Jesus seems to open it up. How does it feel to be a part of this expansive people and kingdom?

3 Peter seems to draw links between Jesus and Moses, intimating that God had a plan all along. At the same time, Peter focuses on the responsibility of the Romans and others. How do you think about this balance of God's sovereignty and human responsibility? Does Desi's exploration (pp. 231–232) help?

4 Try reading Acts 2:33–36, Psalm 110 and Philippians 2:5–11. What themes about the king do you see flowing between the passages? Have you thought about the ascension as a biblical theme like this before?

5 In a possible echo of our explanation of Hannah's song (1 Samuel 2:1–10), we are seeing that the kingdom of God is simultaneously deeply personal and utterly global/universal. How have you thought about the personal/universal balance of God's kingdom before?

(Q) 2 Corinthians 15:1–58
19. The return of the king (pp. 241–251)

1 1 Corinthians 15:3–4 repeats the phrase 'according to the scriptures'. That's been the aim of this BST volume and study guide, to encourage us to think about the king and the kingdom 'according to the scriptures'. Has this study challenged any of your previously held beliefs about the kingdom? How would you explain the kingdom in a few sentences, 'according to the scriptures'?

2 Hope is rooted in the resurrection (15:12–19). Is that true in your experience, or do you need to re-centre your faith in the resurrection of Jesus? 'Jesus' resurrection is the linchpin that holds everything together' (p. 242).

3 As we move through the passage, and the chapter in this book, we
   start thinking about 'the end'. How does it change things for you to
   see it as the end of everything evil, rather than the end of the world
   or of time?
4 Paul continues on from the present conflict to our future hope
   (15:35–49). Ponder these words. How does that promised hope
   affect you?

ⓠ Revelation 21:1 – 22:5
20. The unshakeable kingdom (pp. 252–262)

1 John uses contrast in Revelation to make the point. Where God was
   not, now God is. Have you thought about these contrasts before?
2 Revelation includes a great deal of promise-fulfilment, like Isaiah
   65:17–19 and 25:6–8. How does the tangible, abundant language
   of delightful banquets on earth compare to views of heaven and the
   kingdom of God you may have heard before?
3 There is a challenging call to purity running through the biblical theme
   of the kingdom of God. How does Revelation 21 contribute to this?
4 'The whole of history is moving towards a great, unending climax that
   marks the consummation of the kingdom that Jesus Christ came to
   establish' (p. 262). Why not close this study by praying the Lord's
   Prayer, and asking for God's kingdom to come?

Copyright acknowledgments

Listen to God's Word
speaking to the world today

The complete NIV text, with over 2,300 notes from the Bible Speaks Today series, in beautiful fine leather- and clothbound editions. Ideal for devotional reading, studying and teaching the Bible.

Leatherbound edition with slipcase
£50.00 • 978 1 78974 139 1

Clothbound edition
£34.99 • 978 1 78359 613 3

The Bible Speaks Today:
Old Testament series

The Message of Genesis 1 – 11
The dawn of creation
David Atkinson

The Message of Genesis 12 – 50
From Abraham to Joseph
Joyce G. Baldwin

The Message of Exodus
The days of our pilgrimage
Alec Motyer

The Message of Leviticus
Free to be holy
Derek Tidball

The Message of Numbers
Journey to the Promised Land
Raymond Brown

The Message of Deuteronomy
Not by bread alone
Raymond Brown

The Message of Joshua
Promise and people
David G. Firth

The Message of Judges
Grace abounding
Michael Wilcock

The Message of Ruth
The wings of refuge
David Atkinson

The Message of 1 and 2 Samuel
Personalities, potential, politics and power
Mary J. Evans

The Message of 1 and 2 Kings
God is present
John W. Olley

The Message of 1 and 2 Chronicles
One church, one faith, one Lord
Michael Wilcock

The Message of Ezra and Haggai
Building for God
Robert Fyall

The Message of Nehemiah
God's servant in a time of change
Raymond Brown

The Message of Esther
God present but unseen
David G. Firth

The Message of Job
Suffering and grace
David Atkinson

The Bible Speaks Today:
New Testament series

The Bible Speaks Today: Bible Themes series

The Message of the Living God
His glory, his people, his world
Peter Lewis

The Message of the Resurrection
Christ is risen!
Paul Beasley-Murray

The Message of the Cross
Wisdom unsearchable, love indestructible
Derek Tidball

The Message of Salvation
By God's grace, for God's glory
Philip Graham Ryken

The Message of Creation
Encountering the Lord of the universe
David Wilkinson

The Message of Heaven and Hell
Grace and destiny
Bruce Milne

The Message of Mission
The glory of Christ in all time and space
Howard Peskett and Vinoth Ramachandra

The Message of Prayer
Approaching the throne of grace
Tim Chester

The Message of the Trinity
Life in God
Brian Edgar

The Message of Evil and Suffering
Light into darkness
Peter Hicks

The Message of the Holy Spirit
The Spirit of encounter
Keith Warrington

The Message of Holiness
Restoring God's masterpiece
Derek Tidball

The Message of Sonship
At home in God's household
Trevor Burke

The Message of the Word of God
The glory of God made known
Tim Meadowcroft